D1239029

Dollars for Reform

Dollars for Reform

The OEO Neighborhood Health Centers

Isabel Marcus
University of Texas at Austin

LexingtonBooks
D.C. Heath and Company
Lexington, Massachusetts
Toronto

RA
418.5
P6
M37
1981

Library of Congress Cataloging in Publication Data

Marcus, Isabel
  Dollars for reform.

  Bibliography: p.
  1. Poor—Medical care—United States. 2. Federal aid to community
health services—United States. 3. United States. Office of Economic Opportunity, Comprehensive Health Services. 4. Medical policy—United States. 5.
Evaluation research (Social action programs)—United States. I. Title.
RA418.5.P6M37 1981   362.1'0973   79-2198
ISBN 0-669-03092-9

Published simultaneously in Canada

Printed in the United States of America

International Standard Book Number: 0-669-03092-9

Library of Congress Catalog Card Number: 79-2198

To Herman Marcus and Dorothy Gabel Marcus
whose contributions are unending

Contents

Preface and Acknowledgments

This book represents an extended personal odyssey. My work on it first began in the Department of Political Science at the University of California, Berkeley, under the supervision of Aaron Wildavsky. His understanding task-mastership was the most intellectually challenging and rewarding experience during my entire graduate career in the Berkeley of the "glorious" 1960s.

I was aided at that time by employment as a consultant on an Office of Economic Opportunity (OEO) neighborhood health center consumer-education project supervised by Dr. Alberta Parker, a faculty member at the School of Public Health at the University of California, Berkeley. She generously opened many OEO doors for me.

And, of course, the writing of this book could not have been undertaken without the extraordinary cooperation of the Office of Health Affairs staff as well as local health-center clientele and administrators. They are too numerous to mention in print. This book truly is their endeavor as much as my own.

The first draft of the book was completed while I was a first-year law student at Berkeley. The literary style of the original manuscript reflected the conflicting intellectual demands of legal prose and social-science analysis. The book remained untouched until I assumed my teaching position at the University of Texas, Austin, as an assistant professor in the Department of Government and a visiting assistant professor in the School of Law (January 1977). By then, ten years had passed from the agency's peak interval (1966-1968), and I was confronted with the searching question: What intellectual contribution can this analysis make? The burgeoning interest in implementation studies convinced me that a revised manuscript might be useful.

Many persons and several institutions facilitated the writing of the original manuscript and the subsequent revision. Three typists deserve unstinting praise: Mary Millman (now a lawyer in San Francisco), Mary Helen Solis, and Mary Alice Castello. Each typist has become a personal friend.

To the Department of Health, Education and Welfare I am indebted for a doctoral fellowship that allowed me to complete my work during my first year of law school. During this time, I also received travel funds from the Health Services Research Program of the Institute of Business and Economic Research at the University of California, Berkeley. The University Research Institute of the University of Texas, Austin, also invested a modest sum to assist me with typing expenses.

Then, there are personal acknowledgments of support: To my children, Erica and Justin Pritchard, for their unstinting love; to my former husband, Roger Pritchard, for his conscientious assumption of extra child-care responsibilities during the original data-gathering phase of the study and to my many dear friends in Berkeley and Austin who saw me through the crises that punctuated the decade.

Introduction

The name *War on Poverty* reflects both the optimism and the blindness of the 1960s. The United States had never lost a war, so the title was evocative of success. The United States had always engaged in a war for good cause; inequalities caused by poverty would be eliminated by waging the war.[1] The U.S. public could recall the camaraderie and spirit of sacrifice generated during a war; the racial conflicts and tensions that surfaced during the 1960s could be healed by a focus on the war effort; distinctions of caste and class could be buried along the way; national rhetoric and national commitment could mesh. Discounted were the possibilities that there might be interests with a stake in the continuation of poverty in U.S. society, that the poor might not be able or equipped to take advantage of whatever opportunities for access were made available, that a class could be singled out for special treatment without arousing keen resentment among others,[2] and that the general predisposition against change could be overcome.[3]

During its relatively short life, the War on Poverty, and more specifically its administrative vehicle, the Office of Economic Opportunity (OEO), was the object of critical scrutiny from the right and the left.[4] To the right was an administrative quagmire; to the left it was anything but a "root and branch" operation.

Assisted by the advantages of hindsight, scholars and civil servants have written numerous accounts and analyses of OEO programs and their legacy. Some accounts have been written by often rueful "insiders," others by academicians from a wide variety of disciplines. It is not surprising that the literature covers the intellectual spectrum from castigation through challenge to earnest apology.

For scholars and policymakers concerned with significant efforts at reform in U.S. society, the seeming confusion generated by this range of commentary has produced an unanticipated benefit. An analytic review of the various explanations for the problems encountered by the War on Poverty and the prescriptions for remediation that flow from those explanations reveal the limitations and deficiencies in various types of public-policy analyses.

One group of commentators follows the "defective policy formulation" approach. They argue that the premise for the War on Poverty was unsubstantiated and possibly conflicting assumptions concerning the causes of poverty, that these assumptions became the bases for federal policy to alleviate or eliminate poverty, and that the consequence for the entire program was an ambiguous set of policy objectives that ultimately intensified conflict between the poor and the rest of the population. In Moynihan's trenchant prose, "A program was launched that was not understood and not explained, and this brought about social losses which need not have occurred."[5]

The prescriptions for remediation of the deficiencies pinpointed by this analysis are relatively straightforward: clean up the formulation end of the policy process; be more sensitive to underlying assumptions; develop adequate data to test these assumptions; be aware of any major inconsistencies or contradictions among the assumptions and anticipate the likelihood of heightened conflict and lack of direction at the implementation stage if the inconsistencies or contradictions are not resolved at the policy-formulation stage.

At first glance, it is difficult to pick a quarrel with this analysis. Indeed, it is satisfying at an important psychological level because it takes us back to the alleged genesis of the difficulties. A faulty beginning marked by egregious errors at the very least compounds later difficulties and, more likely, lays the foundation for failure or, at best, limited success. In an era of heightened self-consciousness, the unself-conscious fare poorly.

Upon closer scrutiny, this explanation suffers from several major deficiencies. Basically, it is a regressive post hoc explanation, which encourages avoidance of a thoughtful analysis of the rest of the policy process. Defective policy formulation as the major explanatory variable for program failure is post hoc because its existence is largely determinable after implementation has been unsuccessful. Only with the advantage of hindsight can one determine whether all assumptions were explored adequately and the inconsistencies or contradictions eliminated. Defective policy formulation as the major explanatory variable for program failure is regressive because it assumes that even if policymakers are sensitive to potential formulation defects and make good-faith efforts to avoid them, should the program fail, the policymakers simply were not sensitive *enough* to potential formulation defects.

The initial underlying assumptions of the formulators, when translated into program terms, are said to set forces in motion. Little if any attention is paid to shifts in policy assumptions by successors or policy implementers. "Genesis" explanations, especially when a fatal flaw can be discerned, are static explanations.

Another group of commentators follows the defective-organizational-strategies approach. They maintain that War on Poverty programs were fraught with major organizational problems, which undermined any potential for program success.[6] The inability to develop stable bases of support in low-income communities as well as to implement effective staff-client relationships, the failure to establish crucial and systematic service linkages with other social-service agencies, and the lack of an adequate information system to guide the service function are cited as instances of deficiencies that contributed to overall program precariousness and failure well before the political agenda had changed in Washington.

And, reminiscent of Moynihan, the prescriptions for remediation of the deficiencies pinpointed by this analysis are relatively simple and straightforward: clean up the administrative implementation end of the policy process; build support constituencies; firm up links with existing resources; develop better information systems.

Again, one would say at first glance that it is difficult to pick a quarrel with this type of analysis. Indeed, the analysis is appealing because it provides us with concrete, task-oriented prescriptions. But the deficiency is that this analysis addresses troubling and troublesome surface phenomena without exploring their origins and possible connections. Only a better, more "rational" administering vehicle for a program is needed.

A variant of the defective-organizational-strategy approach argues that the political conflicts generated by the War on Poverty resulted, at most, in reluctant support of poverty programs and, more often than not, in antagonism and hostility from important local and national figures.[7] Conditions of token cooperation or resistance led to the failures and eventual demise of OEO.

The prescription for remediation of this alleged deficiency, though more elusive than heightened awareness at the formulation stage or more appropriate organizational strategies, is still uncomplicated: find and use better political brokers to head off or mute conflict.

Yet again one would say that it is difficult to pick a quarrel with this level of analysis. It is attractive because it fits some of our most tutored political sensibilities. But the deficiency in this explanation is that the element of political fortuity is so heightened that policy-process analysis, except for a catalog of often situation-specific political gaffes, appears to be irrelevant or unimportant.

If there is persuasive merit to the expressed reservations regarding the explanatory value of these different, though by no means exclusive, policy-analysis perspectives, are other, more satisfactory perspectives available? Implementation-process analysis is one appealing candidate. It does not preclude recognition of the impact of the policy-formulation stage; nor does it exclude criticism of organizational deficiencies and political sophistication. Rather, it encompasses them while recognizing that program-implementation difficulties or deficiencies may rest on other considerations as well.

There is, however, an overwhelming common theme emerging from the flood of public-policy implementation case studies which inundated the social sciences in the late 1960s and early 1970s. As Eugene Bardach noted, "The character and degree of many implementation problems are inherently unpredictable."[8] Despite the most carefully designed efforts, programs inevitably are forced off course and may well founder on the dangerous shoals of "underperformance, delay and escalating costs."[9]

Assuming that these conclusions are accurate (and up to this point there has been no persuasive counterstatement), we are left with several alternatives. One is the pessimist's route—to throw up our hands in despair and allow bureaucracies to either muddle along or argue for the dimunition of their role through a "less administrative" approach "in which people make decisions for themselves in their own best interest, but in which the sum total comes out as a net increment to the social good."[10] Such an approach focuses on general rules to guide decisions and then counts on existing "natural" economic and social forces such as market conditions, incentives, and bargaining power for their execution.[11] The underlying assumption is that the use of such market forces eliminates the real-world impossibility of always or even frequently having superior people and superior plans to achieve desired goals.[12]

Another alternative is to rely on fixing—repairing the damage done during the implementation process.[13] Such an ad hoc strategy has as its prerequisite highly motivated and committed personnel who possess political acumen.

Yet a third alternative looks to better design efforts for the implementation process. This approach does not eliminate recognition of the fortuity of events and circumstances as they impinge on the implementation process. Moreover, it recognizes the value of fixing when a situation allows it. The contribution of this alternative lies in a focus on improving design. This, in turn, suggests that bureaucrats may be able to improve their implementation efforts if they incorporate the knowledge that implementation studies provide or, at least, are able to anticipate the difficulties that these studies detail.

Reliance on this third approach should be preceded by an important caveat. To examine and measure a program by criteria internally generated from its own ideology and often overblown rhetoric is intellectually unprofitable for implementation analyses. Such a procedure inevitably leads to the threshold question: Why has this program not measured up to its pronouncements? And reliance on a threshold question framed in this manner is all too unlikely to uncover many insights except the recognition that the activity of policy formulation involves exaggeration.

The alternative is to start with a minimalist, more neutral perspective by framing the threshold question thus: Why and how did anything happen at all? From this perspective, it is possible to go beyond the appearance of quick success or abject failure to explore the difficulty of "translating broad agreement into specific decisions, given a wide range of participants and perspectives, the opportunity for blockage and delay that result from a multiplicity of decision points and the economic theories on which a program is based."[14]

This distinction between the "prisoner of the program's rhetoric" and the minimalist positions as the starting point of the analysis is far from a semantic one. Whether articulated or not, the mind set of the analyst is crucial to any intellectual inquiry. The minimalist position is not mere indulgence in skepticism; rather, it is an effort to minimize the impact of preconceptions regarding a program or policy.

This book explores two major components of the implementation process: the dispensing of federal dollars and the monitoring of their use. It is an analysis of often painful, continuing choices and their attendant difficulties. The choices involve the following:

1. Institutions or individuals to whom the dollars are dispensed;
2. Conditions under which the dollars are dispensed;
3. Strategies to achieve maximum impact with the dollars;
4. Techniques to monitor the use of the dollars;
5. Approaches to evaluate the effectiveness of the dollars.

The major argument of this book is that social-change demonstration agencies, like other bureaucracies, must cope with sets of choices in the implementation process. The major distinguishing feature of the choices is that they are generated by the very nature of the social-change demonstration operation. And, paradoxically, these choices are likely to undermine the agency's social-change reform agenda by the difficulties and dilemmas they create.

It should be noted parenthetically that informants interviewed for this book rarely if ever pointed out dilemmas or even major contradictions in the implementation process. They tended to see problems generated by the program as capable of solution if only there were greater quantities of various resources—time, staff, or dollars. The contradictions or dilemmas emerged from analysis of the data they provided.

Two mutually inclusive lines of explanation for this gap in perception are suggested in this book. One explanation looks to the qualities and experiences of the reformers themselves. In this instance, young, intense medical-care reformers, fresh from Peace Corps experiences in which relatively limited dollars assisted by personnel commitment and creativity often achieved impressive results, dominated the domestic health-care reform endeavor. These reformers appeared to underestimate the staying power of entrenched, high-status, professionally dominated institutions. But, rather than accepting their personal specific ingenuousness as a controlling explanation, it might be more profitable to consider the possibility that reformers, generally speaking, are likely to operate with such a gap—that the harsh realities, even if they are recognized, must be played down or set aside; otherwise, the vision may never be implemented, and the reformers might remain immobilized.

The other explanation looks to the properties of the situation itself—to the incompatibilities among cultures, to the resources available, to the expectations generated, to the goals set and the incentive system used. This approach, while not denying the role of the actors' motivations and intentions, stands for the proposition that the best of intentions and the highest of motivations, though a consideration in any analysis, cannot adequately explain implementation dilemmas. In fact, ironically, the dilemmas of the situation appear with greater clarity when the disparity between the logic of social-reform demonstration endeavors and the reformers' motivations is explored.

Choices in the implementation of a reform endeavor are embedded in an ideological context. In chapter 1, the ideological context in which the neighborhood health center operated is explored.

At the inception of the War on Poverty, health care was not viewed as a major focus on reform. Although the causal connection among health care, health status, and poverty was recognized as a part of the poverty cycle, low priority was given to an activity as expensive and prolonged as medical care. A combination of fortuitous circumstances and ideological flexibility allowed health-care reformers who hoped to develop and administer high-quality, new health-care delivery institutions called neighborhood health centers to generate a sympathetic response within the OEO for a demonstration program. The neighborhood health centers were to address themselves to such broad health-care delivery reform issues as (1) the development of a totally new relationship between providers and consumers where the professional takes responsibility for program aspects of the operation while the new institution becomes truly responsive to and under the control of the people it serves; (2) the development of new health roles and careers; (3) organizing around an interest kind of need as a basis for successful community action in other substantive areas; (4) providing a physical and organizational focus for other kinds of antipoverty activity; (5) the modification and refinement of institutional and organizational arrangements to ensure personalized care, family care, or care that will conform to high-quality standards and be attractive to professional personnel of high caliber.[15]

Choices in the implementation of a reform endeavor also are embedded in a structural context. Chapter 2 is a formal account of the rise and fall of efforts to bring the rediscovered poor into the medical-care mainstream or, at least, to demonstrate how this goal could be achieved through innovative social-service programs by the Office of Comprehensive Health Services located in the OEO Office of Health Affairs.

Because they were funded by the War on Poverty, these new health-care institutions were designed to serve the poor—that clientele within the medical-care delivery system most heavily penalized by the distorted allocation of health resources in relation to human needs and by waste and inefficiency along the way. But the centers were designed with the hope that others who might not be the direct beneficiaries of OEO largesse would be encouraged to confront pressing problems of health-care delivery in the United States. In contrast to other OEO programs focused on the poor and their specific needs, the health-care reformers hoped that their success in providing innovative, high-quality, comprehensive care at reasonable cost to the poor would force major structural changes in the delivery of "mainstream" medicine.

The first major policy choice for a demonstration agency with a mandate to purchase the delivery of social services involves the judicious dispensing of dollars. From among all the potential recipients of its dollars, an agency must develop some standards of stricter scrutiny to narrow the range of choices, with full recognition that this necessary action may have a significant impact on the direction of reform. Chapter 3 details this process.

Prior OEO experiences suggested that dollar infusions into low-income target areas in an unorganized fashion, while generating a plethora of groups and projects, did not necessarily produce coherent, sustained, or sustainable results. Dollars could just as easily produce chaos.

Claiming that the development and administration of a new health-care institution were far more complex endeavors than other OEO community-oriented undertakings, the Office of Health Affairs purchased the development of new health-care institutions from existing providers. Despite the fact that remarkably few provider institutions had demonstrated or proved any capacity to develop and sustain significant health-care reforms, the agency appears to have assumed that dollars could overcome institutional resistance to change—a classic U.S. perspective—that anything can be accomplished with sufficient dollars.

In addition to the assessment of project-sponsor capability, the agency, and eventually Congress, had to determine eligibility for receipt of the services provided by the health centers. The second half of chapter 3 explores the agency's effort to avoid the welfare-eligibility stigma and its eventual, tragic loss of control in this policy area.

Because reform-demonstration dollars are highly limited and controversial, demonstration agencies must do more than assess sponsors' capabilities to deliver the goods. They must develop strategies to achieve maximum impact with the available dollars. Chapter 4 outlines these strategies, which can be divided into two types: maximizing or legitimating and risk-avoiding. Maximizing strategies focus on the direct impact of federal dollars to sustain the momentum for a reform program operating within a limited time frame. For example, the agency calculated that higher-status or impeccable sponsors for some projects would ensure the rapid and efficient delivery of high-quality comprehensive health care. Or the agency targeted some projects as "showplaces'' for impression-management purposes and directed public and bureaucratic attention to them.

Risk-avoiding strategies attempt to avoid the dilution of the impact of project dollars through their diversion to largely unproductive endeavors such as fiscal siphons or contruction of facilities. Like maximizing strategies, they are premised on the desperate recognition of the cruel constraints of time.

In the broad sweep of the implementation process, choices among categories of project sponsors and among strategies to achieve the greatest possible impact with limited reform dollars are merely the beginning of the endeavor. In programs that challenge status quo arrangements, the escalating intensity of conflict is likely to mean that Washington is called on more often to intervene in seemingly irreconcilable situations.

The devices available to a government agency for dealing with such conflict levels are limited. Direct agency intervention is costly, time-consuming, and often ineffective in resolving deeply rooted local conflicts that tend to generate intermittent crisis situations. One alternative is the development of institutional forms to contain, if not resolve, the conflict. However, the surface simplicity of such an alternative is deceptive. The power distribution within the local project and between the local project and Washington is unstable and changes over time. Fundamental political questions of institutional accountability emerge predictably and are viewed quite correctly as direct challenges to the status quo. Chapter 5 focuses on these questions by analyzing the issue areas of employment and the development of governance mechanisms for the centers.

The dollar-dispensing process is complemented by the dollar-monitoring process. Conventional wisdom would have it that the possession of dollars is the key to federal power. Theoretically, an agency that desires to retain power in order to enforce its own controversial reform agenda (or to control conflict) can attempt to monitor programs by defining the dollars and controlling the dollar flow.

But local projects develop their own agendas and vested interests, which, from Washington's perspective, are irrelevant to or in conflict with the longer-range reform perspective. Local differences may be vital, but major reform issues transcend parochial concerns.

The transcendental nature of these major reform issues fuels an agency's attempts to secure compliance with its reform agenda. And the major vehicle for securing compliance in a fluid bargaining situation is a panoply of fiscal sanctioning devices. Chapter 6 assesses the effectiveness of these devices brought to bear on projects where noncompliance with the reform agenda or lack of capability to manage a program is apparent and, in fact, has continued for a prolonged period.

While the agency worries over the dilution of its agenda and the loss of control over projects through dollar dispensing, it is faced simultaneously with problems of long-term fiscal viability for its projects. Since the demonstration endeavor promises only limited funds for a brief period, an agency and its projects must eventually turn to other financing mechanisms as supplements and eventual replacements for demonstration dollars. Conventional funding specifications, however, are geared to fitting the needs and categories established by those entrenched social-service projects that the demonstration program challenges.

Ironically, the degree of project success may be largely irrelevant to agency efforts to ensure this external financial support. Because demonstration programs both look different and operate differently from more routine programs and because they may be perceived as threatening to the already established conventional clientele of entrenched agencies, they will be unlikely to "fit" satisfactorily. Moreover, a demonstration program has a transient quality. It may not be worth assisting from other sources' vantage point, since there is no guarantee of long-term congressional interest in or approval of controversial programs. When, in addition, the demonstration endeavor serves a marginal, politically powerless segment of the population, the available federal funds from entrenched agencies are even less likely to be made readily available.

There is one more imperative operating on a demonstration agency, and it entails a further set of choices. A front-line demonstration agency must prove to a skeptical world that its programs are effective. Chapter 7 is an account of the dilemmas that this set of choices generates. Ideally, evaluations show results, preferably of a quantifiable nature, that reveal a favorable cost-benefit ratio. Even if we assume that the necessary information for making such a calculation is readily available (which it often is not), there are still major policy issues to be decided. The choice of calculus for costs and benefits is a highly political issue; for a controversial demonstration agency, survival can be at stake. Given the limited time frame during which a demonstration program must do something significant and different, projects are likely to reveal the chaos and uncertainty that social change generates rather than quantifiable results of effectiveness demanded by an impatient Congress or executive branch.

But the *creation* of a set of viable institutions is not enough. Effectiveness means that the new institutions must be able to have a *sustained* impact on the system. The agency cannot rely on the assumed success of some of its projects to sustain its impact on the social-service sector it is attempting to reform. It is subject to other, often contradictory imperatives dictated by the logic of a demonstration endeavor: continuing expansion, replicability of projects, and remaining in the vanguard.

To prevent its predatory bureaucratic competitors from parceling out its resources, a demonstration agency is under extraordinary pressure to expand rapidly. In effect, it may be forced to compromise the quality of program sponsors in order to retain its numerical momentum. But rapid expansion must not compromise the alleged ease of replicability of projects or the reform agenda itself, even though the capacity and commitment to reform are limited—often surprisingly so—among an increasing number of prospective grantees.

In effect, the agency is damned by the logic of its endeavor. Expansion, replicability, and the maintenance of the reform agenda are harsh simultaneous imperatives that can create major dilemmas. In the world of bureaucratic competition, projects must be not only viable but also replicable, the demonstration logic runs, lest they be isolated experiences with little or no applicability to other situations that appear to be fundamentally similar. If they are isolated experiences, then the demonstration dollars merely reveal that the demonstration project can work in a particular situation.

Effectiveness, moreover, must be considered in a rapidly shifting time frame during which the enthusiasm for the new waxes and wanes quickly. Caught between demands for results and the need to be continuously innovative in order to maintain its position, the agency, by its very nature, cannot give projects the continuous, long-term attention that is probably necessary for ensuring viability and a sustained impact on the system. To avoid being ignored or cut back, the agency must, after an all-too-limited time, ignore its projects and spawn a second and third generation of attention-getting ideas. Reform endeavors are too likely to become trials without commitments.[16]

A number of informants maintained that reform and social change were local or grass-roots phenomena and that federal administrators, despite their reform intentions, could never be local change agents. "When we rush in and try to become local change agents," one astute staff member commented, "we fail, because there is no way in which a federal official can be one. What can happen is that we can bring in a local change agent who wasn't on the scene previously; in a sense it's like serendipity in bio-medical research." Another staff member noted: "We make bets that they [the local people] will create social change, and we reinforce them because we think it's worth it. We frequently turn out to be wrong. People leave; people turn out not to be good or not to be able to make the local situation happen because they're chased out. Our bet that they could work was wrong, and now we ask whether the new people are change agents." "It's easy to have grandiose dreams of power from Washington," said another informant. "It's easy to be a critic or an advocate, but it's a different 'bag' to develop programs. You end up saying 'we've got a great program out, but the people out there are lousing it up.'"

If federal reformers cannot be agents of local change, can they be the bearers of change in a much less ambitious manner and on a lesser scale by acting as catalysts through demonstration programs? Can they facilitate change at the local level by their limited prodding and intervention in local affairs? Leverage through federal dollars, more realistically assessed, may consist of assisting the establishment of the legitimacy of the demonstration endeavor in some situations and effecting incremental changes, rather than quantum leaps, in others. "The idea of demonstration money doing wide scale things is not valid; we [the agency] can do limited things quickly," one staff member reported. The element of fortuity or of a committed, sensitive, and sophisticated agency staff person may create agency clout within a local project among parties to the grant or with outsiders such as third-party agencies. Can they facilitate change by their slow pushing for expansion or redistribution of resources and a change of emphasis in policy at the national level? Such questions are far easier to formulate than to answer.

To date, there has been no viable solution to the problems of providing adequate health care for the poor and to the larger issue of major reform in the health-care delivery system. The talents and skills that were developed or liberated in the burst of energy and creativity generated by the War on Poverty have not been translated into a coherent program of reform. But at least the issues have been raised, and it is hoped that the dilemmas and contradictions are better understood.

Pressman and Wildavsky suggest that when a program is characterized by "many contradictory criteria, antagonistic relations among parties and a high level of uncertainty about even the possibility of success, it is not hard to predict or explain the failure of an effort to reach its goals."[17] At once, they are both correct and incorrect. If one examines the criteria, nature of the relations, and level of uncertainty in a demonstration program, an explanation of failure and a spurious sense of discovery are obtained. However, such an examination may fail to explore the systematic bases for these properties—the defects in principle—the incompatible imperatives that create dilemmas and that damn demonstration reform endeavors from their very inception.

A word should be included here about the research method used in this book. In choosing to look at the issue of the implementation problems encountered in efforts to purchase institutional change in health-care delivery, it seemed evident that persons involved at both federal and local levels should be interviewed. Although no formal random sampling was undertaken, most of the major federal actors and a number of local projects were visited. No formal questionnaire was used in these encounters. Informants were encouraged to describe their own experiences. Nevertheless, it would be inaccurate to leave the reader with the impression that there was no underlying structure to these encounters. The initial research categories developed from my own perceptions and experiences as a consultant to an

OEO project were modified and revised through the data collected in these interviews. Through comparison of interviewees' perceptions and experiences fed back into successive interviews, the categories of analysis were modified and revised. From these categories major premises and arguments were generated.[18]

Not surprisingly, the interviews were an extraordinarily rewarding and enjoyable source of information. In many instances, I sensed that incumbent and former staff members, who had devoted so much time and energy to the program, were pleased to share their experiences. Because I promised each interviewee total and complete anonymity in this book, I have been unable to quote sources by name. I did find many of the interviewees' comments, insights, and experiences so rich and revealing of the quality and flavor of the experience that I wished to convey them to the reader. Consequently, I have included some of the most quotable material without identifying the source in order to preserve my original research commitment.

There is one caveat for the reader. To the seeker of rational, classical, sequential decisions and policy prescriptions, this book will be unsatisfying. There are no simple comments or explicit answers to the many issues raised. It is illusory to see social policy only as making an inroad on a problem; there are dynamic aspects to any policy such that it also expands the problem, changes the problem, and generates further problems. If the analysis is valid, however, the difficulties that plague policy planners and implementers (procedural ambiguities and complexities, unintended consequences, enigmas, and dilemmas) will appear with greater clarity and with more than mere utility as descriptions though with less force than a premature, full-blown theory of implementation.

Dollars for Reform

1 Conceptual Underpinnings of Reform

Before 1960 poverty was simply not a direct and open subject of national, political concern. People who formulated programs to aid the poor had to do so in the name of other and more politically attractive causes (reviving the economy, preventing juvenile delinquency, rebuilding central cities).[1]

Contemporary readers who can readily avail themselves of social statistics regarding poverty need to be reminded that prior to 1965 almost no official statistics on the extent of poverty existed. Also "no detailed information spanning two or more years on a sizeable number of families or households was available until the early 1970s. The only comprehensive statistics available during the 1960s were snapshots of the overall distribution of income. . . . And they were rarely accompanied by any explanation of why income was distributed as it was."[2] But a series of shifts in U.S. society between 1960 and 1965 led to changes in the political mood.[3] In his first State of the Union address in January 1964, President Johnson announced an unconditional War on Poverty.

Health Status and Poverty

During the initial policy-formulation phase for the Office of Economic Opportunity (OEO), advisers to Presidents Kennedy and Johnson did not include health programs among the poverty agency's priorities. While poor health status has been recognized as an *important* variable in the perpetuation of poverty, it is by no means the only variable:

> It has been said that "the sick get poorer and the poor get sicker." In spite of the existence of a complex set of inter-relationships of heredity, distribution and availability of medical facilities and services, behavior toward health care, environmental conditions, and socioeconomic factors, which are difficult to distinguish, there is an undisputable association of increased morbidity and mortality with poverty.[4]

But recognition of the association between poverty and illness is not tantamount to a policy prescription that the improvement of poor people's health status necessitates reform or expansion of medical facilities for the poor. Even if health is viewed as an enabling condition which helps lead to what is now labeled an improved "quality of life,"[5] among scholars and activists committed to improving the health status of people in the United States, an extended, heated debate has raged over the impact of health-care services compared with that of employment and educational opportunities on health status.[6]

At the early policy-formulation phase, economic growth through full employment was viewed as the key to mitigating and eventually eliminating poverty. Cash assistance was viewed as possibly necessary, but temporary sustenance for the able-bodied; after education and training, only those still unable to benefit would need cash assistance or in-kind transfers. It still was assumed that most people could earn their way out of poverty.[7] At a more practical level, it has been argued that the underlying reason for emphasis on the human-capital approach "was that job programs cost money, and a great deal of it. To undertake the massive public-works programs . . .—which alone could have quickly created the jobs that were lacking—would have required at least an additional $2-billion to start, and perhaps $10-billion a year within a short time. . . ."[8]

But it soon became apparent that economic growth might not alleviate the myriad handicaps endured by the poor.[9] An explanation was needed for the failure of economic growth to narrow the gap which appeared in the crude statistics available to policymakers.[10] Social theorists began to conceptualize poverty as a self-perpetuating cycle with income disparity generated by unemployment or underemployment as merely one component. A new set of explanations was provided to account for a social problem.

Once the cylic nature of poverty was acknowledged, the debate among academicians and social activists shifted to the relative merits of the "culture of poverty" school (emphasizing the adaptive and rooted properties of culture as a pragmatic adjustment to external and internal stress and deprivation) and the "environmental" school (emphasizing the modifiability of behavior when the individual is confronted with a changed environment). To the extent that the War on Poverty developed the notion of "community action" which emphasized "a comprehensive attack on all of the inter-related causes of poverty,"[11] it can be said that the refinements of the debate sensitized policymakers to a diffuse and broad range of considerations.

As Blumenthal reminds us, most of the analysis is now so well accepted that the "original language sounds hackneyed and repetitive: the 'powerlessness' of the poor, their need for 'identity,' the 'cycle' of 'escape' and rebellion. But at the time [these] theories altered the entire intellectual framework of anti-poverty efforts."[12]

This more generalized sensitivity and awareness to the interrelationships among poverty issues was reinforced for health-care policy-formulation purposes by reports from existing OEO programs regarding the health status of program participants. Administrators discovered that poverty-program participants often had a below-average health profile when compared with similar age groups in other segments of the population. Recruits for OEO job-training programs were more likely to have chronic disabilities than their peers in more advantaged segments of the population. Preschool- and school-age children were more likely to have uncorrected, sometimes severely handicapping impediments. In effect, health status affected performance in those OEO programs which were designated as the vehicles to move people out of poverty.[13] To the extent that the quality of educational and employment performance was connected with poor health status *and* the evident absence of adequate medical care, agency policymakers and implementers were forced to confront directly issues of health and medical care affecting low-income populations.

Many persons would agree that sensitivity to a broad range of policy considerations on the part of individuals concerned with the formulation of public policy is commendable and desirable. The basis for this approval is the belief that such sensitivity develops insights that will improve the quality of policy formulation. Quite understandably, liberal professionals concerned with the delivery of social services to the poor were delighted with the heightened sensitivity that the dialogue promoted. Victorian assumptions that the poor were responsible for their own lot were being challenged. If the new social theorists were persuasive, institutions premised on these late nineteenth century beliefs would lose their strategic position of dominance in the "welfare" system.

Dollars and Structures

While the insights that new or heightened sensibilities bring are fundamental to any reform endeavor, they may remain splendidly remote from the policy formulation process if they cannot be meshed with available dollars. Every realistic innovative idea as well as every remedial effort has a price.

OEO policy maker interest in the inadequacies of the existing health-care system for the poor was reinforced by the availability of public funds for medical care. The large amounts expended both for Medicaid as well as Medicare in the early sixties constituted a precedent for public-sector involvement through financing in the delivery of medical services to defined groups within the general population. Of equal importance for policy formulation purposes, the data collected by 1965 pointed to the inflationary spiral in medical care fees generated by dispensing federal dollars from these programs into the health-care delivery system. It was apparent that more public dollars did not purchase more care or even better care for the poor or the aged.

Recognition that money can reinforce outdated ideas or be used for selfish ends is not tantamount to denying its usefulness. Such recognition may speak to using it in new ways. The underlying behavioral premise easily can remain untouched. To prod people and institutions to undertake activities and programs which they otherwise might fail to do required sizeable amounts of money. Dollars were a powerful incentive for change.

The unsatisfactory inflationary experience identified with Medicaid did provide a straightforward object lesson regarding the relationship between dollars and the direction of change. To increase the effectiveness of public dollars dispensed for the purchase of health-care services for the poor, the service delivery institutions needed reform. Or, alternatively, new institutions that were more responsive to clientele needs had to be created. Structural change was viewed as the means to achieve more effective, efficient, and equitably distributed health-care services.

The emphasis on structural change and, preferably, new structures was not impeded by the melange of beliefs regarding the nature of poverty shared by social reformers. Nor did proposed social reform strategies pose conceptual barriers. Rather, they encouraged enormous flexibility which sceptics and critics claimed bordered on the ambiguous.

> If the causes of poverty are circular, then intervention at any point may be effective and the more the better. At the same time, neglect of any one aspect of the problem is excused by the indirect influence upon it of actions elsewhere.[14]

From such a perspective it became difficult, if not impossible, to determine the relative importance of different proposed interventions or to anticipate their impact on the poverty cycle.

"Broad aim programs" and more narrowly defined "specific action" programs flourished simultaneously on the policy drafting boards and within actual programs.[15] The former were characterized by a nonspecific change-for-the-better justification. By virtue of their ambitiousness and magnitude, they involved unstandardized large-scale interventions. The latter, as their title suggested, were designed to achieve specific aims. They were more likely to claim that they could demonstrate cause-effect relationships which would be of major assistance in effective policy formulation in the future.

Action was the order of the day. "Something must be done" and "all bases must be covered" were the War on Poverty imperatives. Political and bureaucratic needs were accommodated in the flourish of activities.

Admittedly, in a "high energy" reform endeavor, it may be exceedingly difficult to force the issue of closure on programs. And with the advantage of hindsight, there is a tendency to fault individuals caught up in the sweep and excitement of the action at the time. As a framework for systematic, directed policy formulation and program planning, such conceptual diffuseness and attendant lack of closure may be a source of endless frustration; as a reference point for reformers concerned with maintaining great amounts of flexibility in their operation, it appears to have been ideal.

The demonstrated need for better health care became the justification for intervention in the poverty cycle by reformers interested in health care. New structures embodying expanded notions of health-care delivery and claiming the capability to intervene effectively in both the cultural and environmental components of the poverty cycle could be developed and tested.

To establish the significance and innovative nature of their proposed structural changes, the reformers were careful to distinguish between narrow, conventional *medical care*, which was limited to care provided by physicians or other health practitioners and which was dispensed in doctors' offices, hospitals, and nursing homes, and more expansive *health care* which encompassed dental care, mental health services, home health care, health education, nutrition, environmental health, transportation to and from health services, as well as other activities to promote good health.[16]

The proposed new structures were conceptualized as health-care institutions. They were designed to avoid carrying over old problems of rigidity and inefficiency into new organizational structures. They incorporated various reform-oriented ideas which had been circulating around the health-care field, including clinics as freestanding dispensaries; the "floating hospital" or the more extensive use of home care for patients; prepaid health-care cooperatives in which consumers played an important role; comprehensive, family-centered medical group practices which would make more efficient use of medical expertise; and the expansion of preventive health-care services.[17]

The basic characteristics of the neighborhood health center were:

1. Focus on need
2. A one-door facility, readily accessible in terms of time and place, in which virtually all ambulatory health services were made available
3. Intensive participation by and involvement of the population to be served, both in policy making and as employees
4. Full integration of and with existing sources of services and funds
5. Assurance of personalized, high-quality care and professional staff of the highest caliber

6.   Close coordination with other community resources
7.   Sponsorship by a wide variety of public and private auspices[18]

Many of these characteristics were designed to address directly the health-care delivery failures in existing institutions serving the poor. Health centers were more than financing mechanisms, and hence distinguishable from health insurance.[19]

Among the most preeminent advocates of the structural reform of health-care institutions, there never was any consensus regarding the scale and scope of the proposed OEO health-care reform endeavor. This absence of consensus, however, in the field of health care may be relatively unimportant if, as Fein suggests, we are dealing with an unchanging situation in which image is more important than reality:

> Because some (even if relatively little) medical care deals with matters of life and death, because of fear, because of infatuation with science and technology—as well as because medicine oftentimes does help . . . persons have come to believe that medical care services and intervention by the physician make significant contributions to health.[20]

The proposed scale and scope of the program and estimates of the anticipated impact of the new health-care structures varied widely. Many of the claims seemed genuine and persuasive, although with the advantage of hindsight they may appear to be somewhat unsophisticated.

At one end of the spectrum were the "sweeping reformers" who believed that the development of new health-care delivery structures could and would provide such attractive, high-quality care at reasonable cost that the middle-class who found their medical bills spiraling would want to expand the health-center program to their communities. These reformers argued that Congress would then be convinced to provide incentives for restructuring the entire medical-care delivery system rather than to perpetuate the status quo by increasing subsidization through Medicare and Medicaid. Along this line of reasoning, developing quality comprehensive care for a particular category of persons with particular federal dollars was the immediately available means to a far more ambitious end.

Somewhat more narrow in their focus were the "advocates of the poor" school who grappled with unresolved issues of equity and equality.[21] Is equity realized when equal numbers of dollars or services are available for the health care of different persons, or when equal numbers of dollars or services are utilized, or when equal health outcomes are achieved? Human dignity included the right to a decent existence, they reasoned. No one should die for lack of financial resources to obtain adequate nutrition or medical care. Furthermore, no one should suffer desperation or pain for lack of health care that money could buy.[22] Adequate, accessible health-care facilities for low-income persons had to be developed, and conventional institutional practices had to be changed to embody greater sensitivity to low-income patients. But the debate did not produce a resolution of the fundamental equitable issue.

Although usually identified with more radical intellectual trends, these individuals often relied ultimately on the traditional economic justification for government intervention as a remedial action for nonefficient allocation of resources, or, in other words, a market failure. But they went beyond such traditional justification for the provision of medical services to the poor when they argued that external imposition of health care as a priority for the poor was inadequate unless the poor "participated in" and ultimately "shared in the control" over a visible, high-quality, economically viable major service in the community. Only then would a low-income community be able to sustain a sense of some control over its own destiny—a sense which they claimed was lacking in poor communities but existed in middle-class ones. Disruption and conflict could be functional for the achievement of long-term goals. Moreover, community input in the designing and managing of health-care facilities would provide low-income persons with the skills to participate in the fast-growing health-care industry.

Despite their difference in emphases, both the sweeping reformers and the advocates of the poor endorsed the broad-aim approach to structural reform and innovation. From their perspective, ambitious, unstandardized, large-scale interventions were far more likely to have an impact on the system than specific aim endeavors.

More modest in their beliefs regarding the scope, scale, and anticipated impact of health-care delivery reform were the "gradualists," who argued that the reforms should be focused and limited in order to have maximum impact on the existing system. They argued that a specific-action orientation might hasten the spread of certain crucial reform components such as group practice, team medicine, the use of paraprofessionals, and "meaningful" consumer input leading to more broad-based accountability of health-care institutions.

An alternative to the typology developed above (namely, sweeping reformers, advocates of the poor, and gradualists) is Alford's classification of (1) market reformers aiming at the restoration of market competition and pluralism through innovative biomedical and technological research, (2) challenger bureaucratic reformers concerned with the "corporate rationalizing" of such a complex industry, and (3) equal-health advocates seeking free, accessible, high-quality care with an emphasis on community control of facilities.[23] In his analysis, the OEO neighborhood-health-center movement could and did absorb the energies of these three types of reform groups, jockeying for power within the health-care system because the centers emphasized efficiency and coordination of resources as well as innovation in delivery techniques and increased access of previously excluded or marginal population groups.

Despite the disparity in perspectives regarding the desirable or manageable scale and scope of the reforms as well as their anticipated impact, the health-care reformers displayed consensus regarding the use of research and development (R&D) demonstration programs as the most politically feasible and acceptable vehicle for developing and implementing change. Research and development—the search for new knowledge and its reduction to practice—is a familiar creature to politicians and administrators in Washington. It connotes rationality and scientific endeavor combined with carefully thought-out management techniques.

Used initially for federally subsidized scientific and/or military research, R&D was transferred to the area of innovative design of social-service delivery systems under the rubric of demonstration programs. To counter allegations of nonscientific amorphousness, the programs were said to focus on specific policy issues and to serve targeted populations. The anticipated upshot of success (however it was measured) was "large scale adoption and major shifts in the aims, styles, resources and effectiveness of major social service organizations and programs."[24] It was assumed that rational beings would adopt and expand on the discovered right answers.[25] And it was believed that rationality would outweigh the political liabilities that these demonstrating programs were likely to generate—unequal distribution of money and resources, distraction from coherent national policy, and overemphasis on success.[26]

Health-care reformers were blessed by the fact that in the health-care field, research has always been an acknowledged legitimate vehicle for increasing medical knowledge, which in turn is equated with progess—an unquestionable scientific "good." Medical research enjoys a high status among professionals and laypersons alike and, therefore, a concomitant high degree of autonomy from funding sources. The funding pattern was, and continues to be, the granting of public funds on the basis of personal, professional, and institutional affiliation prestige as well as the nature of the research proposed. Use of "buzz" word research bridged the gap between more familiar medical research and demonstration programs for the delivery of health-care services. But, as Piven points out, medical research is solution-oriented, and when the term is transferred to the delivery of services, a confusion ensues between acknowledgment of a problem and a policy solution.[27]

From a more skeptical perspective, Piven conceptualizes the demonstration notion as a strategy of influence between levels of government and between government and voluntary organizations.[28] She is careful to point out, however, that she views this strategy as a means of deflecting discontent, providing short-term concessions, and avoiding substantial and enduring improvements by limited commitment within a limited time framework and for a limited area of population.

Reformer reliance on demonstration programs is consistent with the flexibility characteristic of OEO programming. A broad, eclectic view of the nature and causes of poverty allowed for or justified a wide range of remediation-oriented government-sponsored interventions of either the broad- or specific-aim sort. Since strategies for mitigating or eliminating poverty in either broad- or specific-aim projects were untested, an R&D demonstration effort appeared preferable to a final commitment to a particular program approach, especially when jurisdictional reach was in flux and organizational capability in at least some instances was uncertain.

But exactly what was being researched, developed, and demonstrated? Whereas a concrete end product such as a cure or palliative usually can be pinpointed for laboratory or teaching-hospital research funding, the end product of a social-service delivery demonstration effort focusing on structural (and ultimately behavioral) change is far more difficult to articulate and describe in great detail. The persistence of the question, however, resulted in the rather nebulous claim that *doing something important in a different way* was the basis for the endeavor.

The obvious threshold question is: What is *important*? Reference to the conceptual underpinning of the War on Poverty was of limited utility; its diffuseness could provide no clear-cut answers. Since the policy provided no guidelines or boundaries, policymakers and implementers tended to rely on their own perceptions of what was possible as the basis for determining what was important. For OEO health-care reformers, the delivery of better health-care services to underserved target areas was *needed* because of the *failure* of others to provide adequate care. It was *possible* to accomplish this task despite the mess or the vacuum which both the private and public sectors created or reinforced. And it was *important* because people suffered directly from the absence of health care. A skeptical observer might add that it was needed and possible and therefore was important.

Starting from the deficiencies of the existing medical-care delivery system (fragmentation of services, high costs, failure to use preventive-medicine techniques, and the insensitivity of many medical professionals and institutions to the needs of their clients), the reformers claimed not to be certain or close-minded about possible solutions to these problems, given their recognition of the range of deficiencies, needs, and priorities in different low-income communities. In the slightly exaggerated but nevertheless reasonable comment of one informant, the health affairs staff preferred to "let a thousand flowers bloom." It was an article of faith that the hardiest and best projects would survive because they were deserving. Not only would they meet local needs, but also they would serve as an inspiration and example to other communities which might not receive demonstration funds. Moreover, even those projects which were less successful could not be discounted totally because the existing facilities for the medically indigent were so bad that anything created by the agency was better than the status quo and therefore was *important* and different.

2 Organizational Context of the Dollar-Dispensing Process

Staff Recruitment Patterns

In 1965 a small health component was established in the Community Action Program (CAP) Office of Program Planning. It went beyond existing federal medical-insurance and medical-care delivery programs to address "both the financial and nonfinancial obstacles standing in the way of improved health in poor neighborhoods."[1]

The small, high-powered staff consisted of Ruth Hanft, an economist, John Frankel, a dentist with ties to the Public Health Service, health-care reformer Richard Weinerman of Yale, and Lisbeth Bamberger Schorr. As the agency became aware of the need for expanded health-care programs, additional staff were recruited. The choice of staff type made at this critical juncture of the program's history had a profound impact on the entire direction of the program.

The first OEO director, Sargent Shriver, has been characterized as an "inspirational leader."[2] Whatever limitations existed in his capacity for administration, he was able to attract enthusiastic, articulate young talent to the agency. The intensity and excitement of the experience can be best summarized as the "exhilaration derived from the view from the top."[3] Since Shriver previously had been the director of the Peace Corps, he had access to talented, highly motivated young people who had worked in Third World countries setting up health-care programs. He also had connections to Dr. Julius Richman, a highly esteemed medical school academic with impeccable credentials among health-care reformers.

Not surprisingly, the professional staff recruited for the crucial expansion phase were former Peace Corps physicians. They had strong ties to prestigious academic mentors identified with health-care reform. But they had little or no experience in developing or implementing domestic health-care programs. To compensate for this deficiency they included their mentors as well as other highly respected, reform-oriented medical consultants for the neighborhood health center program.

Within a short period of time the medical professional staff and their consultants established an "inner circle." Those early staff members who lacked medical training were expected to be mindful of the boundaries established by medical professional solidarity.

The medical professional staff-consultant relationship is of special importance for an understanding of OEO health-care policy formulation. The consultants were relatively sophisticated, battle-scarred veterans of earlier health-reform efforts who operated in a small, well-developed network. In the past, many of these reformers had found their efforts to promote change in the medical-care delivery system frustrated either by outright hostility from mainstream organized medicine toward government involvement in the delivery of medical-care services or by lack of medical concern about the health problems of the poor. Consequently, despite the expenditure of enormous amounts of energy and time, the reformers had enjoyed little previous success in their dealings with the Congress or different federal bureaucracies.

From the older medical consultants' perspective, OEO's commitment to health care offered a unique opportunity. The agency appeared to have freedom, dollars, and vision.

The cue or "buzz" words surfacing in the reform literature of the 1960s are revealing: *intensive, developmental, mobilization of resources and expertise, activating or stimulating change.* These are action words. They convey the sense of government serving a pioneering and inspirational role in social policy—a role previously associated with universities and foundations.[4]

The contrast with the major dispenser of government dollars for health care, the Department of Health, Education and Welfare (DHEW), was striking. DHEW suffered from nightmarish bureaucratic fragmentation; no clear policy position was likely to emerge from such a structure. Along with the fragmentation came complex regulations for each of the agency's many programs and complicated funding procedures which turned the dollar dispensing process into an obstacle course. DHEW staffing patterns and preferences ensured the perpetuation of such a situation. Career medical civil servants trained in public health and medical-care administration dominated the agency. In part, OEO staff attributed the continuing failure of DHEW to develop solutions to problems connected with the delivery of high-quality, reasonably priced medical care for all people in the United States to the lack of imagination of these civil servants. Finally, DHEW demonstrated great reluctance to challenge the American Medical Association (AMA) whose opposition to government sponsored or subsidized comprehensive health care for any group in the population was well known.

OEO senior staff were quick to point out the contrast in bureaucratic styles. They claimed that their prior Peace Corps service sensitized them to different cultural responses and to complexities in interpersonal relations rather than to civil-service management-oriented considerations. Several doctors in key positions preferred staff with psychiatric training because such persons were capable of "genuine" concern for people and could cope with conflict more effectively. Informants remarked that they were pre-pared to set aside the certainty available from the traditional corpus of knowledge on health-program development and administration for the ex-citing uncertainty of "learning as we go." The appropriate analogy was to a good clinician who possessed the capacity to listen to patients with greater sensitivity, who would make a diagnosis based on a broad range of variables, and who could prescribe remedies appropriate to the situation.

This self-confident, optimistic senior staff group prided itself on operating at a government level high enough to influence policies and deci-sions relating to the delivery of medical care, while claiming to remain "responsive" to grass-roots situations. (An important senior staff person was praised as the highest-level bureaucrat to visit a local project and have community people shout at him.)

As the agency developed, the staff continued to view themselves and their operation as *progressive*, a term which often was equated with *an-tibureaucratic*, or, in the words of later battle-scarred veterans, *doing the maximum within bureaucratic limits*. It was apparent that this self-definition of entrepreneurial capacity was a source of great pride among a number of key senior-staff informants and was used extensively by them to distinguish their operation from every other federally funded health-care delivery endeavor, despite the dilution of these prized qualities through staff expansion, turnover, or staff disenchantment over the likelihood of large-scale significant reform.

A small group of program analysts were the administrative core of the neighborhood health center program's operation. These analysts were young, highly motivated, overwhelmingly Caucasian women and men who had no special medical expertise or prior management experience. In the spirit of the sixties they were willing to "take risks," even if, as several female analysts reported, they had to confront sex based discriminatory behavior and harassment directed toward them. Each analyst was assigned responsibility for several projects. In some situations, the analyst became a project advocate; in others, the analyst developed into an adversary. In either case, the analysts usually visited projects several times during the year and tended to have more complete information than agency leader-ship.

A number of informants characterized the early days as a "golden age," possessing the quality of working with an "extended family." This family encompassed not only the small staff of the agency but also some of the key high-status medical professionals associated with the first eight grantees. As in many families, there was a commonly shared belief that all those involved in the family wanted to do good and were trustworthy and that consequently elaborate rules and regulations to govern behavior (of grantees) were unnecessary.

But the corollary of the intense emotions as well as the spirit of camaraderie which the extended-family concept generated was the profound, unbuffered sense of betrayal which developed as the initial staff and grantee group developed into a larger organization concerned with selling the neighborhood-health-center concept to a much wider constituency. Some of the early staff who did not possess medical degrees but who initially were acceptable as members of the "family" felt slighted and rebuffed when medical professional expertise became a major hiring criterion for senior staff. Moreover, as the program expanded and the "buddy" system between the agency and the grantees broke down, the agency discovered that grantees might be neither likeable nor trustworthy.

Over time, the excitement of the reform effort subsided. After a while, the enterprise even became tedious. As Pressman and Wildavsky note,

> The advantages of being new are exactly that: being new. They dissipate quickly over time. The organization ages rapidly. Little by little the regulations that apply to everyone else apply also to it. . . . Youth has gone and middle age has come, hopefully more powerful, certainly more experienced, inevitably less innovative.[5]

Survival in the bureaucratic world is not guaranteed by enlightened, enthusiastic staff. An agency needs protection. To the reformers the OEO seemed to have been given such protection. Its director, Sargent Shriver, was a presidential assistant. Rather than operating in a niche within a conventional Cabinet-level department such as Health, Education, and Welfare (HEW), the agency had direct access to the President. And President Johnson is reported to have said, "this thing can't survive less'n everybody knows when they're hitting it, they're hitting me. I'm your protection."[6]

Supplementing structural autonomy and a guarantee of political protection from the president was the prospect of large amounts of dollars. The vast outpouring of federal dollars aimed at ensuring adequate medical coverage for the aged and the poor had failed to encourage new and efficient institutional arrangements in the medical-care delivery system and had only increased the demand for services at inflated costs. Medicare and Medicaid had become an unbalanced strategy of demand stimulation.

With the advantage of hindsight it is easy to fault the reformers for assuming that these available federal dollars would be re-allocated to the neighborhood health centers as they proved themselves. At the time, sufficient criticism had been directed toward both major federal programs which could lead them to conclude that the government was committed genuinely to changing some of the most undesirable aspects of the existing medical care delivery system. Moreover, the reformers like many others were prisoners of the widely held belief that the resource pie was every expanding. New funds in large amounts would be available.

Program Expansion

Between spring 1965 and June 1966, the Community Action Program Health Office funded eight health-care projects for low-income communities as R&D grants.[7] These awards were made to institutions with connections to highly influential health-care reformers. (See the discussion on strategies for agency visibility in chapter 4.)

In November 1966, the small CAP health unit underwent a dramatic change when specific legislative authority for a neighborhood-health-center program was enacted. A Comprehensive Health Services (CHS) program was set up, for the development and implementation of programs focused on the needs of poor persons residing in urban or rural areas having high concentrations of poverty and a marked inadequacy of health services.[8] In establishing programs, CHS was to be guided by the criteria that health services should be readily accessible and responsive to the needs of residents of the target area, that area residents should participate in their delivery of services, and that delivery of services should be carried on under competent professional supervision. Along with the legislative mandate came $50.8 million in grant money—enough to fund thirty-three new projects as well as to re-fund the existing eight.

The legislative history reveals no opposition to this significant expansion. There are several explanations, none of which are mutually exclusive, for this lack of controversy. First, the initial program (eight projects and $10 million) was hardly noteworthy within the OEO budget and virtually unnoticeable in comparison with the billions spent on health care and research by HEW and the Veterans Administration. Second, potential opposition from the AMA to reformist ideas of prepaid group-practice-type medicine had been neutralized by senior staff within the OEO who had made it clear to the AMA that the projects would not interfere with existing private practices of AMA members. Third, the confident staff of the proposed agency appear to have convinced such key congressional figures as Senator Edward Kennedy that the provision of health services *sui generis* might be an effective and possibly less controversial intervention in the poverty cycle.

One year later, the mandate of CHS was expanded to include health-workforce development as well as such controversial activities as family planning, alcholism, and narcotics addiction.[9] The Office of Health Affairs was established, and within it the neighborhood health center program was to be administered by CHS.

Despite this expansion, the amended Economic Opportunity Act reveals increasing pressure to dilute the impact of the War on Poverty in general and health services in particular. One indicator of these pressures, as far as health issues are concerned, was the provision allowing projects in rural areas to provide simpler, less comprehensive services than urban projects. While such a stipulation arguably reflects the grim reality that it is often far more difficult to provide extensive comprehensive services in rural areas where the population is scattered and the existing facilities are few, the political rationale for this clause lay in the agency's need not to antagonize certain powerful members of Congress from rural areas whose constituents proposed health projects falling short of the agency's reform-oriented criteria. Another even more telling indicator of these pressures was congressional replacement of the broad OEO eligibility criterion of residence in the target area with the old welfare rule of individual-income eligibility. (See chapter 3 for a more extensive discussion of this issue.) Finally, Congress' enactment of the Partnership for Health Amendments of 1967, which provided additional funds to HEW for comprehensive community-health projects, signaled congressional disenchantment with the OEO health-care program. Centers under HEW's aegis were to place less emphasis on the innovative nonmedical services included in the OEO projects.

Program Decline

During the late 1960s and early 1970s the political mood of the country underwent a drastic change. Public loss of faith in the virtues of government intervention was apparent.[10] Both the efficacy and effectiveness of government action were open to challenge.

Not surprisingly, congressional appropriations reflected popular unwillingness to commit increasingly large increments of dollars to broad-based government interventions such as OEO. It became the target for a coalition of Southerners and conservatives.

While OEO was able to sustain existing programs, "it ceased to function as an active force in shaping legislation affecting the poor."[11] The OEO's own laconic outlining of the fiscal fortunes of the agency reveals the extent and impact of this loss of agency function:

In fiscal year 1967, $50.8 million was obligated for the Comprehensive Health Services Program. About $41.5 million was for new projects, $9.1 million for re-fundings and $.2 million for supporting activities.

Funds were available for a limited number of new efforts in fiscal year 1968. Six new operational projects received just over $6 million. Three planning projects received about $0.9 million and contracts of about $4 million were obligated. Over $25 million was awarded in re-funding actions. In all, $33.2 million was expended for CHS activities.

The President's budget for FY 1969 requested $90 million for the Comprehensive Health Services Program. However, cuts in the OEO budget decreased this amount substantially. Just over $52 million was finally expended. Only 2 new operational projects were initiated; planning grants (utilizing Research and Demonstration funds) were made to help restructure hospital outpatient departments in Boston, Cincinnati, Minneapolis and Newark. The 1969 Amendments, enacted on December 30, 1969, extended the program for 2 additional years.

The President's original budget proposal for fiscal year 1970 also included $90 million for the Comprehensive Health Services Program, including $10 million for new efforts. It was indicated that additional efforts would be concentrated on applying the Program Guidelines to new settings and conditions. Primary attention would be focused on restructuring hospital outpatient departments, additional rural projects, extensions of existing and new group practices and manpower development.

During the year, 27 new projects were funded. About $2.0 million was used for technical assistance and related contracts and $59.5 million for refunding actions. Total obligations approximated $74 million.

The President's budget for fiscal year 1971 included $110 million for the Program. $40 million was for new developmental and demonstration projects. Priority is to be given to the development of community-wide networks of comprehensive health services serving populations of 100-200,000 persons in areas of concentrated poverty.

The President's budget also anticipated that responsibilities for re-funding $30 million of existing projects are to be transferred from the Office of Economic Opportunity to the Public Health Service, DHEW. This action affected about 16 projects.[12]

The curtailment of OEO health centers through failure to provide adequate funds is consistent with the broad program thrust of the Nixon administration. Despite the rhetorical emphasis on education and training, it was reported that "of the $16 billion spent on the poor in 1969, just over $3.5 billion was spent on education, Manpower, community organization and social services."[13] The articulated priorities for the OEO were "more efficient management systems in programs, greater regionalization of progress, and the transfer of control of operating programs to departments of government."[14]

Nixon's special message on August 11, 1971, informed Congress that OEO needed to continue its innovative role without hindrance. To free its bureaucratic energies he proposed a transfer of some of its programs to more conventional operating agencies. Along with the Job Corps and Headstart, the Neighborhood Health Center (NHC) program was mentioned as a likely candidate for transfer. The 1971 congressional appropriations contained provisions for the transfer of a number of viable health centers to HEW.

Many agency staff and local project people voiced concern over the proposed fate of the health centers. Beyond bureaucratic proprietary interest in continuing the flow of federal dollars and programs through the OEO, there were independent bases for resistance to the transfer. The Department of Health, Education, and Welfare was the conventional bureaucracy that had created the need for OEO health programs. To transfer the fledgling centers to the bureaucratic sprawl of HEW, still the captive of mainstream organized medicine, was a serious setback for health-care reform despite the existence of HEW's Comprehensive Health Planning Center program modeled on the OEO.[15] Moreover, HEW's regional structure meant that regionally based bureaucrats with little experience in dealing with health centers, and possibly with a differing philosophical perspective, would assume responsibility for monitoring projects; OEO-style "nurturance" was unlikely.

In a symbolic effort to reassure OEO staff, a memorandum of understanding was signed between the director of OEO and the secretary of HEW.[16] The memorandum set out policies consistent with OEO policies to be followed by HEW in supervising the transferred centers. This was said to serve as "guarantee" for existing projects. Also HEW agreed not to approve the transfer of a project grant during the next three years from an existing grantee or delegate agency to another grantee or delegate agency without the former's agreement or without a fair hearing for termination for cause.

The memorandum also contained an elaborate set of criteria for the selection of projects for transfer, although OEO staff articulated an awareness that a complete transfer of health-center operations was merely a matter of political time.

> III. (a) the selection of projects, for which responsibility is to be assumed by the Secretary (hereinafter referred to as the "selected projects") will be made by the Director with the concurrence of the Secretary on the basis of the following criteria, provided that the total of the grants required in the fiscal year ending June 30, 1971 for the support of the selected projects may not exceed $30 million:
>
> 1. whether the project provides a broad scope of services which is in, or is approaching full operational status:
> 2. whether the project has a sound basis of community participation and relationships;
> 3. whether major demonstration features of the project have been developed and assessment begun;
> 4. whether the project has previously received grant support from the Department of Health, Education, and Welfare (HEW) or bears a close and mutually beneficial relationship to HEW programs; and
> 5. whether the funding for a project facility is within the scope of HEW authority.[17]

Cynics or realists might observe that such bureaucratic guarantees among parties lacking equal bargaining power are worthless. In the case of the health-center program, such an observation is borne out at least in part by federal data regarding the number of operating projects. Even if the letter of the agreement was not violated, that is, the original OEO centers continue to exist, despite a number of favorable evaluations, the absolute number of OEO- and HEW-generated projects and the amount available per registrant for existing programs declined sharply. In effect, "the spirit of that agreement did not hold and the neighborhood health center program stagnated. For several years the Nixon and Ford administrations requested substantial cutbacks in the number of centers supported and the level of funding. Congressional opposition prevented such cutbacks, but the program was held at a constant level of funding despite the rapid increase in health care costs."[18]

The subdued tenor of those times is reflected most profoundly and painfully in the congressional testimony of the director of the Office of Health Affairs:

Mr. Perkins (D. Ky.) . . . I would like to put one final question to you, Doctor Bryant, if you feel that the $195 million is going to do the job, for the people in the ghettos that really need these services and the rural people?

Dr. Bryant: Well, of course, Mr. Chairman, the problems that we have in providing health care to poor Americans are immense.

I think that the figures that are here are proportional to what I see as accomplished, a dual sort of role for the Office of Economic Opportunity.

I do not think that this committee or the Congress ever had this in mind that the OEO would be the end all as far as providing the health care to all of the poor in this country, but I think the role we have had to develop and demonstrate new ways of approaching the problems, I am trying to figure out the best way to provide health care to the poor.

I think in that role, the figures we have requested in the present budget for 1972 are appropriate figures.

I would not by any means indicate that that sum of money, $195 million (in 1971) will solve the problem, but as you know, there are a number of other activities underway, primarily under the auspices of the Department of HEW, both doing some of the kinds of things we are doing; however, the largest amount of money is in Title 18 and Title 19 of the social security amendments. That is where billions of dollars are expended, and this will at least remove some of the financial barriers for the poor to receive medical care.[19]

Between 1971 and 1973, no new neighborhood centers were developed by the Office of Health Affairs. Funding for centers still under OEO's aegis remained constant despite the increasing costs of medical supplies and services as well as expanded utilization.[20] The OEO funded fifty-five comprehensive health centers at a cost of $95 million during fiscal year 1972 and forty-one centers at a cost of $74.3 million during fiscal year 1973. In 1973 the President ordered and a federal court upheld the transfer of OEO programs to HEW.

In 1972 Richard Nixon was reelected. His landslide victory had a marked effect on OEO programming. The first Nixon administration maintained OEO programs at the 1969 level (less than $2 billion). By 1973 the second Nixon administration was prepared to move directly against the agency. The 1974 budget proposal contained no mention of funds for OEO; as his first act, the newly appointed OEO director ordered agency staff to begin to dissolve their programs. It was the intervention of a federal court which prevented the director from defying Congress' clear intent to continue the program until 1974.[21] Unable to destroy the agency by frontal attack, the Watergate-preoccupied Nixon administration dumped the "problem" back into the Congress' bailiwick.[22]

The congressional response was predictable: OEO programs were dismantled by being absorbed into existing conventional bureaucracies, spun off into independent public corporations, or allowed to die a bureaucratic death. The Ford administration recommended and Congress supported cutting funds to $155 million for 1977 and eliminating twenty centers.[23] Moreover, it made several unsuccessful attempts to transfer decisions regarding the funding of centers to state governors.[24]

The OEO, established in the White House to wage the War on Poverty, has been abolished; it has been replaced by the independent, low-profile Community Services Administration (CSA) within DHEW.[25] The 1967 message of a chastened Sargent Shriver rings prophetically true: "The war on poverty is not fought on any single, simple battlefield, and it will not be won in a generation."[26]

3 Putting Together a Program

At least in theory, a flexible mandate from Congress to an agency regarding the dispensing of federal dollars is a boon. In such a situation, administrative discretion replaces significant formal, externally imposed, and possibly politically generated constraints on a vital administrative activity. Upon empirical examination, however, broad administrative discretion is by no means synonymous with the absence of significant constraints on administrative activity. It merely replaces one set of advantages and liabilities, which the dispensing of federal dollars brings, with another.

The mandate from Congress for the Neighborhood Health Center (NHC) program required the dispensing of health-care dollars to institutional grantees. The rationale for the congressional choice is apparent. Aware of the development of a burgeoning federal sector since World War II and its well-publicized unresponsiveness to the poor, Congress, in passing War on Poverty legislation, attempted to divert the flow of federal dollars to the "grass roots" rather than fuel the expansion of the federal bureaucracy. As part of the War on Poverty, the NHC program was party to this "grass-roots" rubric.

Moreover, in the health-care delivery field, the political necessity for dispensing funds to grantees was readily apparent. The history of organized U.S. medicine from the 1930s to the present has been punctuated by well-organized and funded lobbying efforts to prevent the federal government from direct involvement in the delivery of comprehensive health-care services.[1]

Once Congress chooses to mandate the operation of projects to grantees, it is faced with yet another choice: the development of a classification of persons or institutions eligible for receipt of project funds as grantees. Since the congressional mandate did not contain such a legislative classification for the neighborhood health centers, the agency was free to develop the necessary administrative classification.[2] The section of the OEO Healthright Program Guidelines entitled "Who May Apply" reveals the enormous degree of discretion retained by the agency in the dispensing of health-care dollars:

> Any public or private nonprofit agency is eligible to receive financial assistance for developing and carrying out a comprehensive health services project. These projects, wherever feasible, shall be included in community action programs so as to avoid duplication, promote efficiency, better

21

assist persons and families having a variety of needs and otherwise achieve the greatest possible impact. A political jurisdiction recognized by OEO as a community action agency is an eligible applicant.

Agencies assuming responsibility for development and administration of a project undertake a commitment to carry out a major anti-poverty health effort for a substantial period of time. Investments in manpower and in facilities for these projects are considerable. Continuity of effort and services must be maintained in order to achieve the anticipated return and benefits.[3]

In effect, only private, profit-making health-care enterprises were barred from applying for health dollars. Such a prohibition is consistent with Erdmann's comments on U.S. beliefs regarding medical organizations, namely, that nonprofit status makes medical-care organizations substantially immune from corruption of their health-care goals and, conversely, that the profit motive in medicine has a powerful corrupting influence.[4]

When administrative discretion is not constrained substantially by agency guidelines, it would be reasonable to assume that funds are more likely to be dispensed on merit criteria. In theory, the best proposals and the most competent, qualified local personnel should be funded, especially when program emphasis is on diversity, competitive effort, and the appearance, if not the reality, of projects being initiated locally.[5]

But the funding of projects by a new, controversial social-change agency is, by the very nature of the enterprise, a high-risk activity. Agency dollars, even if they are free from congressionally imposed constraints and rigid administrative guideline requirements, are like risk-venture capital. Expending such capital is an endeavor fraught with pitfalls and potential liabilities.

One sound maxim, appropriate to risk-venture situations, is that the conscientious holders of capital, fully aware of the nature of the enterprise, may want to be involved with the best, most reliable institutions and people—those with a "proved track record in delivering the goods"—in an effort to minimize the risk. Bold rhetoric aside, as the controversial dispenser of such capital, the Office of Health Affairs (OHA) appeared to recognize implicitly the wisdom of this maxim, although interview data with key early staff reveal that relatively little attention was paid to the consequences attendant on this crucial initial policy-implementation determination.

The Strategic Choice: Deliverers of Health-Care Services

Basically, there were two different types of federal grantees: new nonprofit community corporations (often the outgrowth of the Community Action

Programs) or existing health-care provider institutions (medical schools, hospitals, health departments, and established group practices). Both types of grantees brought advantages and liabilities to the NHC program.

The major experience of OEO with nonprofit community corporations lay with the highly controversial Community Action Program (CAP). Despite the proclaimed commitment of the OHA staff to the "longer-range" goal of establishing effective nonprofit community corporations to administer health programs, many key individuals displayed a lack of enthusiasm for existing community corporations. According to one staff informant whose observations were echoed less graphically by others, the CAP corporations were living with "one foot on a banana peel and the other in the grave."

Staff informants recognized that the highly controversial nature of existing CAP community corporations led to their heightened vulnerability. They anticipated that the mistakes of the existing CAP community corporations would be magnified and used successfully by opponents of the NHC program to challenge the concept of any meaningful community participation, much less control, in a local health center.

The major thrust of their criticism, however, was that community corporations lacked the organizational capability to deal with the complicated problems generated by developing new health-care delivery structures. The local CAP might be able to handle relatively simple programs such as emergency food distribution; it might provide storefront medical care. But it did not have the capability to ensure the delivery of quality care.

The primary explanation for this perceived lack of capability was that existing community corporations had few (if any) community notables with medical training on their board. Given the very limited number of minority-group physicians in the entire country, this deficiency was not too surprising. But to senior agency staff with medical backgrounds, it constituted a serious drawback. To their minds, laypersons were hardly qualified to identify relevant health-care resources, to implement health programs, and, in particular, to monitor for "quality control."

Lacking medical professional input, these boards, according to agency staff, incurred an additional liability. They would lack legitimacy in the local medical professional community. Their lack of legitimacy would affect the extent of local medical establishment cooperation and active involvement. Such cooperation and involvement were considered essential to the center's immediate survival and longer-term success in Washington.

Recognizing the highly limited time frame under which the agency operated and aware that congressional enthusiasm for the program might evaporate within a few years, agency staff conveyed a feeling of futility when assessing local CAP efforts. "If we let them [the community corporation] try to run programs to learn what they have to do, it might destroy the neighborhood health center. There wasn't time for that kind of thing in a demonstration program," one staff member commented.

Seeking to avoid the political liability of identification with CAP and its community corporations in any way, key senior staff eliminated non-profit corporations as serious contenders for health dollars, especially in the early years. Instead, the staff informed established medical-care provider institutions who received agency funds that the development of non-profit community corporations to administer the local projects was one of the longer-range aims of the program, and that Washington was prepared to assist in the achievement of this goal. Such information appears to have been proferred in a more general manner; there is no evidence of an explicit or even an informal developmental timetable for the transition from provider institution sponsorship to nonprofit community corporation.

The absence of timetables for the transfer of control from providers to community corporations was the basis for criticism from community activists. It was viewed as a manifestation of the agency's basic unwillingness to commit the centers to "community control" when faced with the skepticism, if not hostility, of the medical establishment at the local level. Undoubtedly, there is an element of truth to these claims. In fact, a fairly convincing argument can be made for the proposition that the medical professional socialization of key senior staff affected their perceptions regarding the capabilities of community groups, even where local medical-establishment hostility to community input was not a paramount issue. But in all fairness, it should be said that consideration of the developmental pace of projects on a case-by-case basis was consistent with agency staff beliefs that the commitment to demonstrate the effectiveness of new structures in a wide range of locations and under differing handicaps necessitated open-endedness in expectations regarding the transfer of control at both agency and local levels.

In sharp contrast to vulnerable, controversial community corporations were a wide range of existing established provider institutions respected by the medical professional community. Medical schools, hospitals, local health departments, and nonprofit local group practices or medical-care foundations were already in the business of training medical personnel or delivering medical services. They had extensive prior experience in managing large sums of money and in recovering third-party reimbursements. Since the new health centers would be both complicated and expensive, agency staff reasoned that provider institutions with their knowledge, experience, and ability to recruit medical professional staff were the "workable," if not "natural," delegate agencies.[6]

This position is reflected in one of the early policy papers drafted by the agency:

The model program will be sponsored by an existing, qualified medical institution willing and able to organize, provide, and supervise professional services of quality, within a framework of objective evaluation. . . .If a Community Action Program (CAP) with an appropriately unified background is already in existence in the selected neighborhood, such a CAP may serve as grantee for the neighborhood health service. The identified sponsoring institution would then contract with the CAP to organize, supervise, and provide the health services in the neighborhood health center as projected herein. . . .

The sponsoring medical institution may be (1) a public hospital, (2) a voluntary hospital, (3) a university medical center, or (4) a comprehensive group practice organization. In each instance, eligibility for sponsorship will depend upon adequacy of services available, and evidence of comprehension of the objectives of the program, together with evidences of practical ability to carry out these objectives on a continuing basis over the long term. The sponsoring institution need not be in or immediately adjacent to the neighborhood to be served.

Choice of the sponsoring institution will be made on the basis of investigation and deliberation by a committee on appraisal, composed of qualified persons living and having their professional interests outside the geographic area to be served. Such an appraising committee must make thorough study of either (1) a single institution that has expressed interest in becoming a sponsoring institution; (2) if more than one institution has applied for sponsorship of a center within a given neighborhood, the committee shall study all institutions so applying, with a view to selection of one; or (3) if either the federal agency or the government of the state in question has determined to set up a neighborhood health center within a specific service area, and no institution has applied for sponsorship, the committee on appraisal shall study one or more appropriate institutions with a view to recommending one whose interest in sponsoring the proposed neighborhood health center will be solicited.

It will be of crucial importance to avoid sponsorship by any institution toward which an appreciable number of persons within the selected neighborhood feel hostility because that institution has failed in the past to provide good medical care in a sympathetic environment, or because it has rejected persons applying for medical care, on grounds that have appeared unreasonable to the applicants.[7]

For agency senior staff with medical training, provider institutions, especially prestigious ones, were known and reliable and could assist in the legitimation of the program, a key consideration for a controversial innovation. There was a sense of ease and comfort in dealing with other professional colleagues even if provider institutions had resisted reform in the past. "If you didn't have a gap between what the institution wanted to do and what you wanted to do there would be no need for money." one staff member remarked.

Perhaps it was this very sense of comfort which led to an underestimation of the complexity of the linkages and fiefdoms within the health-care system as well as to the failure to recognize the high degree of impermeability to change of professionally dominated institutions. ". . . The overwhelming fact about the various reforms of the health system that have been implemented or proposed—more money, more subsidy of insurance, more manpower, more demonstration projects, more clinics—is that they are absorbed into a system which is enormously resistant to change."[8]

The deep desire for immediate success, with its corollary heavy emphasis on *technical* success in the actual delivery of services, tended to color staff perceptions and policy choices.[9] That the target of institutional change not only participated in the project but also basically governed it as well posed no articulated conflict-of-interest situation as far as the key agency staff were concerned.

Agency staff further rationalized the choice to dispense dollars to established providers by claiming that a "twofer" effect would be achieved. Not only would new, legitimate health centers be developed, but also federal dollars would become the vehicle or incentive for further change within existing, established medical-care institutions. To an outsider, such claims may contain a leap in logic amounting to a leap of faith in provider institutions. For medically trained agency staff with extensive contacts primarily among liberal supportive health-care "market reformers" and "bureaucratic reformers," such an assessment was realistic.[10]

But existing medical provider institutions, especially those serving low-income communities, were burdened by liabilities which could and did have consequences for the direction of the entire demonstration endeavor. Established provider institutions serving low-income communities were viewed by their patients as insensitive to the problems and needs of the poor. Complaints of long waiting hours, of being shuttled from clinic to clinic, of impolite medical and nursing staff, of eligibility forms which had to be completed before treatment was administered, and of failure to explain medical conditions satisfactorily were widespread among indigent patients. Medical care studies confirm the existence of such patterns specifically identified with facilities for the poor, especially minority-group poor.[11]

> The reason the medical systems have not reached the poor is because they were never designed to do so. The way the poor think and respond, the way they live and operate, has hardly ever (if ever) been considered in the scheduling, paperwork, organization and mores of clinics, hospitals, and doctors' offices. . . .These faults result in a vicious cycle which drives the poor away from the medical care they need.[12]

In effect, provider institutions came to the program with tarnished reputations. Over time, their practices toward the poor had not changed, and now the providers were the recipients of even more federal dollars designed to demonstrate that they had the capacity to deliver better health care in a more sensitive and humane manner. Low-income informants recognized the irony in the situation and claimed that the providers, unlike the poor, were being "rewarded" for past failures.

Compared with the anticipated political liabilities incurred from contracting with new untested nonprofit community corporations to administer a health center, possible patient hostility toward existing providers seemed to pale as a major issue. Legitimation of the enterprise in the eyes of Congress and of the relevant professional community and a relatively high degree of assurance of quality control were the bottom line considerations in dollar-dispensing choices.

But a predisposition toward established provider institutions as federal grantees carried with it an additional, more significant liability even from the agency's perspective. A new health-care structure delivering quality care is unlikely to have a bargain price tag. And agency staff discovered that established provider institutions, habituated to ever-increasing government largesse in their coffers, charged comparatively high prices for their expertise.

Expectations of provider institutions tended to mesh with the attitude of some of the early key senior staff toward extensive, if not extravagant, funding to purchase provider interest in and compliance with the agency's reform agenda. One staff member noted:

> The basic philosophy was to spend lots of dollars to get people to change their minds. . . . Medical students needed to be attracted to these kinds of situations [health centers] so there would be cushy deals for medical students during the summers. I didn't like it, but the Director had gone to medical school and I hadn't. In some centers he believed that the docs could be bought to do what they ought to do for blacks and the agency was willing to pay high.

"[Our] beliefs led us to be the victims of those whom we were dealing with. Admittedly, a federal demonstration purse has a certain amount of slippage, and even failure advances knowledge. The agency bought its way into the legitimators so that it could say 'we're in with the medical establishment,' " another staff member reported.

But even relatively large amounts of dollars for individual projects were not the major financial incentive for provider-institution participation in the program. A key incentive for most institutions was the overhead costs, which were incurred by the federal grantee in the administration of a project.

For medical provider institutions confronted with spiraling operational costs and highly limited ways of generating adequate capital, such overhead dollars (usually comprising 20 to 30 percent of the total contract) were a boon. Many provider institutions were said to be willing to do business with the federal government in order to acquire sizable overhead costs. These extra dollars were used to subsidize such underfunded components of their operations as laboratories or libraries.

One center administrator rationalized the situation, claiming "The hospital [delegate agency] does get financial benefits from direct and indirect overhead costs which come to 8.8 percent of all salaries and wages . . . but it is locked into a formula and a hospital is a very expensive operation. . . .Moreover, it is involved in large training and research efforts. It may not collect as much as it is supposed to from other sources."

Calculation of the indirect overhead-cost rate and the range of provider activities subsidized by these dollars was a subject of great concern and intense negotiation between Washington and the provider institutions. Providers, especially universities, hoped to negotiate a standard rate each year which was higher than OEO's 20 percent rate (borrowed from the National Institutes of Health). The agency was pressured by the Association of University Treasurers to raise the rate, and ultimately the staff found a loophole which allowed for separate rate negotiations with each provider institution.

Among agency and local center staff, concern was voiced over provider insistence that the rate be constant or upgraded annually because costs were fixed or mounting. Given that start-up costs for a new project may be considerable, it appeared less reasonable for provider institutions to continue to demand the same fixed institutional overhead percentage of the grant after the project had been operating for several years. One center administrator dealing with a provider institution which itself was convinced that it was losing money with 20 percent indirect overhead costs commented, "If you take a small new grant of $30,000 to $40,000, the 26 percent figure may be accurate. But if you get $2 million, there is not a linear relationship. We couldn't see what we were getting for that big a hunk of overhead."

The provision of indirect overhead costs in government grants has been touted as an incentive for participation in publicly funded programs. Undoubtedly, this claim is accurate. But it must be recognized that the provision of such costs can lead to less desirable consequences as well. Grant applicants in the health-care field tended to display a casual "what's selling this year" approach to federally sponsored programs and to draft proposals to meet federal program stipulations. Often little attention was paid to the merits or even the desirability of undertaking a project. An endeavor such as the NHC program was merely "a new focus of academic research and education promoted by the availability of federal funds and articulated by liberal professionals developing their own identity."[13]

Moreover, the institutional overhead system contained no incentives to modify overhead costs over time. As long as the overhead costs were useful to a provider institution, it was unwilling either to lower the rate or to cut back on the absolute amount of dollars, thereby freeing federal dollars for other health centers. When the overhead costs or, rather, the project itself was no longer useful to the provider institution, it was likely to want to disassociate itself completely from the project. Typically, such local situations were ones of enormous confusion and turmoil, if not outright disaster. Moreover, in these situations a reliable, potential alternative federal grantee was not waiting in the wings.

While it would be inaccurate to assume that the overhead system always was causally related to local project difficulties, it must be noted that the overhead system encouraged provider retention of the project, which often put the provider at loggerheads with community activists and local neighborhood-health-center staff chafing under provider rules and administrative practices. For example, provider institutions needing the overhead dollars predictably would be less willing to train low-income consumers to participate significantly in the center's governance or to relinquish control over the center to a nonprofit community corporation, despite the agency's reform agenda and longer-range commitment.

Once the decision was made to give preference to established medical provider institutions, a further choice related to the agency's drive for high visibility and credibility had to be made. Among providers, some types of institutions were more preferable or desirable federal grantees. The agency could favor medical schools, hospitals, medical societies, health departments, or prepaid group practices.

Consistent with the policy decision to seek reliable risk-capital guarantors, it appeared that some provider institutions were more than ordinary reliable guarantors. Their capabilities for providing high-quality medical care were unquestioned; their reputation in medical circles was impeccable. Agency dollars dispensed to such providers might have far greater impact for the entire program, since involving high-status provider institutions would legitimate the program in the eyes of the medical profession, upgrade its status as a reform effort, and counter objections from both the medical profession and the poor that agency funds were merely subsidizing poor people's medicine. Lacking such status connections derived from a close association with an outstanding provider, the local center might also fail to attract better-qualified personnel. In effect, the principles on which mainstream health care operated—status, prestige, and dollars as prerequisites to quality care and legitimacy—were incorporated into the new health-center program.

An appropriate metaphor for these policy considerations is suggested by a pebble thrown into a pond of still water. The pebble makes a splash, and its impact generates a set of ever-widening circles totally out of proportion to the pebble's size. Like the pebble in the pond, agency staff reasoned, "impeccable" sponsors of health-center projects would assist the agency and the centers in making a "splash."

Medical Schools

Medical schools and their teaching-hospital affiliates were preeminently desirable as participants in the NHC program. Both enjoyed high status as purveyors of education and possessors of the most advanced medical knowledge.[14] They had extensive dealings with the federal government, particularly since the 1950s, and claimed to have the capability to manage large sums of money.

A number of the foremost medical schools feared that a commitment on their part to the operating of a neighborhood health center would drain their capabilities. They were unwilling to participate in the program.

Other medical schools and teaching-hospital affiliates were more responsive to the idea. These tended to be characterized by at least one of the following properties: key, liberally oriented, entrepreneurial medical-care delivery reformers on the teaching faculty; extremely limited endowments; extensive pressure from students to become more involved in the routine care of low-income clientele. Despite the presence of a few liberal reformers and students in these institutions, the commitment of many of their key teaching and administrative personnel to the NHC reform agenda was open to question.

Medical schools were identifiable clearly as bastions of that heightened sense of professional expertise which recognizes no lay influence and no substantive patient contributions to medical treatment.[15] In contrast, neighborhood health centers were designed to reduce exaggerated professionalism through such reforms as team medicine (using doctors, nurses, social workers, and community outreach workers for case conferences on patients), the development of paraprofessional job classifications and career ladders, and the creation of institutionalized channels for community input into the centers' operations.

Although some medical schools contained a department of community or social medicine stressing preventive medicine and the total ecology of disease,[16] academic medicine tended to emphasize concrete and specific research, care for acute rather than chronic conditions, a general orientation toward diagnosis, and cure of highly specific diseases and the individual patient.[17] Their teaching-hospital affiliates, while providing invaluable high-quality care for interesting and unusual teaching cases, displayed little interest in the discharged patient. OEO health-care philosophy and neighborhood health centers themselves, in contrast, emphasized preventive, comprehensive, continuous health care marked by recognition that social and cultural conditions not amenable to *conventional* medical care often were crucial factors in high morbidity or mortality rates for low-income communities.

When medical schools came forward as grantees, they were suspected of self-serving motives in many low-income communities. One recurrent type of urban situation which encouraged these suspicions involved university-connected teaching hospitals located in changing or changed neighborhoods where the original clientele departed from the area but still used or controlled the hospital. The hospital board was likely to use the opportunity for center sponsorship as part of an effort to mollify low-income-community hostility without displaying any real commitment to reform.

A classic example of this situation was south Brooklyn's Long Island College Hospital serving in its private rooms a paying, middle-class white population, which had long since left the neighborhood, and an impoverished minority-group patient population in its clinics and wards. An informed observer of the New York medical-care scene commented, "The hospital was trying to deal with its future viability in the community. . . .It could use the neighborhood health center to illustrate its 'we are not uncharitable or unkind' posture."

Temple University's teaching hospital faced a similar situation:

> North Philadelphia was a white blue-collar eastern European enclave housing many "able and deserving students of limited means," the group Temple was specifically founded to serve . . . the character of the surrounding neighborhood changed. Much later, two major events occurred in rapid succession in 1964 and 1965 which tended to bring Temple to the attention of its black neighbors. The first was a major civil disturbance which erupted on the doorstep of the main campus at Columbus Avenue. The campus and its communications facilities were appropriated by the police as a command post for its anti-riot activities. The choice was logical because it contained the only non-hospital phone switchboard large enough to meet the needs of the police force. However, in the mind's eye of some community people, Temple had chosen to serve the enemy. Secondly, in November 1965, by act of the legislature of the Commonwealth of Pennsylvania, Temple University became a state-related institution in the Commonwealth system of higher education. With the resources thus made available, Temple immediately began to expand its physical plant . . . Temple's priorities for space utilization were not compatible with those of the community. Temple's growing pains were being felt by the community not only in the area surrounding the main campus, but also one mile farther north around the Health Sciences Center campus. Here, too, angry people who had no other place to go, were beginning to complain about the service in the emergency room, in the out-patient clinics and on the wards of Temple University Hospital.[18]

In the first OEO funding round (1965 and early 1966), three grants went to medical schools, Tufts University School of Medicine was awarded grants for both a rural and an urban project. Undoubtedly, the presence of well-known medical-care reformers Doctors Jack Geiger and Count Gibson in the Tufts Department of Preventive Medicine was a key consideration in the award. The University of Southern California Medical School also received funds for a neighborhood health center. The Los Angeles proposal had the full support of its dean, Roger Egeberg, who had excellent connections in the federal health bureaucracy and later joined HEW as Assistant Secretary for Health. Another grant was awarded to the South Bronx Montifiore Hospital, the teaching hospital associated with Yeshiva University's Albert Einstein Medical College. The hospital's connections with academic medical-care reformers George Silver and Martin Cherkasky buttressed the credibility of the Montifiore proposal.

Following the initial round of funding, medical schools continued to participate significantly in the program. In addition to the twelve medical schools that were either grantees or administering agencies, faculty of twenty-four schools participated in other ways. These thirty-six schools, accounting for more than one-third of the nation's medical colleges, participated in the development of over half the OEO-aided comprehensive health-services projects.[19]

Medical schools also retained a respectable proportion of agency resources. In 1970, the year of maximum expansion for the program, they ranked third in the number of grants (fifteen) following behind new non-profit health corporations (twenty-five) (some of which replaced medical schools as grantees) and hospitals (nineteen). In dollar amounts, however, they ranked second ($17.2 million) only to new health corporations ($22.1 million). Nonprofit health corporations with ten more grants than medical schools received only approximately $5 million more in funds than did medical schools.[20]

Hospitals

Although hospitals occupy a lesser status in the medical professional hierarchy than medical schools and teaching-hospital affiliates, their importance in the health-care delivery system, especially for low-income clientele, necessitated their inclusion as center sponsors. In many communities, hospitals have been the only facility for medically indigent patients; the hospital emergency room often serves as the general practitioner for the ghetto. Hence hospitals are highly visible and usually irreplaceable for low-income patients.[21]

In many ways, hospitals shared the liabilities previously identified for medical schools. Like medical schools, hospitals often were financially hard-pressed and tended to incur increasingly large operational costs and to accumulate deficits. The OEO provision of indirect overhead costs became the incentive for hospital assumption of a project. Like medical schools, hospitals might be unlikely to surrender control of the operation as long as the financial incentive for participation in the project remained significant.

Like medical-school training, hospital care tends to be organized around crises or episodic illnesses rather than the type of preventive comprehensive ambulatory care espoused by the neighborhood health centers. Hospitals, by virtue of their role as the focal, centralized intake point from private practitioners or from clinics, were likely to experience great difficulty in reconceptualizing their role under the NHC program as a satellite or backup operation for the center. They were likely to encourage the hospitalization of center patients rather than rely on innovative ambulatory-care techniques, despite warnings that hospitalization costs for center patients were not included in federal funds for the center.

Moreover, the traditional nature of hospital governing structures tended to reinforce status quo arrangements and practices. Hospitals have "defied conventional public regulation."[22] Their boards tend to be composed of community notables who feel comfortable with high-status medical professionals, while remaining appropriately deferential to medical- and hospital-administration professional competence. In such a situation, it was clear that neither the trustees nor the medical or administrative staff might be committed to the wide range of health-care delivery reforms which the agency sought to have federal grantees undertake.

As with medical schools and their affiliated teaching hospitals, the motives of hospitals were viewed with suspicion by many of their low-income clientele. Chicago's Mount Sinai Hospital, one of the only alternatives to Cook County Hospital for indigent blacks, was faced with such a situation:

> One rather gloomy evening, the upper middle class trustees of a large Northern urban Jewish hospital looked out and found their hospital surrounded by deteriorating housing, the streets filled with angry people, and the stores of some of their best contributors to the last building fund drive (1965-1966) in flames. These same angry people were dissatisfied with Mt. Sinai's emergency room and outpatient clinics. The trustees finally realized that this situation had not developed suddenly. The original clientele of the hospital had long ago retreated to suburban Skokie before the Southern black migration. The original clientele, to a large extent, still used Mt. Sinai for their in-hospital care, for Mt. Sinai continued to be the workshop of their private physicians. The surrounding community, to a large extent, used Mt. Siani for *all* its care because there was no place else to go. The hospital found itself serving two quite different populations, neither of which was satisfied because of the concessions made to the other. If the hospital was not to lose all its support from the well-to-do Jewish community, the black

community would have to be pacified. The vehicle for this pacification program appeared in the shape of an OEO funded neighborhood health center. Here the community could safely be "involved." Interestingly another arm of the establishment was having some difficulty with this community, because it replaced housing much needed by the people, with parking facilities much needed by the company. Sears, Roebuck came forward with an offer to design the neighborhood health center building and to lend the money for its construction.[23]

Even when a hospital defined itself in the same ethnic terms as its low-income clientele, there was no guarantee that it departed from the conventional institutional disregard of accountability to clientele. Nor was there any certainty that it was regarded highly by its clientele or that its motives would be considered above suspicion. In reviewing the troubled history of a center associated with a "black" hospital, one informant recalled, "we made a wrong assumption—that because there was a black hospital, blacks in the community would like it. But the hospital was incompetent in medicine and had no interest in the poor."

During the first funding round, three hospital-delegate agencies were selected. One grant went to Beth Israel Medical Center to finance ambulatory-care facilities for a program under its aegis affiliated with Gouveneur Hospital, a municipal hospital on the lower east side of Manhattan. The other two grants went to two Chicago institutions, Mount Sinai and Presbyterian Saint Luke. The latter project was identified with medical-care reformer Joyce Lashof.

In succeeding years, hospitals occupied a goodly share of agency resources. Until the major push in 1970 to fund new, nonprofit health corporations, hospitals comprised the largest number of agency grants.[24]

Practitioners

The agency staff was aware of the need to avoid skirmishes with the American Medical Association (AMA). Despite its declining membership during the late 1960s and early 1970s,[25] the AMA still had significant control over the supply of physicians and professional control over the production, pricing, and distribution of medical services.[26] Should the center program bear the brunt of AMA hostility, the likelihood of program success would be severely handicapped.

Although agency dialogue with the AMA was framed in the context of the cardinal professional principle of preserving the patient's freedom of choice, the real issue was the extent to which the centers would be federally subsidized competition on AMA members' turf. Recognition by the AMA that the overwhelming majority of center clientele were unlikely to be the patients of its members helped neutralize organizational opposition to the program. Further, guarantees were provided by the OEO that it would not "compte with" the private sector. Generally speaking, the AMA was supportive of OEO efforts during the late 1960s. It even established a committee on the medical problems of the poor. Later, as OEO waned, it became indifferent to the issue.

During its early years, the agency enjoyed staunch support for the NHC program from the National Medical Association (NMA), the professional organization for black doctors headed by a well-known medical-care reformer, Dr. John Holloman. Successive NMA leadership, however, was far less sympathetic to the center concept and voiced concern at the national level that the centers would interfere with members' private practices.

Freed from the potentially devastating handicap of opposition from the AMA and from the likelihood of negative national publicity from the NMA, the agency was able to focus on the role of local organized medicine in the centers. Local medical societies were synonymous with the local medical establishment. They could not be ignored. Nor could the agency risk antagonizing them. "Medical society opposition to these programs (through political pressure or the denial of eligibility for hospital staff and specialty boards as well as the prospect of higher malpractice insurance rates) makes the going fifty times as tough, " one staff member noted. On the other hand, the agency was acutely uncomfortable at the prospect of local societies becoming grantees. Local societies had no prior organizational experience in delivering health care services.

The compromise perspective was embodied in the agency guidelines:

> Local medical, dental, pharmaceutical and other professional associations must be consulted at an early stage of the planning and on a continuing basis. Every effort must be made to establish close working relationships with professional health personnel who are or will be serving the neighborhood. A professional advisory group may be established both to achieve this participation and to review the quality of care provided.[27]

In most communities, the agency followed strategies which encouraged peripheral involvement for local medical societies. These included hiring a strong medical-society person on the center staff, establishing center-affiliated organizations which included representation from local medical and dental societies, and involving local medical societies in program review and comment, thereby furthering the legitimacy of the centers without allowing any substantive medical-society control over the flow of federal dollars.

Despite staff personal misgivings about the capabilities of the societies, publicly the agency did not eliminate the possibility of federal dollars coming directly to them. "We keep medical societies involved by telling them that if they come up with a better program, we have no principled reason for not funding them," one staff member disclosed.

Most local medical societies remained uninterested in the health center because of their own nonactivist stance regarding society involvement in the direct delivery of services. But in communitees where hostility to group medical practice was expressed through the local medical society, a center could anticipate serious difficulties.

A classic example of this situation occurred in the Bellaire, Ohio NHC project. A local liberal group practice medical foundation with union ties was pitted against the medical society which had applied for an OEO grant and had been rejected. The medical society had strong connections to its congressional representative. The upshot was a congressional investigation of the project which uncovered virtually nothing and, like many such undertakings, left agency senior staff resentful and frustrated.[28]

In another community, the county medical society had applied for a grant and was rejected. After the first year of operation, a staunch medical-society man was fired from the center staff. The medical society threatened to scuttle the project and brought in the state's congressional delegation as well as the university board of regents. One staff member commented, "things got so bad there we were ready to pull out the grant, though there was support and pressure from minority group doctors on our behalf."

Local NMA chapters often were openly hostile to the idea of a neighborhood health center located on their turf. With the advent of increased Medicare and Medicaid funds, these doctors had an even greater interest in expanding their private practices and opposing center activities or the reforms for which the center stood.[29] "Black doctors protect you" and "if we weren't here, no one would be" were their appeals to ghetto dwellers.

Relatively speaking, local NMA chapters were powerless in the larger medical-care delivery system. Black physicians usually had difficulty in capturing government dollars. Either they could not raise the dollars necessary to qualify for federal matching funds or they were untutored in sophisticated methods of grantsmanship and lacked significant access to the political system.[30] But in some communities, where NMA chapters made strong bids to control the flow of center dollars, the agency was forced to neutralize its opposition through compromises which, in some cases affected the reform agenda. In Detroit, for example, black professionals allied with the black community forced the local health department grantee to hire black physicians on a part time basis for the center staff. Both the agency and the grantee opposed this practice for sound reasons. They believed it would have a negative impact on the continuity and comprehensiveness of center health care delivery.[31]

Another source of provider sponsorship was the small number of medical group practices (prepaid capitation or fee-for-service type). Although both types of practice were private and profit oriented, the agency viewed them as a means for structural reform of the delivery system because the most outstanding of these practices were committed to preventive and comprehensive health care and served as models for other group endeavors.

The agency awarded three major contracts to group practices. Two of these awards went to agencies which had long experience in medical-care delivery and were no longer controversial operations (Kaiser Medical Foundation in Portland, Oregon, and Southern Monterey County Medical Group in California); the third award went to a group practice in Ohio (the Medical Foundation of Bellaire) which generated active hostility from the county medical society.

Health Departments

The public sector of the medical-care delivery system, the local health department, was another source of center sponsorship. For the agency, this category of sponsor posed problems. Conventional professional wisdom maintained that there is little (if any) tradition of excellence in medical care delivery under public auspices. One prestigious medical school which was prepared to do nothing more with federal demonstration dollars than restructure its outpatient department informed the agency that it would be ''immoral'' to grant health dollars to the county health department in its stead. Professional snobbery aside, it was the case that the local health department was a vital, albeit last resort health care institution for the poor.

To many medical-care reformers, health departments were plagued by unimaginativeness, vulnerability to political pressures, ''welfare'' attitudes toward the poor, and rigidities accentuated by low civil-service salaries and inflexible job descriptions. Within the agency there was widespread concern that demonstration dollars would be swallowed up in a proliferation of new health-department jobs without any change in the delivery of services to low-income populations. Moreover, the senior staff of OHA, well connected to other sectors of the health-care delivery section through their medical education and Peace Corps experiences, had no history of prior involvement with local health departments.

Nevertheless, several health departments were funded as delegate agencies for health centers (see table 3-1). The Denver Department of Health and Hospitals received one of the first grants awarded by the agency; its director, Sam Johnson, a well-known medical-care reformer, was one of the early developers of the NHC concept. Another grantee health department was located in one of the country's poorest counties (Lowndes County, Alabama, a center for the black power movement in the civil-rights campaigns of the early 1960s). The agency was forced to fund the local health department, despite its often unpalatable attitudes on racial matters,

Table 3-1
New OEO-Aided Comprehensive-Health-Services Project
(millions of dollars)

Administering Agency	1965-1966		1967		1968		1969		1970	
	Number	Amount	Number	Amount	Number	Amount	Number	Amount	Number	Amount
New Health Corporations			8	13.1	3	2.0	2	1.5	12	5.5
Hospitals	4	4.5	7	8.1	2	1.3	4	0.6	2	0.9
Medical Schools	3	4.0	6	10.0	1	1.1			4	2.1
Health Departments	1	1.2	6	6.1	1	1.1				
Group Practices			3	2.0					2	0.8
Other			3	2.2	2	0.7			3	0.4
Total	8	9.7	33	41.5	9	6.2	6	2.1	23	9.7

Source: Untitled OEO document, Washington, 1970.

Note: The totals, by administering agency, are as follows: New health corporations, 25, 22.1; hospitals, 19, 15.4; medical schools, 15, 17.2; health departments, 8, 8.4; group practices, 5, 2.8; other 8, 3.3. This table does not account for refunding of projects in each year.

because there appeared to be no other remotely acceptable provider institution in the county.

The Welfare System at Work: Expansion and Contraction of "Eligible" Recipients of Services

Paralleling the degree of administrative discretion in the choice of project sponsors was the initial degree of discretion in developing classifications of persons eligible for federally funded health-care services. The symmetry in latitude of agency choice for providers and recipients of services reflected the infusion of current, politically acceptable ideas regarding the poor into the policy-implementation process.

During the early and mid 1960s social scientists were beginning to reconceptualize previously held theories concerning the nature of ghetto life. It was an instance of an "unusually successful group dissecting an unusually unsuccessful one."[32] According to the admittedly controversial, revised perspective, ghettos were not simply inhabited by alienated economic individuals who lacked any cohesion and sense of community.[33] Ghettos were communities which had adapted in various ways to the norms and values of the larger society.

Reconceptualized as communities, usually of color, whose members endured disenfranchisement and marginality in the U.S. political and economic system for a far longer duration than the pre-World War II European immigrant poor, these ghettos were seen as possessing viability, vitality, and strength. A new dignity attached to their residents. For planners and other social policy formulators, this revised perspective bolstered proposed strategies for social change premised on the continuity of life within a geographical area.[34]

Influenced by the concept of ghettos as neighborhoods or communities rather than mere traps or social dumping grounds, the OEO choice of client-eligibility criteria was predictable. Faced with the option of geography (all the residents of a defined low-income community) or income (individuals determined to be of sufficiently low income to qualify for social services), the agency chose the geographical, or community, criterion of eligibility. Consistent with the findings of efficient economies of scale at neighborhood health centers, initial agency guidelines required that those seeking funding serve target-area populations of at least 10,000 persons.[35] To the extent that "target area" was coterminous with "community" or "neighborhood," according to the social-science literature, it could be determined by natural geographic boundaries, evidence regarding users of "neighborhood" facilities, cultural characteristics of residents, or residents' perceptions.[36]

Basically, there were three separate bases for agency advocacy of the community criterion of eligibility: the environmental context for health care, the impact of eligibility on low-income persons, and the consequences of income eligibility for the program's operations. The environmental context for health-care-delivery argument relied on the claim that specifically in health matters, income eligibility requirements totally ignored the fact that environmental and social conditions (many of which were associated with poor health status) were not confined to persons within a poor community *below* a limited specified poverty income; rather, these conditions tended to characterize an entire neighborhood regardless of marginal income differences. Moreover, communities characterized by such environmental conditions usually had limited access to medical care whatever the marginal range of income variations among individuals might be.[37]

From this perspective, it was irrelevant whether better "results" would be obtained by treating the "near poor" who were on the threshold of entering the mainstream of U.S. life versus the moral appeal that justice required treating only the "poorest of the poor" who were least able to purchase medical care. The poor might be more needy, but should they be given preference, the near poor would become even more unequal and suffer greater hardships.[38] Basically, the shared character of low-income communities made the gap between the near poor and the poorest of the poor insignificant for purposes of the provision of adequate health-care services to meet local needs.

Another line of reasoning focused on the impact of income eligibility on individuals themselves. For low-income persons, medical-care payments represented a greater loss as a percentage of income than for middle-income persons. Individuals with highly limited resources, when faced with a multiplicity of demands, might well choose to forgo or postpone health care and expend their income on what they viewed as more immediate, essential, and pressing needs. Such a situation has the characteristics of a lottery in which some will be heavy losers.[39]

Moreover, scrutiny of existing individual income eligibility standards developed and used by other agencies revealed that they did not take health needs into account in establishing these standards. Not only was it difficult, if not impossible, to determine what an individual's or family's health needs might be during the course of a given year, but also it was difficult to estimate with any degree of accuracy the cost of that care.

This combination of the failure of the income eligibility standard to address the twin issues of the impact of medical-care payments on family income and assets as well as the failure of a standard to be reflective of health needs was a damning indictment of the income eligibility system.[40] Even if the environmental arguments could be brushed aside, narrow income eligibility classifications appeared to accomplish very little.

The third thrust of the agency's defense of the community criterion of eligibility focused on the consequences of the imposition of an income eligibility standard for the NHC program itself. Income eligibility standards would cast neighborhood health centers as poor people's clinics in the eyes of the medical profession and the poor. Such casting would limit the centers' ability to attract well-qualified medical professionals with a long-term commitment.

For the poor, social service income eligibility touched on raw nerve. Income eligibility was identified with welfare bureaucracy, a system considered highly repressive by its clientele.[41] It served to distinguish the poor from the middle classes who were far less likely to have the experience of being told they were ineligible for a program or benefit. It was, in effect, an announcement of personal failure to society. Should income eligibility be established, the agency maintained, the net result would be the failure of the poor to distinguish innovative OEO health programs from other conventional welfare programs.

Not only would the program be stigmatized in the eyes of providers and consumers, but also it would be divisive within a community. Income eligibility would exclude neighbors who shared the same lifestyle and values, but had a marginally higher income. Communities, the basic structural unit of the program, would be divided into participants and nonparticipants. Community residents who assisted in the organization of the project and were employed by it might then become ineligible for service. Such "artificial" divisions were bound to handicap the effective functioning of the center in a neighborhood or community.

Communitywide eligibility, in contrast, kept open various options with potentially beneficial consequences for the projects. If the neighborhood health centers were to attract other federal or local health dollars burdened with differing eligibility standards, it was best to be as flexible as possible to allow maximum coordination of alternative funding sources with the centers.

For the first two years of the OEO operations, the geographical eligibility criterion was policy. The OEO legislative mandate merely required provision of readily accessible services to residents of poverty areas. "Since no technical capability existed for estimating quickly from the census, or any other source, the characteristics of the poor according to more complex definitions," initially the figure of $3,000 was chosen as the "poverty line."[42] Like other numbers used to establish eligibility for government benefits, the "poverty line" in some important ways was unrelated to the reality it chose to define. The computations failed to take into account urban-rural differentials in the cost of living, the rate of inflation, and the effect of disabling illness on a low-income household. Supplementing income criterion in the pinpointing of poverty areas were other poverty indicators such as housing conditions, density of population, and school dropout rates.

Admittedly, the argument alleging arbitrariness in individual income eligibility could be used against a community eligibility standard as well. At some point, after all, a community's boundaries were defined arbitrarily, and beyond that boundary but in close proximity there might be persons sharing the same income level and lifestyle who would be excluded from the program.

Though exclusion rather than unwelcome inclusion was the anticipated issue for the community eligibility criterion, in fact the latter situation did occur. The definition of the community had to be expanded beyond local perceptions to accommodate administrative requirements. In one project, the director who requested a budget increase was told that the agency could not authorize the requested augmentation unless the community target area was enlarged. According to the project director, "for demonstration purposes it [the project] had originally been small; it was a defined universe with everyone counted. OEO told me 'you've got to do it [enlarge the target area] or the funds will remain the same.' I had to go back and tell the community about 3,000 additional new target-area members [from a distinctly different community nearby]."

The counter to these claims was simply that this "arbitrariness" was much less significant than the oppressive, demeaning income eligibility criterion. In addition, the benefits accruing from the geographical criterion far outweighed the isolated instances of failure to mesh completely with local perceptions.

For the agency, implementation of the geographical eligibility criterion was facilitated by the fact that most of the early applications for grants came from providers associated with urban ghetto communities in which there were visible high concentrations of the medically indigent. Given patterns of residential segregation by race and income, the likelihood of serving a large number of obviously nonpoor was greatly curtailed. According to one staff member, "When we had to give definitions [a politically defensible mix of those in the target area] for utilization of a neighborhood health center, we said that 80 percent had to be under the poverty line. However, no checking of this figure was made by us in the grant itself." And there is no evidence that in the early years the OEO General Counsel's Office made independent checks of these figures, although it kept insisting that programs serve the poorest in any target area first, to protect the agency from congressional criticism.

The ethos of the early and mid 1960s which was reflected in the War on Poverty enabling legislation allowed OEO to operate with a liberal rather than a restrictive clientele definition. When the political climate changed, however, the agency's discretion in clientele definition was removed, and an important component of the agency's initial demonstration flexibility was eliminated.

By 1967, mounting pressure regarding the costs of implementing the War on Poverty led to a congressional change in rules. The requirement for individual eligibility criteria was written into the law and developed into guidelines by OEO.[43] With a stroke of the congressional pen, program clientele were redefined. The agency's commitment to community-based care was eliminated. Some low-income residents of poor communities became the ineligible "near poor." (Only health-center emergency services were available for individuals having incomes above the guideline specifications which allowed centers to choose from either the standards of the state Medicaid program or the OEO poverty index, whichever was the highest.) The poor were reminded of their ultimate political powerlessness.

Perhaps the best way to illustrate the nightmarish situations which congressional establishment of individual eligibility posed is to review a rather extensive section from a General Accounting Office (GAO) audit of OEO's Chicago neighborhood health centers:

The Mile Square Center, which began operations in February 1967 as a research and demonstration project, initially required only that a person live in the target area to be eligible for free care. In June 1967, the center revised its eligibility requirement by adopting a standard for free care which was based on family-income levels applicable to persons living in public housing. This standard was more liberal than either the OEO poverty-line index or the income standard of the State of Illinois Medicaid Program.

After revision of the OEO guidelines in March 1968, the center was required to adopt by November 1968, the start of its next grant period, more stringent standards governing the persons who would be provided free care and a fee schedule for persons not entitled to free care. In response, the center adopted, and OEO approved, a list of seven standards for determining a person's eligibility for free care and a fee schedule calling for a payment for each visit of $0.25 to $7, depending on family size and income level for those persons in the target area who were not eligible for free care under the seven standards. The average cost of services at the center has been estimated by the center at about $33 a patient-visit.

Our fieldwork was completed before the revised standards were to be effective; therefore, we were unable to review the center's experience in applying the standards. However, our analysis of the standards showed that their application would probably result in an inequitable distribution of free care among persons in substantially similar economic circumstances.

For example, one of the standards provides that all persons who were registered at the center as of October 1, 1968, and all members of their families be eligible for free care. In contrast, all persons and members of their families who were not registered as of October 1, 1968, would have to pay a fee for each visit to the center in accordance with the approved fee schedule unless they qualify for free care under one of the other six standards.

The other six standards, when applied, may also result in similar inequitable treatment. For example, a family of four having an income of up to $6,900 and living in public housing is eligible for free care, whereas a family of four not living in public housing or qualifying under one of the other standards is ineligible for free care if its family income exceeds $3,600.

Also, the fee schedule adopted by the center permits persons who are not medically indigent by State standards to receive care at the center at relatively low cost. As shown by the following table, the income levels of persons eligible for care on a fee basis at the center exceed by as much as $3,600 (for a family of eight) the income levels of persons who are medically indigent under State of Illinois Medicaid income standards.

Number of Persons in Family	State Standard for Medical Indigency[a]	Mile Square Center's Fee Schedule	
		Range of Annual Incomes	Range of Fees per Visit
1	$1,800	$1,801 to $ 4,830	$0.25 to $5
2	2,400	2,401 to 5,520	0.25 to 5
3	3,000	3,001 to 6,210	0.25 to 5
4	3,600	3,601 to 6,900	0.25 to 5
5	4,200	4,201 to 7,590	0.25 to 5
6	4,800	4,801 to 8,280	0.25 to 5
7	5,400	5,401 to 8,970	0.25 to 5
8	6,000	6,001 to 9,660	0.25 to 7
9	6,600	6,601 to 10,120	0.25 to 7
10	7,200	7,201 to 10,580	0.25 to 7
11	7,800	7,801 to 11,040	0.25 to 5
12	8,400	8,401 to 11,500	0.25 to 5

[a]Maximum annual incomes under State title XIX (Medicaid) standard.

We believe that the liberal fee schedule may attract to the center a significant number of persons who would not be considered medically indigent under the State standard. A center survey of 533 of its patients, selected at random, showed that about 34 percent had family incomes in excess of the State standard for determining medical indigency.

The center's project director stated that the standard making all members of families from which a member had been registered as of October 1, 1968, eligible for free care was warranted so as not to destroy the center's emphasis on family-centered care. The project director stated, also that she had recognized and had advised OEO headquarters officials of the inequities that could result from application of the other standards of eligibility for a single community, such as the one for public housing residents. The project director stated, however, that the center's advisory council had spent a great deal of time discussing eligibility standards and that the public housing standard was the one decided upon by them.

The project director stated also that she considered the income standard under the State Medicaid program to be unrealistic in "today's" medical market and that the center's experience with the amount of illness and cost of medical care made her believe that the income standard of public housing was not unduly liberal.[44]

Simultaneously, the agency and the individual projects were exposed to far greater political risks. Restrictive individual eligibility required more extensive monitoring of center clientele and provided increased opportunities for evasion and scandals which would impinge on agency and project credibility.

In 1970 the center clientele were redefined yet again to allow some of those persons above the poverty line (up to 20 percent in any community) to use the center on a sliding-scale fee. This was soon abandoned as unfeasible, and direct on third-party payments were required of nonpoverty patients, although partial-payment schedules were established for the "near poor."[45]

While both Washington and the local projects were united in their opposition to income eligibility, once it was mandated by Congress, differences between the OEO and the local projects were bound to develop. From Washington's perspective, every income eligibility cutoff point was arbitrary; allowing a greater range of eligibility did not address the critical policy issue of the provision of community-based medical-care services. For the local projects faced with a congressional *fait accompli*, increasing the income eligibility level might assist the centers and the providers in coping with immediate pressure from the target-area populations. From Washington's perspective, congressional allowance of partial pay scales for center clientele was a partial policy breakthrough having greater long-range effects on the financing of health-care services than short-term shifts in arbitrary income eligibility requirements. From the perspective of the low-income consumer, such partial pay scales were less desirable than a slightly increased income eligibility. And from the center's perspective, the development of partial pay scales was an enormous bureaucratic effort with small likelihood of success because of strong local pressures not to enforce collection of partial fee payments.

Despite valiant efforts by the agency to salvage the concept of delivering health-care services to the broadest possible base in a given geographic area, the initial community-based perspective of the program had been seriously diluted and compromised. Political demand for medical care among those with little effective market demand was subject to congressional manipulation. And partial-payment schedules for the near poor merely served to reinforce the program as essentially poor people's medicine.

4 Agency Strategies for Program Visibility

"Compared to ongoing programs in education, housing or health, the Great Society agencies in the ghettos were relatively insignificant and impermanent institutions."[1] The OEO-funded institutions such as the neighborhood health centers lacked the initial advantages of more conventional, federally funded social-service programs.

To compensate for their newness and relative insignificance, various OEO programs developed strategies to draw favorable attention to their efforts. They perceived that they had to produce visible, impressive program results within a short time[2]—even though "relatively little money was spent, relatively few people were affected, the real problem was hardly touched."[3] The initial health-care policy choice of dispensing dollars to "reliable" provider institutions (discussed in chapter 3) was one strategy which was intended to produce positive, concrete results quickly. Expertise and status appeared to be prerequisite to the successful development and administration of a neighborhood-health-center (NHC) project.

But "reliable" providers alone could not ensure the program of the desired visibility. Other strategies had to be developed which would aid agency efforts. These strategies included the avoidance both of siphons and of the regionalization of the program, the channeling of resources, and the attempt to develop multiple constituencies.

Avoiding Siphons: The Community Action Program and the OEO Regions

Elementary bureaucratic wisdom recognizes that the greater the number of organizational channels through which the flow of agency dollars must course, the greater the dilution of the dollar-dispensing agency's visibility. If the dollar-dispensing agency is secure in its funding and protected by its clientele, visibility may not be a paramount concern, and a multiplicity of bureaucratic channels may be relatively unimportant. But if the dollar-dispensing agency is controversial, and therefore vulnerable, then external bureaucratic layers siphon off limited agency resources and divert public recognition from its endeavors. Siphons may have their own programs for which they are seeking additional dollars. Even if they do not wish to divert the dollars, siphons often develop their own ideas regarding the implementation of the original program and may use their own guidelines to modify the direction of program implementation.

One major siphon within the OEO was the Community Action Program (CAP). It was conceptualized as the multipurpose vehicle for political involvement, organization, and (eventually) achievement of change by the poor on their own behalf. It would provide the means to "fight for an end to alienation, institutionalized dependency, failure, withdrawal, and frustration."[4] This vision of the poor organizing and leading a struggle against the injustice of the status quo assumed that not only would the poor better their lot by involving low-income communities in determining priorities, in planning, and in implementing programs, but also the very nature of U.S. society would be transformed for the better by that struggle.

Funds were granted to a large number of new local CAP agencies which were supposed to reflect a broad cross section of the local political structure, social and welfare organizations serving the community, and residents of the target area to be served. Paradoxically, the poor suddenly were thrust into the position of becoming fund raisers for their community.

These new local agencies, it was argued, could develop relevant programs because they involved the actual or potential clients or often their "representatives" in the development and operation of programs. Moreover, because the local Community Action Agency (CAA) included representatives of existing service agencies as well as politicians, the local CAA could be said to have "touched base" with all the crucial external forces impinging on the community and needed as allies; the CAP notion was an effort to develop a representative structure responsive to a troubled target area.

Rather quickly it became apparent that the grass-roots programming aspect of CAP carried with it enormous liabilities as well as assets. Some programs were embarrassing failures. Other programs were said to "raise the level of perceived and validated discontent among poor persons without actually improving the condition of life among the poor in anything like a comparable degree."[5] Members of Congress were deluged by complaints and allegations from hostile low-income constituents demanding commitment and action and from angry local civil servants who apparently had viewed the program simply as a "means for coordinating at the community level the array of conflicting and overlapping programs that proceeded from Washington in ever increasing numbers."[6]

Not surprisingly, as pressures mounted, the Washington CAP office which Congress held accountable for the activities of local CAPs became merely one casualty in the assault on the entire community-action concept. It was an instance of blaming the victim.

The major initial congressional response to these pressures was a modification of the OEO program in 1966. The undifferentiated funds authorized for CAP were packaged into various categorical programs such as legal assistance, emergency food, and health affairs. Packaging provided Congress with increased leverage over the total OEO appropriation; Congress could specify sums for various favorite programs and require more precise program definition.

Packaging generated intense efforts by various OEO programs to deal with members of Congress who were sympathetic to the aims of specific programs rather than the community-action concept. The Office of Health Affairs (OHA) staff engaged in a public-relations campaign to cement ties to key congressional sympathizers. They promised concrete, visible, documented program results for federal dollars instead of a number of small, often politically volatile programs organized by CAP. Congressional fears concerning the quality of services in the center were assuaged by the emphasis on medical professional input into the program.

Freed from the political liability of AMA opposition (see chapter 3), the OHA staff could highlight in glowing terms the seemingly politically "neutral" aspect of health programs to some members of Congress. "In Watts, the angriest, most militant leaders can sit down with a very conservative professor of medicine, and their differences seem to melt away because they are talking about a real problem in which their interests coincide."[7]

Finally, the agency staff could remind Congress of health-center program compatibility with popularly accepted Victorian distinctions between the deserving and the undeserving poor (those whose impoverishment was the consequence of unforeseeable events and those whose poverty was the result of laziness or an unwillingness to work hard). At least the deserving poor were likely to become reliable, productive citizens if their health problems, which might be the source of their impoverishment, were attended to by competent medical professionals.

With 1966 categorical funds at their disposal, OEO staff was provided with the fiscal base to establish the OHA as an independent operational unit. Within the OHA, Comprehensive Health Services (CHS) was charged with development and implementation of the NHC program.

The vestigial remnant of the struggle to free the NHC program from CAP's aegis can be found in the conduit role assigned to CAP as grantee agency in the Comprehensive Health Services (CHS) guidelines:

A. Relationships to Community Action Agencies

Except in unusual circumstances, in any community which has a recognized community action agency (CAA), the local CAA should serve as the grantee and the health care institution should administer the project as the delegate agency. An agency which proposes to operate a comprehensive health services project should submit the proposed project plan to the local CAA for application to OEO.

If a potential operating agency seeks direct funding from OEO, it should submit with its application the following material:

1. A description of the efforts made to submit the program through the local CAA.
2. A description of the response to such efforts by the local CAA.
3. An explanation of why the applicant believes it is necessary to secure direct funding from OEO.
4. A description of procedures for coordination and program linkages with the CAA.

Whenever OEO receives an application for direct funding of an operating agency rather than fundng through the local CAA, it will contact the local CAA for a statement of its position on the application. OEO will determine how to fund the project, if approved, on the basis of the information received from the applicant, the CAA and other interested parties. This procedure also applies to refunding applications.

When the grant is made to a CAA, an agreement is required between the CAA and the health care institution which is to be the operating and delegate agency. The provisions of the OEO Standard Contract Form for the conduct and administration of Community Action Program components indicate the general requirements for such an agreement.[8]

The local CAP function was limited to formal sign-off of federal dollars upon Washington's request. Indirect costs allowed to the local CAP were minimal and did not constitute a significant drain on health-center program resources.

The other major potential fiscal- and power-duluting siphon which the agency sought to avoid was the OEO regions. Although OEO's initial operation was Washington-based, over time the agency was confronted with the same arguments against centralization of functions which always have haunted social-service bureaucracies—effectiveness and responsiveness to a wide range of local situations.

As OEO operations expanded, pressure to establish regional offices mounted. In 1967 the OEO capitulated. Quite predictably, a struggle between the regional offices and OEO headquarters ensued over program control and the allocation of resources. Regional offices pressed for political, not mere administrative, decentralization.

Since all CAP programs operated through OEO regions and since, in theory, all neighborhood health centers had CAP grantees, the regional offices sought to control the NHC program. Publicly, the OHA staff viewed the regionalization issue as a nuisance. It had low priority for an operation which was developing a service as valuable as health care. Privately, they were concerned about the likelihood of regional responsiveness to parochial demands emanating from powerful local interest groups. For the health-care reform agenda, responsiveness to such demands would be a retrograde step.

In the struggle to avoid health projects being subjected to regional control, the OHA staff were assisted by the fortuitous accession of other OEO programs to decentralization. Consequently, less pressure was put on the health-program operation to decentralize. But short-term breathing space was not reassuring for the staff. To avoid the reemergence of regional bureaucratic appetites and pressures, the Washington staff mounted a campaign to ensure regional recognition and acquiescence to the proposition that professionalism was needed in the administration and delivery of health-care services and that only Washington possessed that expertise. After a protracted struggle in Washington, the OHA emerged as the only office within the OEO operation that managed to avoid regionalization.

Channeling Resources

The production of visible results required more than the avoidance of such siphons as CAP and the OEO regions. Visible results meant affirmative results out of proportion to the relatively modest NHC budgets. While informants were unable to specify clear criteria for determining when results were disproportionate to dollars spent, the tenor of their remarks suggests that they were referring to both the *rapid creation of new medical-care* facilities which served *sizable numbers* of clients and the delivery of *high-quality, reasonably priced care*. (According to medical-care delivery experts, between 10,000 and 30,000 clients was the desirable range for a successful neighborhood health center.)

To assist in the creation of impressive, visible results, the agency made several key resource channeling decisions. First, given the billions of dollars flowing annually into the health-care system, it was imperative not to subsidize existing medical-care services which already had alternative funding sources or which, by their size and nature, would consume OEO dollars without much payoff or, in some instances, even without a trace. Second, to heighten agency and project visibility, it was necessary to avoid extensive planning grants and to concentrate on funding operational situations. Third, to maintain the image of sizable effective interventions in the medical-care delivery system, it was desirable to fund large-scale ambitious projects. Finally, since visibility ultimately depended on the actual delivery of services, it was appropriate that the agency and the grantee find adequate facilities for the delivery of services within a short time.

Avoiding Subsidies to the Status Quo

The need for high visibility and the commitment to demonstrating new forms for the delivery of health care meant that precious OEO dollars ought not to be spent on subsidizing other federally funded health-care services. The reverse situation was far more desirable. Under the rubric of coordination of existing resources, the agency sought to capture other federal dollars, thereby freeing demonstration dollars for innovative delivery practices. To this end, the OHA guidelines contained a section devoted to coordinating health funds and services:

> OEO cannot fund services for which support is already available. OEO funds are a "last dollar" resource to help fill gaps in existing services.

> The comprehensive health services project should be integrated or coordinated with all existing publicly supported health services in the area. This includes Children's Bureau Maternal and Infant Care projects and Children and Youth health projects; Public Health Service health services projects; Regional Medical Programs; mental health services; vocational rehabilitation services, etc. The comprehensive health services project shall negotiate with each of these resources to have their services delivered to the neighborhood's families through the comprehensive program—or, in the case of highly specialized services, in close coordination with the neighborhood program.[9]

> Arrangements must be made so that the comprehensive health services project is linked with related anti-poverty efforts, such as manpower and education programs, neighborhood service centers, Head Start programs, etc. These linkages should facilitate employment, education and other steps to self-sufficiency of residents of the poverty neighborhood.[10]

Supplementing these instructions to capture program funds were a set of guidelines regarding the capture of dollars available through existing federal and state third-party reimbursement programs.

> In addition, the comprehensive health services project should work out with appropriate local and State agencies arrangements whereby all Federal, State and local programs (including particularly welfare medical care payments for persons on public assistance and for other needy persons) which now provide funds for health services are integrated within the comprehensive health program. (See the Joint Statement of the Department of Health, Education, and Welfare and the Office of Economic Opportunity concerning "Coordinated Funding of Health Services.")[11]

From a theoretical perspective, the guideline instructions were reasonable and consistent with the centers' objectives. But the likelihood of capturing funds from other programs was minimal. Dollar dispensing means power and influence for an agency. As the OHA staff husbanded its funds, so did other agencies. Consequently, "coordination" remained a bureaucratic hope rather than an administrative reality.

Reimbursement from third parties for services delivered by the center appeared equally reasonable and consistent with center objectives. And collecting dollars from sources whose sole function was to dispense dollars for services rendered by others appeared to be a less controversial and difficult undertaking than capturing the program dollars of other social-service bureaucracies. Again, the gap between the brave bureaucratic hopes in the guidelines and administrative realities (detailed in chapter 6) was an enormous one.

The resource channeling strategy adopted by the OHA was evident in its position regarding two other issues: local project payment for center patient hospitalization and the calculation of the rate for grantee indirect overhead. In both instances, the resource channeling strategy pitted the NHC reform agenda against harsh economic realities.

Hospital care is the most expensive form of medical care. Not surprisingly, hospitals consume a disproportionate share of available medical care dollars for low-income families.[12] Nevertheless the hospitalization rate for low-income families is proportionately greater than for the rest of the population. One identifiable source for this disparity is the health status of the poor; they are more likely to develop chronic disabling conditions requiring hospitalization. The other identifiable source for this disparity in the rate of hospitalization is the tendency of low-income persons to wait until they are seriously ill and may require hospitalization before seeking medical advice as well as the limited ambulatory-care facilities available in publicly supported hospitals.

To demonstrate that reliance on hospitalization was excessive and could dilute the impact of the preventive, comprehensive, ambulatory care approach of the neighborhood health centers as well as to prevent spiraling hospitalization costs from consuming the bulk of precious demonstration dollars, the Congress and the agency chose to minimize the issue of center responsibility for clientele hospitalization costs.

In its report on the Economic Opportunity Amendments of 1966, which first authorized CHSP, the Senate Committee on Labor and Public Welfare stated that "the actual cost of institutional care is not to be financed under the provisions of this section except in *highly unusual circumstances*." [*underscoring supplied*.] The Committee did not state what those circumstances were to be. In February 1967, OEO issued guidelines which repeated the Committee's statement but did not further define what those circumstances would be.[13]

To ensure comprehensive care when NHC ambulatory facilities could not meet patients' special needs, centers were encouraged in the agency's revised guidelines to develop linkages with hospitals as backup facilities.

> Specialized diagnostic procedures must be definitely arranged for elsewhere by the staff. Where services are provided through a Neighborhood Health Center, the Center must provide a direct link to a hospital for diagnostic or therapeutic needs which cannot be met by laboratory and X-ray facilities and the personnel of the Center. In-patient care must also be arranged, with the patient's Health Center physician maintaining continuity of care. Arrangements between the hospital and the Center must assure high quality, continuous, personalized care for the hospitalized patient, consistent with the hospital's best practices (which may in the past have been applied only to "private" patients).[14]

There is a noticeable absence of discussion in these guidelines regarding center assumption of responsibility for patient hospitalization costs. The silence is understandable. It is indicative of the policy dilemma faced by the agency.

Nevertheless, the issue of hospitalization costs continued to haunt the agency. The GAO Chicago report provides an excellent case illustration of the problem:

> OEO had not sufficiently defined the circumstances in which its funds could be used to finance hospitalization costs, and, as a result, the Mile Square Center had established a policy of using OEO funds to finance hospitalization at the Presbyterian-St. Luke's Hospital, its sponsoring hospital, to the extent that OEO funds were available, whenever center physicians considerd hospitalization to be necessary.

> At the close of our fieldwork, efforts were being made by OEO health officials to have the center establish priorities to most effectively use the limited funds that were provided to it for hospitalization costs but OEO had not yet sufficiently defined the specific circumstances in which hospitalization costs could be paid with OEO funds. . . .

> The center's initial grant proposal stated that Cook County Hospital was the only institution available for hospitalization of the medically indigent in Chicago but that, as a result of overcrowding, hospitalization at the Cook County Hospital could not be guaranteed even when the physician believed it necessary. The proposal stated that, unless adequate funds were provided to ensure hospitalization, when deemed necessary by the center staff, in a hospital where the staff could supervise the care, the concept of comprehensive care was in jeopardy.

> The center's first grant approved by OEO in June 1966 prior to enactment of the 1966 amendments provided funds for hospitalization costs, as requested by the center, for patients not covered by third parties, such as private insurance companies, Medicaid, and CCDPA. In approving the grant, OEO placed no further conditions on use of the funds provided for hospitalization.

During the center's first grant period, the director of OMC, on behalf of CHRF, made arrangements with Cook County Hospital whereby center patients, for whom there were no third parties available to pay for hospitalization, would be referred to Cook County Hospital by the center. The center, however, chose not to accept such arrangements even though it recognized that the Presbyterian-St. Luke's Hospital probably could not meet the entire demand for hospitalization as registrations at the center expanded toward its target of 20,000 persons.

For the center's second grant period, which began in October 1967 subsequent to the enactment of the 1966 amendments, OEO reduced the $500,000 requested by the Center for hospitalization to $250,000 but it left the specific circumstances under which hospitalization costs would be incurred to the discretion of the center. A center official informed us that, to provide for the continuity of care of its patients, the center continued to refer its registered patients to the Presbyterian-St. Luke's Hospital as necessary.

In July 1968, about 2 months before the scheduled close of its second grant period, the center requested OEO's approval to use an additional $150,000 of the available grant funds to cover costs of hospitalizing center patients at the Presbyterian-St. Luke's Hospital during the remainder of the grant period. This request, however, was not approved by OEO health officials on the basis that CHSP is to emphasize comprehensive ambulatory care and it would take the major portion of funds allocated to CHSP to provide for all necessary hospitalization of patients for whom no third-party reimbursements are obtainable. OEO health officials recommended that the center establish priorities to most effectively use the funds that had been provided for hospitalization. . . .

In approving the center's third grant proposal in November 1968, 21 months after the center opened, OEO approved $300,000 of the approximately $600,000 requested by the center for hospitalization at the sponsoring hosptial. Again, OEO approved the grant without defining, or requiring the center to define, the specific circumstances in which these funds would be expended. To encourage the center to establish priorities for use of the approved funds, however, OEO provided in the grant for a monthly limitation on the amount of funds that could be used for hospitalization.

Further, OEO health officials discussed with officials of the Cook County Hospital, just prior to approval of the grant, possible cooperative arrangements—including the hospitalization of neighborhood health center patients—between the neighborhood health centers and the hospital. The OEO health officials believed that the Cook County Hospital officials were receptive to these arrangements and directed center officials to continue negotiations in this regard.

However, significant additional use of the Cook County Hospital, particularly if additional neighborhood health centers are established in other poverty areas in Chicago, may not be a solution to the problem of financing hospitalization costs of the medically indigent who are not covered by third-party payment programs. At the time it submitted the Mile Square Center's third-grant-period proposal, CHRF estimated that 30 percent of

Chicago's 1.33 million poverty population was medically indigent and not covered under any third-party payment program.

Also, the Cook County Hospital is the one charity source of medical care available to the medically indigent in Chicago, and a November 1968 Chicago Regional Hospital Study, funded by a grant from the National Institutes of Health, HEW, reported that the Cook County Hospital, traditionally an acute-care facility, was overcrowded. The study suggested that some type of payment arrangement be established whereby other hospitals could be reimbursed by the Cook County government for treating the medically indigent who would normally be referred to the Cook County Hospital.

However, on the basis of a 1967 survey of hospital facilities in Chicago that showed a shortage of hospital beds, private hospitals located in or adjacent to the poverty areas may not be able to meet the demand for hospitalization if it is to be provided to the medically indigent on a widespread scale, especially on the "as necessary" basis established by the Mile Square Center.

In discussions with OEO health officials, we were informed that, in general, due to the importance of local initiative and the demonstration nature of the health centers, they did not intend to define the specific circumstances in which hospitalization costs could be reimbursed with OEO funds.

. . . OEO, in its comments on this report, informed us that:

> The staff of the Mile Square Center believes that standards for continuity of care and high-quality service require maximum effort to care for patients at the affiliated, backup hospital [Presbyterian-St. Luke's Hospital]. Similarly, the Neighborhood Health Council has indicated strong resistance to the use of Cook County Hospital. They have been working strenuously [sic] to find a solution which will maintain high-quality standards and overcome the limitations imposed by available funds and restrictive local, state and national policies. After extended efforts, a feasible solution to this need is in sight.

> . . . The OEO staff has implemented its responsibility to restrict the amount of OEO funds budgeted for hospital care. At the same time, the staff has looked to local experiences to guide the development of the most effective policy guidelines. In this respect, as in others, the evolving experiences of the CHS projects have provided important new learning.

> The draft Audit Report notes the continuing attention which has been given this matter by both Center and OEO staff in the administration of this project. In fact, the amount of OEO funds budgeted for hospital care has been reduced over half.

> On the basis of local experiences to date in the operations of CHS projects, the following factors have been identified as key consideration in the allocation of limited OEO funds for hospital inpatient care:

1. Quality and acceptability of the local public hospital
2. Scope of the State Title XIX program
3. Policies of the local voluntary hospitals
4. Efforts of the local CHS project to limit needs for hospitalization.

Although OEO has taken steps to restrict the amount of OEO funds budgeted for hospital care at the Mile Square Center, it has not developed standards as to the circumstances under which the restricted amount is to be used by the center. Such standards on a national level are necessary to implement the intent of the Congress that OEO funds be used to provide hospitalization only in highly unusual circumstances and to ensure equitable treatment to participants in all CHSP projects. Therefore we continue to believe that the Director of OEO should define the "highly unusual" circumstances under which OEO funds may be used to finance the costs of hospitalization.[15]

One final area in which the agency attempted to achieve strategic visibility with its dollars and to avoid subsidies to the existing system was in the negotiations for overhead costs to provider institutions. As chapter 3 suggests, overhead costs often were a significant incentive for involvement in the program itself. Agency staff were aware that overhead dollars could free provider institution dollars for other conventional functions. The health center, like a medical-school department of community medicine, all too often could become a mere appendage in an institution which persisted in operating in a conventional "professional" mode.

Planning versus Operational Grants

The shifting sands of intellectual faddism had brought to the federal bureaucracy a flood of ideas regarding remediation of the condition of the poor in U.S. society.[16] Sorting and preliminary testing mechanisms were needed. One such program mechanism was the planning grant, designed to clarify project direction and development before it underwent full-scale operation and risked costly operational mistakes. Planning grants provided a modicum of visibility to a program while protecting a federal agency from the consequences of a ghastly, highly publicized mistake.

But the price of this protection was viewed by the OHA staff as an excessively high one. Planning grants were resource consumers without any immediate, visible impressive results. They encouraged delays in implementation, clearly the more difficult task. And ultimately they tended to put off the best people who, activist Washington staff asserted, became serious and committed to a project only when it actually was operational.

Consequently, agency policy, especially between 1965 and 1968, was to work closely with prospective sponsors to develop the grant and then to fund the operational stage. In late years, however, planning grants were awarded. In 1970 sixteen planning grants were awarded; in 1971 the number was increased to twenty-one.

This policy shift is explained by two considerations. By the fifth year of program operations, there were relatively few outstanding applicants who were committed to the agency's reform agenda or who displayed the capability to manage and implement the reforms. But even if such qualified applicants had existed by 1970, the focus of federal health-care funding was shifting. Congress and the administration were now interested in developing coordination mechanisms for existing medical services through community health networks [the precursor to the more ambitious community efforts undertaken by HEW in the Health Maintenance Organization (HMO) program]. Agency funds were cut back. Less dollars, a new more modest focus, and the loss of the most innovative Washington staff combined to effectuate the policy shift.

Finding Readily Available Facilities

The issue of facilities acquisition offers an excellent insight into the enormous, unanticipated, practical difficulties handicapping a demonstration endeavor in its race against time and in its efforts to prevent the dilution of the reform agenda. A prerequisite to the delivery of health-care services to a large target-area population is the existence of a sizable facility. If it is a demonstration program, the health-care delivery project operates with the imperative that facilities must be developed rapidly, must be visible, and, if clientele have other sources of care, must be satisfactory to clientele so that they will participate in the program.

Facility construction is a source of significant constraint in a demonstration program. Construction costs are "sunk costs."[17] Brick-and-mortar-investments tie up resources and reduce organizational freedom. Facility construction tends to soak up limited, precious demonstration dollars. It delays vitally important program implementation.

Initially, agency staff looked to the renovation of existing buildings for health centers within the target areas. They reasoned that renovation could speed the creation of operational programs as well as serve as a symbolic encouragement and source of inspiration to the low-income neighborhood. Community persons, on the other hand, tended to view this outlook as evidence of the agency's acceptance of the myth that the poor would be content with less than the rest of the United States. They wanted the "civilized environment" associated with middle-class mainstream medicine—private, quiet, and air-conditioned.[18]

Agency staff who had no previous experience in facility construction soon discovered that renovation was an expensive proposition. "We searched through the South Bronx and Watts to lease places. In the South Bronx we found a warehouse under the Third Avenue El, but to make it habitable we needed extensive renovations. So we began to find ourselves doing $0.75 million renovation jobs," a staff member recalled.

Again, the GAO Chicago report is instructive and revealing:

> Through the renovation and use of temporary facilities, certain health services were being provided to an increasing number of the Mile Square Center's target-area residents. However, because sponsors of the center had been unable to secure a permanant facility or an acceptable site on which a new facility could be constructed, grant funds had been used to lease and substantially renovate two existing buildings which, because of a short remaining useful life or limited available space, are considered temporary facilities. In addition, primarily because of the space limitations, program emphasis had been placed on the treatment of only certain health needs of area residents, and the provision of all health services through a single comprehensive health facility, as intended, had not been realized.

> At the time of OEO's approval of the center's initial grant in June 1966, arrangements had not been made for a facility to house the center. In a letter dated July 26, 1966, CHRF informed OEO of the preliminary results of an architectural firm's feasibility study in which all existing buildings in the Mile Square Center target area were investigated in an effort to locate an acceptable facility for the proposed center. The study disclosed that only two buildings were available which could possibly be adapted for center use.

> Of the two buildings, the architects recommended the three-story, city-owned structure, centrally located in the target area. The architectural firm's report on its study stated that the need for rapid development of the center to an operational state provided an overriding consideration to the feasibility of using the city-owned structure. The report stated further that the overall floor space available was adequate for early phases of center operation and that remodeling could be accomplished within a much shorter time period than could comparable new construction. In August 1966, a 3-year lease arrangement between the city and Presbyterian-St. Luke's Hospital was established whereby the city-owned building would be made available for center purposes at a rental rate of $1 a year.

> In an October 1966 meeting between officials of Presbyterian-St. Luke's Hospital and the architectural firm, it was emphasized that use of the city-owned building for the center was to be considered a temporary measure. The planned period of use of the building was not to be much more than 1 year after remodeling, and the estimated maximum period of use of the building before demolition or further remodeling would be required was not to exceed 2½ years.

> In October and December 1966, OEO approved the use of funds from the center's operating budget for renovation of the city-owned building. The

center became operational in February 1967 and, as of July 1967, total funds expended for remodeling amounted to about $158,500.

Although the remodeled building provided about 12,000 square feet of space and was considered to be adequate for the initial phases of center operations, CHRF officials were estimating, by the beginning of the second program period in October 1967, that at least 20,000 square feet would be needed to serve the 20,000 area residents who would seek assistance at the center. The OMC director informed us that the traditional space standard for providing health services was at least 1 square foot for each person in the target population.

In applying for refunding of the center for the second program period, CHRF informed OEO that, because of limited facilities, the center was faced with two alternative courses of action: (1) to close registration and, with the existing staff, provide in-depth health services to about 10,000 area residents or (2) to expand the program to reach 20,000 residents. In recommending the second alternative, CHRF emphasized to OEO that additional space and facilities would be needed.

In approving the application for refunding, OEO agreed that health services should be made available to more target-area residents. Therefore, in October 1967 CHRF requested OEO's permission to lease and renovate a building located near the center which would provide an additional 10,000 square feet to be used for dental, mental, and social services and for public health nursing.

In approving CHRF's request in June 1968, OEO defined the provisions under which the additional building, a former warehouse, could be leased and renovated. Because the building had been purchased by Presbyterian-St. Luke's hospital and had an estimated value of $60,000, annual rental was not to exceed $9,000 until cumulative payments totaled $60,000. Thereafter, the hospital is not to levy, on the Federal Government or any of its designees, rental costs for the space occupied in the building, except for charges for upkeep, taxes, and insurance. In addition, OEO authorized up to $330,000 to be used for extensive renovation of the building to make it suitable for center purposes. The renovation was scheduled for completion in February 1969, at which time expanded health services were to have been offered to a greater number of target-area residents.

In its August 1968 application for refunding of the center for the third program period, CHRF informed OEO that, although the additional space to be provided by the renovated building would help alleviate acute aspects of the center's space problem, it would not solve the problem. The application stated that a new permanent facility must be constructed to house all the clinical services but that, despite continuing efforts on the part of many people, acquisition of land for this purpose had not been accomplished.[19]

The search for other funding sources for facility construction proved unsatisfactory. The major obvious source, Hill-Burton hospital construction money, was directed toward ends which were incompatible with the agency's reform agenda. Hill-Burton dollars were administered through the states and were authorized for rural inpatient facilties, whereas OHA usually was concerned with ambulatory-care facilities in an urban area.

Finally, recognizing the symbolic and practical need to construct buildings despite the liabilities that construction entailed, the agency sought a mandate from Congress allowing the agency to provide "anything necessary to support services." And ironically, but understandably, OHA ended up with one of the larger government-supported construction programs within the OEO, although the language of the Guideline Policy Governing Support of Physical Facilities does not mention the term *construction*:

> Whenever the application requests funds for the rental or equivalent acquisition and renovation or for other steps necessary to make available and improve an appropriate physical facility for the provision of comprehensive health services, the request will be evaluated in terms of the following:
>
> a. The suitability and location of the facility.
> b. The efforts which have been made to secure and utilize funds available from other resources including the Department of HUD, the Department of HEW, the Economic Development Administration, public and private welfare agencies and other private sources as well as the applicant and delegate agencies' ordinary sources of funds.
> c. The arrangements which have been made for assuring the continued availability of the facility for the program at the option of the applicant and delegate agencies and the OEO.
> d. The costs of rental or acquisition including the residual value of any improvements to be made to the facility as compared to a fair rental for the term of the use of the facility in the program and the costs of alternative sites in the community.
>
> When funds are approved for provision of physical facilities, the use of such funds must conform with the OEO guidelines with respect to real estate appraisals, site feasibility studies, architectural design contracts, construction contracts, etc.[20]

In implementing its construction program, the agency was aided fortuitously by the passage of Federal Housing Administration (FHA) legislation guaranteeing construction loans for medical group-practice facilities and by the fact that there were relatively few applicants for the funding guarantees. (The principal source of financing was the "Billion-Dollar Fund" established by more than 150 insurance companies across the country for the support of construction activities in urban ghettos.) It turned out that even with the support of FHA, according to one knowledgeable informant,

> It was an enormously complex operation at the local and regional levels to get the centers insured. The local FHA representative didn't know much about it because very few group-practices buildings had been built. FHA

people were technically and professionally oriented, while we were
community- and health-oriented, so there wasn't a lot of common ground.
Centers found that they had to hire intermediaries, primarily lawyers and
consultants, to enter into a dialogue with FHA. In the early years, it meant
a fight in every local FHA office. Basically, old line agencies are geared to
do mass types of things like writing up mortgages and issuing checks.

In addition, there were serious disparities between OHA and FHA financing arrangements which reflected the limited time framework within
which the former operated. The FHA tended to insure more conventional
operations; it required a 10 percent downpayment from a project with the
remaining 90 percent to be repaid in seven years in return for a 90 percent
FHA guarantee. Neighborhood health centers, depending on the political
mood of Congress and the Executive and operating on a yearly basis, had
no assurance that the program would be refunded in future years and could
not commit themselves to such an arrangement. In effect, the centers and
the agency both needed an underwriter. The OEO sought the assistance of
HEW which, in turn, agreed to allow the Public Health Service to certify
the applicant project's viability as a prepaid group practice.

To the bureaucratic headaches generated by interagency dealings were
added the host of problems incurred by becoming a program with a construction component. Some problems were technical, such as determining
retention or removal rights to the facility. Other issues involved the agency
in coping with federal requirements designed to alleviate the consequences
of systemic patterns of discrimination against minority groups. Staff energy
was expended to seek out the highly limited number of black architects to
design facilities. Good-faith efforts were made to utilize minority groups'
construction contractors, but many of them could not meet minimal bond-
ing requirements for federal contracts. Even more insoluble was the
problem of dealing with unions known to discriminate against minority-
group members. Administratively, there were no national solutions to these
issues for the agency. On a case-by-case basis, the staff became involved in
unanticipated program intricacies of the most complex sort.

To the difficulties of coordination efforts and to the problems
generated by systemic racial discrimination were added the headaches of involvement in real estate transactions. A world of local real estate politics
surfaced to haunt the agency. Agency staff discovered that real estate ap-
praisals were not objective, neutral devices. They could be geared to the appropriate context; a burned-out piece of ghetto property could be considered useless land, thereby necessitating a low appraisal and a low selling
price, or prime community property, with the resulting higher appraisal and
selling price. Local promoters and entrepreneurs, aided by federal requirements that government real estate transactions be made public, tended
to engage in profitable speculative deals through dummy corporations with
a consequent discernible inflationary impact on local real estate.

In sum, the agency's unavoidable involvement in facility construction cost it both time and money. More importantly, it raised thorny political issues with communities and with other federal agencies, thereby drawing agency staff into activities for which they lacked technical expertise and largely were unprepared.

Such a conclusion, buttressed by hindsight, ought not fault individuals within the agency. On reflection, one might more accurately conclude that reformers involved in social-change demonstration projects which, almost by definition, are built on expansive general ideas are likely to assume that management considerations are routine and relatively unimportant. But over time such considerations may force an agency to dispense resources into program components it ignored or minimized.

Making "Big Splashes"

To produce visible results, the agency had to avoid resource-consuming activities with limited payoffs. In addition, it had to supplement avoidance strategies with affirmative strategies to get maximum mileage out of each dollar dispensed. To this end, the agency used the "making big splashes" strategy to heighten the impression among critics and allies alike that the agency was "doing something big." In sharp contrast to the typical funding pattern of social-service agencies, which encouraged hundreds of relatively small, unambitious starts by scattering operational seed money around the country, OHA decided to pour larger amounts of dollars into fewer projects.

The first eight demonstration projects (funded before the 1966 congressional earmarking of OEO funds) received a total of $10 million. The following year, thirty-three new programs plus the existing eight received $50.8 million. On average, each project received at least $1 million, reflecting both the agency attempts to continue the big-splash policy and the high cost of establishing a quality ambulatory-care facility.

These big splashes, the agency reasoned, would be far more likely to attract the support and commitment of prestigious medical provider institutions. Big splashes would be more likely to provide high-quality medical care. Big splashes, if successful, would be more likely to serve as a visible source of inspiration to other communities to replicate the demonstration project. Money, prestige, and success were inextricably tied to one another.

Successful big splashes, which for a combination of reasons (their size, the amount of dollars invested in them, their symbolic political significance, and the caliber of their leadership) were showplace projects, could blanket out the less successful projects. The Martin Luther King Neighborhood Health Center in the Watts section of Los Angeles was one such big splash. The agency had expended a great deal of time and money on the project which served a sophisticated urban black population. It was the first center to be transferred from provider institution sponsorship to the control of a community health corporation; it was the first center with twenty-four-hour emergency service. OHA used the project to illustrate the potential of the health center idea. The center in Mound Bayou, Mississippi which served a rural black population was infused with symbolic political significance. It had received extensive publicity from its inception and when it became apparent that the Nixon administration might capitulate to the political forces seeking to destroy the center, a nationwide magazine was persuaded to write a story detailing the center's heroic efforts to provide health care to a visibly deprived population.

Finding Political Supports

A major theme in studies of bureaucracy is agency survival and growth through the development of a political base or clientele to muster support and to deflect opposition.[21] Such political supports for an agency may come from within the government or from a sector of the public which stands to benefit from agency programs and dollars. These political supports assist in making agency programs visible and generate excellent publicity for its endeavors. Especially for a relatively small-scale, highly controversial undertaking such as the neighborhood health center, political supports may amplify the impact of agency visibility strategies.

Studies of the political forces operating at the time of the drafting and passage of the Economic Opportunity Act of 1964 reveal that the legislation was drafted and passed by a coalition of highly diverse political forces.[22] The history of the OEO provides evidence that this coalition lacked the cohesion and firm commitment to maintain the program at a high funding level.

The OEO enjoyed a brief moment of splendor and widespread political support in its early days as a new program. New programs are "a commodity on the electoral market." As a political commodity, their exchange value for electoral support is more important than their use value. Once the price is realized in the political market, new programs lose much of their value except insofar as something tangible must be demonstrated at the time of the next electon.[23] The attention span of elected officials is short.

Existing bureaucracies are alternative sources of support to elected officials. Since demonstration agencies often "pick up the pieces" of the efforts and failures of conventional agencies, by definition they are critics of earlier conventional efforts and are unlikely to develop an established inhouse constituency within the conventional bureaucracy. Quite understandably, the criticized old-line agencies are likely to offer only grudging support at best. More likely, they will resist the demonstration effort, alleging that the situation does not need correction or that there is no need for a separate demonstration effort to remedy an admittedly deficient situation. Alternatively, they may be willing to absorb it as rapidly as possible, usually without instituting any significant change in their own operations, because they are not governed by the same rules of competitive economy as industry.[24]

The two most desirable bureaucratic allies, at least from a financial point of view, would have been the Department of Health, Education, and Welfare and the powerful Social Security Administration (SSA), which handles Medicare funds. From HEW's perspective, OEO health programs were, at most, a constant reminder of its own limitations and, at least, a source of irritation and disruption. From SSA's standpoint, OEO efforts were misdirected. The neigborhood health centers emphasized preventive medicine and care for the young whereas SSA's constituency was the aging who needed protection against catastrophic illnesses.

Eventually a new program must confront the gatekeeper-agency, the Office of Management and Budget (OMB). Even bureaucratic support does not ensure a favorable response from OMB, but without such support there is an increased likelihood of potentially damaging decisions. "Those guys have their orders," an agency staff member pointed out. "In our case, it was 'find some reason not to do it,' not 'where or how could it be done better.' Your making the world's best case doesn't make a difference to them. In a sense you need not to believe in your own rhetoric or else you're extremely hurt."

Bureaucratic strategy, then, must be adapted to avoid undesirable results. "It became a matter of a constant act of fancy footwork to keep the people at the White House and at the Budget Office from knowing what we were doing. . . . They didn't understand OEO and had other irons in the fire. We wanted enthusiastic help, but we didn't get it. We decided we had better keep them neutral."

In lieu of, or in addition to, an in-house bureaucratic constituency, programs can rely on support from organized segments of the public. But social-change demonstration agencies, because they are critical both of conventional bureaucracies and of their status-quo-oriented constituencies, are likely to encounter difficulty in generating support from well-established, organized constituencies, especially professional ones.

The obvious major status-quo-oriented health constituencies were the various professional associations within organized medicine. Given the reform nature of the program, such conventional constituencies were unlikely to be supportive. As chapter 3 details, the strategic choice to neutralize AMA hostility to the center program was made during the early years of the program. It was clear that the AMA would not use its resources to provide visibility or active support for the program. Protestations from the NMA were relatively inconsequential. Little appears to have been done to encourage broad support among other prestigious organized provider constituencies such as medical-college associations. Potential grantees were another source of support. Other agencies cultivated a favorable response from potential grantees by encouraging large numbers of formal grant applications for their programs. The result might be a flood of inadequate or unsatisfactory proposals. But politely rejected applicants, hoping for success in the next funding round, were likely to be program supporters.

In contrast, OHA adopted a "winnowing" process which was far less inviting for providers. The agency's rationale for this approach was the avoidance of credibility problems generated by stirring up untenable expectations among potential grantees and within communities when demonstration dollars were so very limited. The agency's lack of definable constituency within organized medicine and its reliance on medical-care reformers and a disparate group of provider institutions with widely varying motivations and capabilities raised the issue of whether a new, more cohesive constituency for the agency could be developed. The only two remaining candidates were the direct beneficiaries of the program, the centers of their low-income clientele.

Each of these two candidates was encumbered with numerous liabilities and few assets. Both candidates were marginal; the centers operated at the periphery of organized medicine; their clientele had been disenfranchised effectively from the mainstream of U.S. life. Both candidates lacked independent financial resources; the centers relied almost completely on the agency for funds; their clientele were classified as eligible for services by congressional mandate rather than any notion of entitlement.

The combination of marginality and dependency of both the centers and their patients created a complex relationship between the projects and Washington. The relationship was marked by hostility and mistrust, generated, in part, by the centers and patients' recognition of their dependency on a distant bureaucracy represented by occasionally visiting staff who were of different skin color or different socioeconomic status or who came from a different part of the country. Clearly, mistrustful clientele, who are marginal to boot, do not make a politically viable constituency.

Finally, both the centers and their patients were preoccupied with activities that required enormous amounts of energy and time. For some centers, managing tensions and conflicts within the community consumed all available energy. For other centers, survival in a hostile environment dictated the choice of energy and resource expenditure. Center patients, likewise, were concerned with survival. Although the provision of health care is a life-sustaining activity, it was not the attention-getting dramatic activity around which people would rally and for which large number of persons would generate support.

5 Problems of Demonstration Program Administration

When a major social-service delivery system is the target of a federally funded program aimed at broad-based reform of dominant institutions and practices within that delivery system, extensive conflict is inevitable. Broad-based reform is synonymous with questioning the prevailing arrangements and vested interests associated with the status quo. Use of public funds raises profound issues of justice and equity, of the distribution and priorities attached to public resources, of the possible expansion of the public sector, and possibly of the scope of citizen participation in institutions.

When the focus of federal reform efforts is health care, the prospect of conflict appears to be heightened. The very structural arrangements of the health-care delivery system appear to reinforce controversies. The politics of medicine is just as much about the power of doctors as it is about the authority of politicians.[1]

Medical professionals are high-status figures possessing specialized, complex knowledge acquired through long, prescribed training. Given the "healing" nature of their profession, it is not surprising that they often consider their self-interest in structuring medical care synonymous with the common good. "Their commitment to 'constructive social harmony' has allowed them in the past to ignore, deny, or suppress the actual meaning of many types of events which produced disequilibrium and disharmony."[2]

Such attitudes and perspectives are highly functional.[3] They create a high degree of occupational solidarity (and concomitant lack of dissent) among medical professionals and the institutions with which they are associated. Other professional colleagues, rather than clients served, are the chief reference group because professional rewards accrue from association with other professionals. Claims to a monopoly of expertise in treatment are successfully sustained by the profession without substantial lay dissent.

Because the medical profession is empowered to minister to some of the most profound needs we share as human beings, it is accorded respectful deference. The corollary is that it can be the focal point for deeply held grievances generated by pain and death. To the extent that reform measures are perceived as questioning some of the privileges and immunities of the health-care profession, they may well encourage the articulation of accumulated grievances by recipients of medical services.

In turn, patient articulation of grievances and proposals for remediation are likely to reinforce professional perceptions that they are being attacked by laypersons. Such controversies are viewed by providers as challenges to highly prized, medical professional autonomy and authority or implicit unwarranted attacks on professional judgment and competence.

In any event, the almost automatic response of most providers to manifestations of discontent is often a defensive/aggressive one. The consequence is that providers tend to choose from a repertoire of tried-and-true strategies for deflecting or undercutting hostility to their privileged position. But once the signal for a legitimated articulation of broad-based grievances has been received by laypersons, the initial provider strategies may be ineffectual. High-status providers and institutions may find themselves subjected to a spiral of demands (perceived as attacks) eliciting their resistance, which in turn is met by more strident demands (again perceived as attacks). Often, this process acquires an internally generated momentum fuelled by seemingly unrelated incidents. The net result, all too often, is the stiffening of resistance to modification or change or, at best, alternating periods of conflict followed by bargaining and accommodation.

When the parties to the conflict are providers and middle-income groups, the likelihood of compromise through *bargaining* appears to be relatively high. The parties are comfortable with the process itself. All groups with a stake in the outcome of the issue have access to the political process.

But when the parties to the bargaining trade-off process are highly unequal in terms of the distribution of influence and power, there are not likely to be feelings of either familiarity or comfort with the process.[4] The gap between worlds is wide and yawning, and few persons are adequately equipped to bridge it. It was in this context that the administrative process for the neighborhood health centers operated at the local project level. It was in this context that agency staff, especially senior staff with medical training, were required to approve or disapprove local actions whose repercussions for project stability were far-reaching.

In the preceding chapters, the role of money is preeminent. If the analysis is accurate, dollars are the incentive for all parties to participate in the project. Reformers saw the dollars as providing opportunities to test new ideas and modify prevailing institutional practices (see chapter 1). Provider institutions viewed federal dollars as a source of financial relief as well as a vehicle for the expansion of services, if not medical empires (see chapter 3). And low-income clientele for the centers, as this chapter explains, viewed federal dollars first as a source of immediate employment, then as a vehicle to challenge existing powerful institutions, and finally as another opportunity for health care. To the extent that a range of common interests to ensure the degree of cooperation essential to program success is necessary, such a diverse range of incentives for participation in a reform endeavor may not provide such a nexus.

Not surprisingly, incompatible or "nonnegotiable" demands arose. These demands were premised on the differing perceptions regarding incentives for participation and were manifestations of differing expectations regarding dollar distribution. Each group (reformers, providers, and low-income clientele) invoked different strategies to press their demands. And each, in turn, exacerbated conflict.

Rather than label different parties' behavior as culpable or blameworthy, it is more fruitful for purposes of analysis to consider their behavior as reasonable or expectable given their interests and the structure of the situation. With the advantage of hindsight, what is strikingly poignant about the enterprise is the tenaciously adhered-to article of faith among key agency staff that sufficient common ground existed to create the prerequisite local conditions for success. In the data, counterindicative empirical evidence paled before their commitment and intensity.

If reform programs generate broad based expectations of change supported by seemingly massive amounts of federal dollars and if program participants have different and often incompatible motives for involvement, resolution or even mitigation of the ensuing conflicts is no easy task. The hostilities originally confined to the parties involved in the program at the local level may spillover rapidly to the federal dollar dispensing agency. The agency then is faced with the unenviable task of attempting to transform opposition to itself into concern for the problem at the local level.[5]

It appears that there exists a fundamental systemic dilemma built into a social-change demonstration agency program. An agency's reform mandate which challenges the practices of existing powerful institutions exacerbates conflict conditions. Exacerbated conflict militates against desperately needed project success, the sufficient condition to establish demonstration program credibility.

Stressing the need for and the failure to achieve that level of cooperation necessary for program success is not an original contribution to the burgeoning literature of policy analyses. What is important to underscore is that the need for such cooperation is heightened because of the expectations placed on a demonstration program and that the failure to achieve that cooperation is inevitable, given the challenge to the status quo which the program poses.

Two major issue areas which provoked exacerbated conflict within the projects and between the projects and Washington provide excellent examples of the structure and dynamics of conflict in the NHC program. These issue areas were employment policies and the structure of NHC governance. Both employment and governance highlight the two most crucial issues confronting a social-change program addressed to low-income persons—the provision of opportunities through the creation of jobs and power over dollar allocation through the establishment of accountability mechanisms at the local level. Conflict over these issues surfaced in virtually every center and remained a source of turbulence for an extended period. Conflict over these issues illustrates the stresses and incompatibilities among components of a broad-based reform agenda at the implementation stage.

Employment

To many persons, the infusion of federal dollars into a community is equated with employment opportunities; to low-income persons, who are likely to be underemployed or unemployed, the equation is particularly clear. The general ethos surrounding the War on Poverty, the emphasis on crusading efforts to remove whole communities from depressed conditions, fueled the perception that federal dollars would provide jobs. And in the health-care delivery field, the OEO guidelines for the neighborhood health centers reinforced the perception that federal dollars would create new, viable employment opportunities:

> As an integral part of the work plan, neighborhood residents must be trained and employed as staff members of the project. Maximum employment opportunities, including opportunities for career advancement, shall be provided to members of the poverty groups being served. A training plan, under competent, full-time direction, shall be included in the application.

> New ways should be sought to develop, train, and utilize a health team that is innovative in both structure and function. The concept of supporting staff should go beyond the traditional roles and might include physician assistants, family health workers, health visitors, community health aides and others who contribute a firsthand understanding of the neighborhood and its people. The program should demonstrate new roles in the health-related professions and test realignments of the orthodox relationships between primary and supporting personnel.[6]

Despite the bold, heartening words of the guidelines, however, the number of jobs available in any health center for individuals with limited training never could meet the extensive, existing employment demands. All too frequently, the early employment commitment made by the provider institution grantees left an array of disgruntled job seekers. They complained of patronage dispensed and old scores settled by whatever community faction preempted the attention of usually unwitting grantees, who were likely to be confused by the rush of job applicants. They also attributed the shortage of jobs to restrictive or conventional personnel practices followed by provider institutions.

Realistically speaking, the conflicts generated by those who were unable to find employment at the center were not capable of solution at the local project level or, for that matter, at OEO headquarters. The local neighborhood health centers, along with every other War on Poverty project, were confronted with the chronic problems of unemployment and underemployment in low-income communities.

In fact, the actual number of positions available was relatively small. In Chicago, for example, the GAO noted:

> Center records showed that, of the 173 employees at the center in August 1968, 94 were local residents. Of these 94, five held jobs paying from $4,980 to $7,560 a year and requiring some skills or previous training. The other 89 held jobs paying between $3,500 and $5,100 a year and generally not requiring previously acquired skills or previous training. . .

> Center officials told us that they had difficulty in filling the higher-paying jobs with local residents because the relatively few qualified individuals in the target area generally had jobs elsewhere. In this regard, our review of job applications on file at the center identified only one instance where a higher-paying job had been filled with a nonlocal resident when applications were also on file from three local residents. Center officials told us that residency in the area was not a job guarantee and that they hired the applicant whom they considered to be best qualified.[7]

Understandably, the very limited number of actual available positions for low-income persons in the centers reinforced local perceptions that the provider institutions, and ultimately the federal government, were unresponsive to local needs.

For those who were fortunate enough to find employment at the center, a different set of problems emerged. One aspect of the agency's reform agenda affecting low-income communities was the training and use of paraprofessionals to assist the medical staff. For example, centers trained and used community outreach workers to encourage individuals to use the center and to serve as an intermediary when necessary between the patient and the medical staff.

But the centers, as innovative reform demonstration institutions, were not plugged into the conventional employment market. With the advantage of hindsight, it is apparent that far too little consideration was given to the development of "realistic" new career models. Again, the GAO Chicago report is illustrative.

> Center officials informed us that, although many of these lower-paying jobs provided experience which might enable the employees to obtain similar positions elsewhere, they were generally considered to be "dead-end" jobs insofar as the center itself was concerned because there was little opportunity for upward mobility at the center. In some cases, however,

the center had promoted employees who were local residents to positions with *higher salary* rates, although the new positions were still *within* the *lower-paying job categories* [*emphasis added*].

The 79 jobs not held by local residents were generally higher-paying jobs requiring some formal training or previously acquired skill. These jobs included, primarily, those held by physicians, nurses, technicians, and executive and administrative personnel. . . .

The center utilized its advisory board to assist in interviewing and selecting applicants and to help locate qualified local residents for unfilled positions. For example, in April 1968 the advisory board members were requested to help locate local residents to fill the following positions: an executive secretary; a driver; and a data coder, who would be given training.

The center had provided training opportunities for target-area residents in such positions as community health aides and had employed trainees in certain technical departments, such as X-ray and pharmacy. In addition, the center had initiated a dental assistant training program for 16 individuals, which consisted of an academic program given by a junior college and a practical laboratory course held in a laboratory made available by the Presbyterian-St. Luke's School of Nursing.

Center officials were hopeful that the American Dental Association would approve the dental assistant program so that the trainees could become certified and eligible for employment outside the center if they so chose.

Also, center officials informed us that the center had arranged for individuals to work part time while attending outside training classes and that a training director was to be hired who would be responsible for developing training opportunities.

OEO health officials stated that training at the center had been limited because of the limited space, the scarcity of employment opportunities outside the center in jobs similar to those held at the center, the increased workload of the director of nurses, and the priorities set by the local community and staff. Also, the officials stated that, at OEO's request, the center had included the position of training director in its third-program-period proposal.

Additionally, as a result of its site appraisal completed in May 1968, the OEO appraisal team recommended that additional training sources be located, upward mobility of nonprofessionals be increased, and center training be integrated with that of the sponsoring hospital.

In this regard, OEO required as a condition of the center's third-period grant that CHRF submit for OEO approval the center's plans for utilization and placement of trainees and for upgrading all nonprofessional employees.[8]

The all too frequent reality at the centers was that "new-careers" positions which provided jobs for community members often had no career ladders outside the center's milieu. In effect, despite their initial attractiveness, they became dead-end jobs, especially for individuals who were unable to acquire some higher-education certificate to affirm their skill-level marketability in an increasingly credentialed society.

Nor were many of even the most liberal of the medical staff at the centers prepared to deal with paraprofessional demands for reassurance and security. Status discrepancies heightened by racial or ethnic differences between professionals and community employees tended to belie the spirit of cooperation and commitment to innovation. Nurses, for example, "experienced difficulty sympathizing with paraprofessional aides who demand equal pay and status after a short course in nursing techniques and a year or so of experience."[9] Conflicts which in other circumstances might be handled in a more conventional labor-management format became the focus for power struggles between the center's sponsor and the community in which the facility was based.[10]

Some scholars have stressed the accelerated pace of the process by which center employees who had been recruited from the community identified themselves with the center and distinguished themselves from the community.[11] The accuracy of this observation is uncontested. Nevertheless, such co-optation did not preclude significant conflict over employment policies.

For the noncredentialed seeking to partake of the status and financial rewards of a health-care delivery system relying on credentials, employment policies were a serious economic and political issue. In striking contrast, for most highly employable, credentialed professionals, the delivery of service was the major concern. Employment was a technical matter to be handled by personnel staff and the senior administrative staff when necessary. But few health-center administrators had the training or skill to deal with labor problems which became major political struggles.

For the federal reformers in their race against time, the heightened expectations of the poor far outpaced agency efforts and ability to break down the firmly entrenched professional barriers. Agency staff often conveyed a deep sense of frustration at the prospect of being caught inextricably between the provider sponsor and the low-income community in employment situations for which no policy solution was available at the agency or local level.

To complicate the employment situation further, conflicts between the center's professional staff and community activists arose over issues interpreted by the professionals as assaults on their clinical judgment and autonomy. For example, demands based on community beliefs regarding the range of medical care available in more affluent white communities were treated unsympathetically by professional staff.

Strikingly parallel to community demands for a modern, middle-class medical facility were community demands for a wide range of on-duty medical personnel. The medical professional worker's claim that certain problems either were infrequent or could be best handled by referral merely exacerbated the conflict. "The health professionals experienced community representatives as unreasonable and stubborn. Community representatives viewed rejection as part of the ongoing refusal to provide equal health services for the black community.

With the obvious advantage of hindsight, it is apparent that the emotional entanglement which punctuated provider/community relations was not susceptible to rapid unwinding. An OEO study found that "providers strongly state that they are unwilling to turn medical and professional matters over to the community group, but not one consumer group (in a study of twenty-seven neighborhood health centers) that we have seen has claimed jurisdiction over *clinical judgments.*[12] Evidence which would counter professional fears of clientele impinging on professional autonomy or integrity appears not to have made any significant impact on center operations.

Often, even when it was evident that the policies challenged by community individuals or groups had little to do with matters affecting professional clinical judgment, the already exacerbated conflict situation set the stage for an escalation of the struggle over more or less apparent symbolic issues. For example, in one center the struggle revolved on the delegate agency's unilateral determination of the holiday schedule for the medical staff. One minority-group center staff person commented, "In our center Martin Luther King's birthday is an accepted holiday and the Jewish New Year is not. We could give the Jewish holiday to our Jewish doctors as an outside business day (which is a practice in our center) but not count it as an additional holiday. If people come to work in our center and we have to give them other things, then they aren't relating to our center." In some centers, demands were made that all medical staff reside within the community, thereby making them accessible to community persons after center hours. In other centers, community activists wanted medical staff to be proficient in Spanish within six months of their assumption of employment. In centers where a minority-group person was employed in a senior administrative position, employment struggles assumed racial overtones. The following experience related by one center staff person was repeated in various forms in numerous other communities: "The crisis all came up when a black administrator with community connections was fired by us [the delegate agency]. There was a big scene with the neighborhood health council and we were picketed. The advisory board claimed that we had no right to fire the guy without consulting them. They called in the feds, who ruled that we had the right to fire him, though they did put us on notice to pay more attention to the council."

The professional counter to such symbolic demands was twofold. Medical outrage often revealed itself in such remarks as "why can't we just give care? These community guys are troublemakers who want patronage:

look what we have done for them" or "A guy goes to school for twenty years, and now people with an eighth-grade education are saying that he can't perform his job or what his salary or his hours should be." Ominous warnings claimed that scarce high-status medical professionals would be unlikely to join a center staff under such "limiting" conditions. Given the intensity of feeling generated by the community's symbolic demands, the professionals' response was viewed as yet further evidence of their insensitivity to the communities in which they were employed.

Governance

Although the bulk of the grants to develop neighborhood health centers were awarded to provider institutions, the centers themselves were viewed as separate institutions by the OEO. In other words, ideally they were not to become mere appendages of existing institutions. As separate new institutions, therefore, centers needed to develop project governance structures. The connection with OEO and therefore with community action meant that governing structures had to involve the community.[13] The rubric for communiy involvement was *maximum feasible participation*.

Despite the vagueness of the term, it was not an ill-chosen one for legitimation purposes. Participation is fundamental to the democratic political process. In theory, at least, it has the potential for being the means for greater redistribution of opportunities and resources. Historically, it has been a basic demand of every major disenfranchised group. Maximum feasible participation might provide employment, the opportunity for low-income persons to educate bureaucrats, the basis for organizing as pressure groups.[14] Hopefully it would legitimate the institutions created by or working with the OEO. Generally speaking, it appeared to be a rejection of the "once commonly held moralistic judgment that poverty is due to personal incompetence and sin."[15]

By probing beneath the attractiveness of the phrase and its short-term utility, it is evident that *maximum feasible participation* is conceptually elusive. As Moynihan points out, it can be interpreted to prescribe the development of power structures on behalf of the poor, the expansion of power structures to include the poor or the organization of the poor to confront power structures and to change them.[16] While these interpretations do overlap at some points, they are distinguishable both conceptually and prescriptively.

The OEO has been faulted for failing to force a definition of the phrase, thereby heightening the confusion and turbulence of the period. This lacuna is subject to multiple interpretations. Some viewed the concept as merely a sham used to assuage the hostility of the poor. Others claimed that the range of OEO efforts precluded the development of a clear, across-the-board formula which could be applied to all programs. A third interpretation was that bureaucratic self-interest lay in the use of an ambiguous concept carrying positive connotations which provided maximum flexibility. Depending on one's view of politics, one or the other interpretation is more satisfying.

With the advantage of hindsight, it might be argued that the CAP experience, which at local levels often involved fierce struggles over issues of "community control" of all CAP programs, should have suggested to the OHA staff that issues of governance and accountability would surface, particularly in mobilized communities with articulate spokespersons. To better understand the lack of sensitivity to this issue by the agency, Altshuler's observations are instructive.[17] He notes that participation is as controversial as motherhood when it is endorsed without excessive zeal. When the endorsement is translated into action, then conflict is inevitable. Other ideals are evoked, and entrenched interests assert themselves. The structure of participation and hence of governance becomes the focal point for the struggle.

As chapter 3 suggests, the general skepticism regarding CAP capabilities manifested by the OHA staff, combined with their own medical professional posture, led them to dismiss the possible lessons which the early CAP years suggested in the areas of governance and accountability. Instead, they focused on strategies to ensure the technical success of the program.

Technical success meant the delivery of high-quality medical care—the legitimate, unchallenged domain of the medical professional. Technical success meant that the center's orientation largely should be a service one. It would meet *real needs* through a *meaningful structure* by bringing together "antipolitical groups," a theory of community organization that reflected both the medical professional's and the agency's desire to minimize conflict. Agency emphasis on initial technical success allowed provider institutions to feel far more comfortable with the centers. To the extent that such emphasis encouraged greater provider ease, it was valuable functionally. But to the extent that the focus on technical success meant the providers could continue to think along more conventional lines regarding the centers as satellites out in the community rather than as serious reform-generating institutions, it was instrumental in the dilution of agency reform goals.

The early rules were established with no community consultation. Consequently, the providers' preeminent position was not seriously challenged. One early senior staff person reminisced that at a meeting a colleague had to remind the agency staff about the need for community participation in the projects. The next day the notion of 51 percent (consumer participation) was written into the guidelines. An OEO consultant's document submitted in 1965 reflects this policy perspective. It proposes that the board of directors of the sponsoring institution appoint a committee to make policy and leadership for the neighborhood health center. There is recognition of the need for committee-member sensitivity to issues of acceptability and availability of services, but not for the reasons which one would suppose. "An indifferent or disputing board will fail to enlist the *cooperation* of *related agencies*, and will be unable to obtain or *hold* the *services* of a competent, working *staff*" (*emphasis added*).[18]

The neighborhood health councils composed of neighborhood residents are considered auxiliary and advisory in function. They are the conduit for information regarding community perspectives on the availability, amenability, and desirability of services and an investigative body for "pertinent problems within the service area."[19] Eventually, they will "incorporate neighborhood residents into the active work of the neighborhood health center."[20]

One common early pattern consistent with the tenor of the preceding excerpts, by which provider institutions with little understanding of the target-area situation created consumer participation for the center, was the route of instant community organization. They turned to ad hoc committees of community "representatives" composed of an existing community elite. The providers failed to recognize that what the existing elite often really wanted was the preservation of their relative status—to be "in" on this big new action, regardless of the degree of real power they may have had at the start.[21] While "instant community organization" may have produced a formal structure for many community persons, it reinforced community scepticism and hostility.

As the program expanded, it became necessary to develop formulas for community participation in the center's governance, depending on the nature of the delegate agency. According to the guidelines,

The establishment and operation of a Comprehensive Health Services Program must involve from the beginning of planning and throughout the conduct of the project, all appropriate elements of the community that share the program's objectives and interests.

1. Arrangements must be made so that the neighborhood residents served by the project have a substantial voice in the policymaking. This can be accomplished by one or both of the following actions:

a. The governing board of the administering agency is structured so that at least one-third of its members are persons eligible to receive services from the project and at least one-half of its members are either persons eligible to receive services or are representatives of community groups, such as social service organizations and labor or business organizations.

b. A Neighborhood Health Council, which acts as a policy advisory board to the administrative agency, is structured so that at least one-

-half of its members are persons eligible to receive services from the
project. Such a council may be either an existing group involved in
anti-poverty efforts or a group especially organized for this purpose.[2]

To meet federal maximum-feasible-participation requirements, provider
grantees preferred to rely on the advisory neighborhood health council (part a
of the Guidelines cited above) rather than develop a new governing structure which would qualify for federal grants. Community participation
through the advisory mechanism was viewed by the providers as a col-
laborative relationship between them and the centers' clientele. But the providers did not envision this collaboration as a relationship between equals.
Even with layperson middle-class advisory/collaborative relations, the providers consistently had operated from a position of strategic advantage.

Health-care institutions had a tradition of collaboration between professionals and nonmedical persons on hospital trustee boards. Community
notables, respectful of and deferential to medical professional experts,
cooperated with the professional administrative and medical staff in
legitimating the enterprise. In effect, health-care institutions developed governance mechanisms which were self-serving. They reinforced medical professional autonomy. Involvement in the distribution of life and death chances in
a population did not lead governance boards to develop as entities which
acknowledged their accountability to patients in a meaningful way.[23]

Both the sponsoring institutions and the OHA failed to recognize that
participation in center governance meant the suspension of a heritage of
disbelief on the part of many minority-group members. "Racial and ethnic
minority groups tend to see 'white' control of major social institutions
resulting in both conscious racism and perhaps unconscious institutional
patterns that are antagonistic to the interests of both minority individuals
and the 'community' as a whole . . . 'white' dominated institutions are
suspect, and delays and hesitancy on the part of these institutions are interpreted, often correctly, as efforts to prevent or delay transfer of power."[24]

Local informants revealed the intensity of existing hostility. Centers
were viewed as institutions generated by whites for their own advantage.
("Blacks see whites as licensed hustlers." "*Maximum feasible participation*
means maximum feasible manipulation.") Centers were usually run by outside professionals ("Low-income groups don't trust outsiders, and the guys
who are trusted aren't qualified to run centers.") Centers had connections
with powerful established medical institutions ("How can we trust the doctors as allies? An ally is someone you could turn your back upon." "We've
been taught that there's a front stage and a back stage to every operation."
"The community often gets 'uptight' about dealing with institutions which
it knows have dealt badly with it. So it may be an accomplishment for the
community if it can say 'Man, you held them up!'")

Once the center was fully operative, the guidelines for community participation required the classical, impeccable, democratic, procedural device of elections to an advisory council: "The neighborhood residents selected for the governing board and health council shall be democratically selected and their terms normally shall not exceed two years."[25] Council size ranged from fifteen to twenty-five members, of whom at least one half were low-income residents from the target area. Other elected members might be community notables whose income exceeded the eligibility guidelines or who might live outside the geographical boundaries of the target area. Participation through the electoral mechanism became equated with a representative form of collaboration in governance. The problem was that it was difficult to discern a *meaningful* governance function for the advisory council:

> The Neighborhood Health Council shall participate in such activities as the development and review of applications for OEO assistance, the establishment of program priorities, the selection of the project director, the location and hours of the Center's services, the development of employment policies and selection criteria for staff personnel, the establishment of eligibility criteria and fee schedule, the selection of neighborhood residents as trainees, the evaluation of suggestions and complaints from neighborhood residents, the development of methods for increasing neighborhood participation, the recruitment of volunteers, the strengthening of relationships with other community groups, and the other matters relating to project implementation and improvement.[26]

To the extent that a sense of participation varies with the immediacy of the linkage between activity and decision, the guidelines did not hold out the promise of meaningful participation in an advisory capacity.[27] Not surprisingly, it was recognized by many as pseudo-participation, a perception which, Benveniste points out, exacerbates alienation.[28] Access, in an advisory capacity, is clearly distinguishable from power.

The effectiveness of electoral mechanisms for representational purposes is aided by an informed mobilized constituency. The existence of such a constituency is measured conventionally in voter turnout. In the advisory-council elections, the voter turnout usually was low and was likely to increase only if friends or neighbors were running for office.[29] One sympathetic center staff person commented:

> While there may be a plethora of formal organizations in the community, fewer than 10 percent of the residents belong; less than 10 percent voted in national elections; less than 4 percent voted in the local poverty election. When our advisory board formed, even after a series of meetings and the use of various publicity techniques, only 52 persons were able to obtain the 25 signatures required to qualify them to become delegates to the election convention. In any formal sense, no one speaks for even a small percentage of the community.

The absence of a mobilized community, in part, was a reflection of the particular difficulties associated with organizing communities around health issues. Individuals tend to limit their contact with health-service providers (especially in low-income communities where there is a clear, understandable tendency to postpone treatment until the condition becomes acute). Those who by virtue of age or infirmity are dependent on health-care providers are an unlikely source of activism. At the community level, other more visible problems may be viewed as likelier candidates for mobilization efforts. "Organizers have to make the difficult case that better health care can be achieved through group efforts."[30] Finally, the correlation between socioeconomic status with differential mortality and morbidity rates may "provide a persuasive case of social injustice, but are not visible enough to energize vigorous organizational efforts at change."[31]

A low turnout for council elections reinforced provider beliefs that the poor were not really interested in center governance. That there might be an arguably sound basis for the community's profound cynicism regarding political involvement in general escaped provider recognition. That there might be an arguably sound basis for the community perception of the apparently meaningless nature of an election to a relatively powerless advisory structure designed to channel community energies toward medical providers' goals escaped provider recognition. That the encouraging of a marginal group to participate in an advisory role had little connection to the immediate pressing needs of the poor escaped provider recognition.

Then, too, the actual performance of the councils often provided further grist for provider perceptions that the target-area residents were unable or unprepared to assume responsibility. As Alford notes, in part, the deficiencies in performance can be attributed to the structural properties of this form of participation:

> The structure of participation maximizes the chances of stalemate by setting up the rules of decision making in such a way as to prevent any major interest from being seriously damaged (the requirement of "consensus"), and by failing to allocate enough power to the decision-making bodies on which community groups are represented. Because these bodies are not given enough power, there is little incentive to set up procedures and create a composition which will lead to effective decision-making processes. Just the opposite incentives exist: to make them large and unwieldy—as "representative" as possible—so that all points of view will be heard but none implemented, save those of the interests who already hold power. The net result is many meetings, speeches, and reports. Committees are set up which plan, coordinate, and communicate—and ultimately evaporate when the planning grant runs out.
>
> One consequence of this particular scenario is that even the professionals who started the project with a sincere desire to "get the community involved" will become cynical about the competence and skills of community groups and leaders. The next time around they will join the ranks of those

who try to make the mechanisms of community representation as fictitious as possible in order to preserve at least some chance of getting a health facility organized, funded, and built.[32]

In other situations, the assumption of responsibility led to genuinely differing perspectives which heightened conflict. In one center, neighborhood violence which affected both black and white staff members prompted staff demands for uniformed, armed security personnel. "The Community Health Council, interpreting uniforms and weapons as symbols of colonialism and repression to which they were opposed, withheld its approval of these measures. Instead, the council members offered to take action to prevent further acts of violence."[33] When faced with several staff members' threats to quit, the center administration expanded the security force despite the council's objections.

In addition, the centers were confronted by a set of problems specific to low-income persons' participation in such structures. Council members often lacked the skills associated with participation in public bodies. Council meetings generally were confused and confusing. Over time, members who developed skills often became salaried center employees or acquired the skills to seek other employment. In either case, they were no longer poor and hence might be disqualified from sitting on the advisory council, despite the usefulness of their acquired expertise. This process of upward mobility has been characterized colorfully as "creaming the poor."[34]

Difficulties emerged in defining the council's area of expertise. In part, this confusion was the consequence of professional control strategies premised on claims to expertise. In part, this confusion was a reflection of the inability of council members to locate authority within the provider institutions. Hospital and university administrators are particularly adroit at being unable to locate individuals with ultimate authority. Such institutions often seem to have infinite capacities for making decisions which are not authoritative.[35] In part, this confusion was a reflection of conflict among existing community political factions who used the council simply as another forum in which to carry on the struggle.

Ethnic splits and rivalries in the target area which led to demands for accurate proportional representation (an especially difficult task in low-income communities where extensive census slippage was known to exist or where a number of illegal aliens were known to reside) caught providers unaware. Community insistence that the composition of the body took precedence over council business often failed to register as a significant issue with providers unless conflict became extraordinarily intense.

In addition, conflicts among preexisting factions within racially or ethnically homogeneous communities surfaced quickly. To their surprise, providers discovered that small amounts of dollars generated major conflicts as political factions perceived the serious limitations on the amount of future dollars available to the community.

One community informant characterized the situation as the "ghetto mentality—let's grab what we can and grab while the grabbing's good." As a consequence, "safe" or "cooperative" councils were subject to challenges to their representativeness by more sophisticated activist community members when it became clear that the center might possess more financial resources than almost any other institution in the community. Another informant described the challengers as likely to be militants and mercenaries or political operators who wanted to cut themselves in on the action.

Agency and provider informants tended to display a surprising degree of naivete regarding degree of diversity as well as the sources of conflict and confusion in council operations. Either out of ignorance or from an endorsement of faddish War on Poverty beliefs, they appeared to assume that a high degree of cooperation or cohesiveness existed in low-income areas.

As conflicts within the council and between the council and the provider emerged, provider anxieties mounted. Councils elected by a low turnout were challenged as unrepresentative by providers, who argued somewhat tautologically that the reason disruptive persons were on the council was that it was unrepresentative of the community. "If there had been the right kinds of elections, the council would have been composed of the right kind of people," one informant cynically noted.

Despite many provider claims of unsatisfactory council performances, organizational development designed to train community representatives did not appear to be a major interest of provider sponsors. The OEO attempted to assist selected centers through demonstration training projects for council members but the program was pitifully small compared to the needs.

Detailing the difficulties and conflicts which emerged in the development of formal governance structures should not obscure the most fundamental issue which the controversy raised—the accountability of a neighborhood health center to its constituency. While satisfactory formal governance structures might be a necessary condition of legitimacy, the responsiveness of the sponsoring providers and the centers to community demands was the sufficient condition.

In the struggle to develop meaningful accountability standards, the mainstream medicine-provider sponsorship of most of the centers became a source of difficulty for the OEO. Some providers did not recognize the legitimacy of community demands; accountability was an "in-house, professional" matter. Even those providers who claimed to be prepared to listen more attentively to clientele demands became the focal point for community suspicion or hostility. These providers offered only involvement in the formulation of broad general policy rather than control over jobs, dollars, and budgets. To community members, control over jobs, money, and the budget was the vehicle for control over the center and therefore institutional accountability to the community.

Jonas argues that these community control demands result merely in community administration of a project.[36] Control of the three basic key building blocks of a health-services institution (capital budget, expense budget, and supply of staff) is key to meaningful control. The argument is an attractive one and merits empirical consideration. But it appears that even community administration provided people with a sense of institutional identification and a vested interest in its operation, although Jonas may well attribute this situation to a lack of sophistication.

Not surprisingly, the lack of or, at best, the casual attention paid to the delineation of accountability standards in the OEO guidelines was interpreted by the providers to mean that they need not reorder their traditional notions of governance and accountability in health-care delivery structures. It also meant that controversies over issues of governance and accountability could continue to be viewed by providers as disruptive of the centers' business—the delivery of health care.

Despite this tendency for provider institutions to demonstrate unwillingness to recognize the validity of community claims and the need for some form of institutional responsiveness to them, it should not be assumed that they knew how to translate this unwillingness into effective avoidance strategies. The majority of the provider institutions were uncertain and frightened of the possible consequences of harsh direct responses to community demands for an expanded role in the center's development or operation. Local project directors were unlikely to have constructive alternative insights. They usually were provider-appointed academic health-care administrators or doctors, white, and, with two exceptions, male with little or no prior experience in low-income communities.

A number of the early directors had been associated with the Medical Committee for Human Rights (MCHR), organized in 1964, to provide health care for volunteer workers in the voter registration drives in the South. These future dirctors saw first-hand the health needs of rural blacks. The idea of combining social reform with health care innovation seemed natural. One of the first project directors, native to the South, recalled that he saw the NHC as an opportunity "to exorcise the sense of guilt at being a white southerner."

With some exceptions, these physician/directors initially were attracted to the job as part of a package which included a mandate to upgrade an existing department within a medical school. Typical of this pattern was a physician who was for the dual purpose of writing a proposal to establish a center and chairing a department of community medicine. Once operational, it was felt the center would provide a teaching experience for students. Another director recruited for similar purposes, accepted the position with the understanding that the existing department intended to "re-orient" itself toward the community.

By the early 1970s, the pattern of recruitment for project directors began to change, and the "second generation" of program administrators reflected more closely the race-ethnicity of the service population and the new issues which the centers were facing. This new group of directors was increasingly nonwhite and nonphysician.[37]

It has been suggested, however, that even if constructive alternatives were readily apparent to local project directors, they may well have had an interest in masking situations and leaving boundaries somewhat unclear. In community-action programs, administrations began to recognize "that tolerance of ambiguity over questions of project control is a primary strategy in mobilizing support."[38]

Perhaps the most instructive illustration of the relationship between governance of the centers, lack of clarity in the guidelines, and the exacerbation of conflict is found in those situations in which community pressure was exerted on both the provider institution and Washington to develop a nonprofit community corporation. Such a corporation would be composed of center clientele or their representatives determined by local elections, local medical professionals, and representatives of community organizations. One informant recalled:

> When it came to the time to make the community corporation the grantee, there was a scary battle. We had made it clear in the negotiations with the delegate agency that it would negotiate away the power over a three-year period. In Washington, people said, "we as an agency stand behind the notion of a nonprofit community health corporation," but when it was about to happen to one of the biggest projects, the doctors in Washington had serious second thoughts. The office was polarized. Did we really mean that the consumer would have that kind of impact? The agency suffered from organizational and conceptual fright buttressed by provider institutions' pressure on the agency to prevent or at least stall the formation of such corporations.

The incident detailed in the preceding paragraph conveys the flavor of the initial effort to develop meaningful participation and accountability structures to the community in which a center was located. Several years after this incident, in one of its publications, the OHA was able to report:

> New neighborhood health corporations have been organized in many areas to assume administrative responsibilities and control. These bodies usually involve both consumers (neighborhood residents) and health professionals on the Board of Directors. The Corporations have gained significant identification in the community. They offer a unique means for expressing

sensitivity and responsiveness to the needs and interest of the various participants. These groups may develop as important new social instruments of shared responsibility.

In 26 projects, such new health corporations have assumed the principal administrative role. There has been a marked trend in recent years to make grants to these local groups.

The responsibilities and activities of the corporations vary. Most frequently the new corporation is the delegate or sub-delegate agency. Some provide services directly; others contract for medical, dental and other professional services. Some will establish one or more subsidiary corporations as related efforts.

The Boards of Directors of the new health corporations range in size from 9 to 48 members, averaging 20. Most commonly (23 of 26), board representation is apportioned, though not always equally, between three groups—the poor, health professionals, and other community groups. The poor or their representatives generally make up ⅓ to ½ of the Board's representation.

The Board of Directors generally makes all major policy decisions and, through individual board members, functions as the Center's patient grievance system. Within the Board, a committee system generally prevails, with a single committee (often the Executive Committee) providing leadership.

The poor members of a board are generally elected from among the population served by the Health Center. While it is difficult to measure their influence on board decisions, the poor are always represented on the major committees. Experience suggests that the older the corporation, the more effective the contribution of poor consumers.[39]

Generally speaking, the agency's stance toward local conflicts over governance and the development of accountability mechanisms was to give projects the benefit of the doubt and to try to maintain a laissez faire posture in the name of flexibility. At best, staff viewed themselves as the broker in a dialogue among the centers, the community, and the provider institutions. Agency informants stressed that they had assumed that some conflict was bound to exist in a social-change demonstration project, although the intensity of the conflicts generated at the local level elicited responses of surprise, dismay, and even anger from agency staff, especially when the agency's broker role became transformed into an active peace-keeping role. As one informant noted, "It's like walking in a mined field. You don't want to step on a mine, and so you take a step at a time to try to get through."

Agency staff claimed to recognize that different centers had to cope with extremely difficult local situations. They maintained that there were often no immediate, apparently satisfactory solutions to problems, that the conflicts generated or exacerbated by the project in a community were part of the "learn as you go" aspects of a demonstration situation. All in all, they conveyed a posture of unusual bureaucratic willingness to cope with uncertainty.

In all fairness, it should be noted that the agency's ability to sustain such a posture was predicated on the demonstration nature of its program undertaking. Experimentation and innovation can mask both internal and external dissent and focus attention on the uncertainty which inevitably accompanies change.

But such flexibility often became a rationalization for failing to act or for playing both sides off against each other. One informed observer at the health-center scene commented: "OEO knows it gave millions of dollars to the university [medical school]. So, it backs off when it responds to community pressures by saying that the council can't control hiring, firing, and budget. Then it says to the university, 'what's the matter with you people? Don't you have any community relations?'"

Clearly, the maintenance of a flexible posture toward local conflicts was advantageous to the agency in many situations. But as an explanation for agency actions, it is only partially satisfactory. As chapter 6 suggests, the agency possessed limited capacity to resolve conflicts. This was a key factor in limiting the agency's ability to intervene effectively. Intervention from Washington not only was time- and energy-consuming for the agency but also could even be counterproductive. For example, in one center where the situation between provider institutions and the community reached a crisis point and the center was closed down for a week, the community was divided and was squaring off with the grantee at the same time. "If we squeezed too hard on the grantee," and informant remarked, "it could afford to say 'out we go' because it was thinking about rebuilding their hospital elsewhere."

In another troubled center, after a five-year period during which the provider delegate agency used the neighborhood health council as a rubber stamp for its decisions, the council demanded a major policy voice as well as a representative on the delegate agency's board of trustees. These demands were rejected. There were confrontations and arrests of the most militant council members. Several activists on the center's staff were fired and arrested. Ultimately, the delegate agency disbanded the council.[40] Community groups sought Washington's assistance and demanded participation in the center's governance. Washington was reluctant to interfere, but when it became evident that the situation had reached scandalous proportions, the agency had no choice, though the provider institution threatened to withdraw from the program.

In fact, the typical local situation in which the provider might be willing to surrender federal dollars voluntarily was likely to be one of enormous turbulence, if not disaster, and one in which a reliable alternative federal contractor was not waiting in the wings.

Given these limitations, it is not surprising to learn that in most situations only when the patient's (center's) fever became terribly high and the inflammation quite serious did the Washington clinicians actually intervene. Crisis intervention for acute episodes characterized Washington's efforts to catch up with situations where the benefit-of-the-doubt outlook was clearly no longer applicable.

6 Problems of Demonstration Administration: The Headache of Dollars

Dollars are the boon and bane of a demonstration agency. They are the basis of its very existence, and they are the cause of its major headaches. They are the ultimate source of its power, and if mismanaged, they may be a major contributor to its demise.

No doubt, all dollar-dispensing federal agencies recognize and adjust to the headaches posed by their major asset. Ministrations to the pain may take many forms, and the relief may be more or less complete. Why, then, should special attention be paid to the headaches caused by dollars for a demonstration agency?

Demonstration dollars are dollars earmarked for the purchase of social change. By virtue of their identification with often controversial policies, they become controversial dollars. By virtue of their controversial nature, they are usually available in much more limited amounts than dollars attached to conventional programs. Paradoxically, limited availability does not correlate with limited expectations regarding their impact. As chapter 7 suggests, demonstration dollars are likely to be surrounded by greater expectations regarding their potential impact than conventional dollars. Demonstration dollars, in effect, are *special* dollars.

Because they are special dollars, they may pose special headaches for a demonstration agency. The etiology of such headaches is found in the problems of demonstration program administration: the struggle to define the dollars once grantees have been picked, the need to control and monitor the dollar flow, and the requirement of program fit with other available federal and state resources. For these headaches, conventional bureaucratic ministrations or prescriptions may fail to provide even temporary relief.

Defining the Dollars

Suppose the agency were able to find the ideal grantees—good, sensitive pragmatic persons with expertise in the delivery of medical-care services, able to manipulate ideas, dollars, and institutions, and attuned to the needs of the new neighborhood health centers. Suppose, further, that the agency were able to find such grantees in reasonably large numbers. It still would not have bypassed one of the major difficulties generated by demonstration program expansion—the differences or incompatibilities between federal and local agendas which emerge during the initial process of defining the federal dollar and which affect future dollar definition rounds.

The Office of Health Affairs (OHA) staff made a genuine commitment to encouraging local initiative and creativity in projects designed to be relevant to individual community needs. Consistent with this commitment, the agency adopted the position that it was unwilling to provide a cookbook formula for an acceptable grant proposal. "When we receive requests for copies of funded project proposals," one agency official remarked, "we will not give them out from this office. If people see one, they think they know what we want. We're trying to get people to write solutions to local problems, and neither the problems nor the solutions are all the same. . . . Just because Watts does something doesn't mean that Denver has to do the same thing. OEO was not there to rubberstamp a program." Informants consistently distinguished the agency's willingness to provide technical assistance in the development of a proposal from manipulation of a formula.

The commitment to creativity in program development and implementation was reflected in the agency guidelines. In the agency's formative year, there was a division of opinion on the desirable degree of guideline specificity. At that stage in the agency's development, it was apparent that the agency could only describe the basic desirable characteristics of a previously untested reform-oriented institution. But even when the program had been operative for several years, agency guidelines still reflected a preference for generality in the description of a center. According to informants, this preference was consistent with the agency's emphasis on innovation, diversity, and project relevance to local situations.

The guidelines identified the following major elements of the center:

1. *Broad scope of services.* Outpatient services must be comprehensive, offered in a single setting, with arrangements for specialized services.
2. *Acceptability and accessibility.* Services must be readily available to users.
3. *Quality of care.* High professional standards must be maintained and quality controls maintained.
4. *Size of population.* Projects should serve between 10,000 and 30,000 persons.
5. *Auspices.* Health services should be provided by qualified professionals with active participation of the neighborhood residents in planning and operations.
6. *Community involvement.* All interested elements of the community should be involved early and actively.
7. *Coordination of health funds and services.* The OEO money is a last-dollar resource, and full integration or coordination with other funds and services is required.

8. *Eligibility criteria.* Emergency care is to be provided without delay, and criteria are to be established and administered in accordance with relevant OEO and local standards.
9. *Personal relationships.* A continuous, personalized relationship between patient and center staff is critical.
10. *New jobs and roles for neighborhood residents as health workers.* Training and new job opportunities are an integral aspect.
11. *Rural programs.* More limited programs may be considered in rural areas.
12. *Coordination with other antipoverty programs.* Links to other poverty efforts are essential.
13. *Reporting and evaluation.* Projects must participate in program reporting and evaluation activities.[1]

Guidelines written from the assumption that minimum definition assists or permits creativity in programs may be useful in some situations or at least not terribly troublesome. They serve as a buffer between the rigidity of codification and the vagueness of oral arrangements. Where the grant has been made to "good risks" and the potential for social change exists, guidelines need not become barriers. Their role in dollar definition is more or less that of a modest reference point. In such situations, the OEO Office of the General Counsel was useful in interpreting the guidelines to allow great flexibility in project operations.

But in situations where a project's potential for success is limited, where the grantee's agenda differs fundamentally from the federal agency's agenda or is incompatable with it, where the center has a weak project director, or where community conflict becomes the preoccupation, guideline flexibility may not encourage creativity. Rather, the absence of clear rules may escalate the local parties' preoccupation with the need for assistance from Washington to solve problems.

For provider institutions and health-center administrators closely identified with them, guideline interpretation by Washington could be a useful backup device. Administrator informants often conveyed, in a strikingly unselfconscious manner, an understandable combination of desire to control situations and high anxiety on contemplating the task. Assistance from Washington through an interpretation favorable to the provider institution was a potential reinforcement for their efforts at local control. Moreover, it mitigated the anxieties generated by a situation in which the unknowns outweighed the knowns.

For community activists, guideline interpretation by Washington was a possible source of advantage to the disadvantaged. The guidelines were viewed as the major piece of paper which articulated the program goals and obligated the agency and ultimately the local project to them. Hence, community activists perceived federal interpretations of the guidelines as a potential reinforcement for their efforts to wrest project control away from provider institutions. Not surprisingly, these activists displayed a concern bordering on fixation with federal guideline interpretation. From Washington's perspective, however, this fixation often was perceived as a mischanneling of precious energy and resources because the guidelines had no legally binding effect. They constituted a book of rules but invited negotiation.

The preceding articulation of provider-institution and community perceptions of the guidelines illustrates one of the paradoxes of demonstration reform efforts. Under the rubric of encouraging creativity, an agency may not foreclose local project options and opportunities through narrowly drafted guidelines. But the very freedom which is viewed from the top as a desideratum can become a source of strain when local parties, in part to allay their anxieties, attempt to force definition to their own advantage. In addition to exacerbating local conflict, local demands run counter to the conventional style of transacting bureaucratic business. Bureaucrats prefer to rely upon such intangibles as the creation of an atmosphere, the development of informal relationships, and the fostering of a series of unwritten understandings rather than specific deals.

It would be inaccurate to assume that agency commitment to the encouragement of local creativity through flexible guidlines flourished at the expense of other agency imperatives. Agency commitment to highly visible, meaningful reform necessitated a judicious blend of agency supervision and monitoring of projects along with the encouragement of local creativity. Agency commitment to the broad, basic reform agenda provided it with an overview which local projects were unlikely to possess. Consequently, the agency was unwilling at times to endorse or encourage local developments which it perceived as inconsistent with the national agenda, even if specific local reforms appeared to be within the guidelines. In a moment of candor, probably not unmixed with some self-serving exaggeration about the rationality of the enterprise, one agency staff member confirmed the existence of such national agendas: "We were looking for certain kinds of projects because we had ideas of comparisons we wished to make. We would negotiate for the project we wanted; unless we could be shown to be wrong later on, we wanted the project to continue that way. We wanted to demonstrate something specific." Another staff member elaborated upon the built-in tension between national and local reform agendas, "You want to let others do their thing, but you know if you did it, it would be right in *your* terms."

Project informants were quick to reaffirm the existence of a national agenda and to be critical of its impact on them. One senior staff member at a center complained:

The agency never says directly what it wants, yet the programs must know how to satisfy the agency. We end up in a quandary over how to satisfy them, and it becomes a guessing game. From a program point of view, the issue is "how far can a program go." There aren't very clear definitions, and after a meeting with the Feds, each one of us would have a different understanding of what was going on. The name of the game is understanding OEO in order to get the dollars.

Center sponsors and clientele tended to view the center as a service-delivery institution in the community, rather than a demonstration effort which *happened* to be located in their particular community. Nor were they likely to see the significance of their project in terms of Washington's national demonstration agenda. Relying on their own perceptions and priorities, they tended not to be passive recipients of federal funds.

One rather battle-scarred former agency staff member, recalling the related problems of identifying increasing numbers of reliable committed grantees and defining the dollars, commented:

You tell a provider that it can have a million dollars. It sets aside what you want to do with the money and starts with its own agenda. The "great programs" are those where the agendas are the same. . . . What you hope to get is a guy committing himself in writing. Then there's a fifty-fifty chance that he'll do things. He probably won't do all he's committed to, but then he can be supervised. After the first funding of a project you're usually stuck with it.

Even in situations where the local provider was of known and relatively reliable quality, Washington was aware that the local agenda might diverge sufficiently from major emphasis in the federal demonstration agenda to warrant close scrutiny and monitoring. For example, one well-known, highly rated provider institution was not noted for its positive attitudes toward clientele participation in the governance of the health center. Its agenda was to develop and expand the use of paramedical personnel. This agenda might well help to double the number of prepaid group practices in the United States. But from the agency's perspective, such a long-term doubling was unsatisfactory if, except for the increased use of paramedical personnel, the delivery of health-care services was largely unchanged.

Even in situations where a reasonably good mesh existed between the provider institution and agency agendas, it was unlikely that the agenda mesh extended to the community. As chapter 5 points out, no matter what the formal designation of the federal demonstration dollars might be, low-income persons in the target area tended to translate federal dollars into employment possibilities. In response to enormous pressures from the unemployed, the underemployed, and the unemployable, often centers where hiring paraprofessional staff as soon as grant money became available and well before the senior medical staff had been hired. A project director commented: "When we first opened up shop, for every person who came in for care, there were forty who wanted a job. Finally, when all the jobs were gone, people were mad." Often community demands were made on the providers and Washington for more jobs and better pay in the name of upward mobility.

From Washington's perspective, employment and training of paraprofessionals were secondary to the service-delivery function of the center. Limited demonstration dollars could not possibly begin to remedy on a broad basis the cumulative injustices manifested in discriminatory employment practices.

Yet another fundamental agenda difference surfaced over the search for additional financial sources for the center. Centers would have to seek state Medicaid funds, especially when OEO resources began to decline. From Washington's perspective, the long-range survival of the centers absent the likelihood of broad national health insurance had to be premised on convincing the states that centers could be a cost-control device for the delivery of health care to the indigent. Washington argued that centers could claim that their costs (including innovative services) were low compared with the costs of clinics and hospitals frequented by the poor.

From the centers' perspective, however, increasing pressure on them from Washington to collect a   diminishing amount of Medicaid dollars from recalcitrant state agencies was a further harassment. It seemed to be a relatively low priority as long as federal demonstration dollars were available. Additionally, the local project administrators were concerned that assertive center efforts to collect reimbursement would generate heightened conflict with local private practitioners who were treating Medicaid and Medicare patients and who, in times of welfare funding retrenchment, viewed the centers as competitors for an increasingly small piece of available public-health-care dollars.

In addition to such general differences as those involving employment and third-party payments, other local agenda differences surfaced from community to community. In each instance, the agency had to weigh the extent to which local agendas, however valid, would dilute the agency's reform agenda, however vague and ambiguous the latter might appear. For example,

> One community wanted $30,000 for dental prosthetics. . . . Most of the community people wanted them because there were lots of older people on the board (who either already had lost or were likely to lose their teeth in the not too distant future). In a dental sense, this group is a lost population. The dental director had to present the choice. If we spend all our time and money making dentures, then your children will not receive preventive care.

The raconteur of this incident made it clear that the agency had decided either not to fund the center's proposed dental program at all if the board remained adamant or to fund a small token portion of the requested prosthetics budget for one year on a "trial basis" with no intention of renewing that portion of the budget the following year.

In another community, environmental health problems were seen as pressing issues for the health center. One sympathetic Washington staff person recalled, "We [the agency] were of mixed minds about the proposal. The center had already demonstrated that health has an environmental aspect. On the other hand, we wanted a big example to show on the Hill, and we wanted to force existing agencies concerned with the problem to do what we thought we shouldn't have to pay for. So we told the community to go slow because there weren't enough dollars." The upshot was that the local project interpreted the agency's response to mean that environmental problems despite their importance and relevance should not be a major health-center concern and were outraged.

In yet another community, people were more concerned about malnutrition than health services per se. In response to community needs, the medical staff began to distribute food like medication and later to write prescriptions for food to be filled at local stores and paid for out of the center's drug budget. The center justified its actions to Washington with the claim that the specific therapy for malnutrition was food. In the long run, Washington remained unpersuaded.

Clearly differences in perspectives and differences in agendas affected the dollar definition and dispensing process. In a number of situations, the guidelines themselves offered no guidance. Agency discretionary authority, local sophistication or political connections, and the publicity likely to result from specific innovations all had an impact on the process.

Controlling the Dollar Flow

Acquiring Relevant Information

Once the dollars have been defined and dispensed, information becomes a key resource for both bureaucrats and local projects. Through information, sense can be made of the environment, and order can be imposed on the relationship between Washington and the local project.[2]

From Washington's perspective, information from the local projects was essential. It would assist the agency in meeting its basic reporting obligations to Congress. The return on dollars authorized by Congress and dispensed by OHA would be measured by the numbers served and services provided by the centers. Information would also assist Washington in developing the capacity to begin to provide informed responses to the larger policy questions raised by efforts at structural reform of the health-care delivery system.

It would be a distortion of reality, however, to assume that Washington was wholeheartedly committed to the enterprise of data collecting. The senior staff, especially in the formative years of the agency, possessed the very action orientation which they sought in local projects—an interest in and commitment to rapid policy development and implementation which far outpaced a concern for evaluation and assessment. They were secure in their belief that the NHC model embodied the best reform ideas. Little or no attention was devoted to the possibility of collecting information to address the significant policy concerns which implementation of the program raised.

Within three years, the agency began to push projects to develop and use data-collection systems. In part, this push embodied agency recognition that Washington could easily be outfoxed. "People in projects are good at hiding dollars," one senior staff member remarked. "We are not so clever at finding them." In part, the push toward better data collection was a response not only to immediate political pressures but also to the structural imperatives generated by demonstration programs (discussed in chapter 7).

Rather than relying solely on the submission of reports and other bureaucratic forms, the agency used program analysts (see chapter 2). Each analyst was responsible for collecting information and monitoring several local projects. To monitor the projects with heightened sensitivity to local issues, most of the program analysts made sincere attempts to develop close contacts with projects.

But Washington-based information gatherers operated under clear handicaps. Despite the efforts of some of the program analysts to convey sympathetic, supportive responses to the local projects and to cast themselves as their advocates, they were viewed as irrevocably being "Feds." Ultimately they were responsible for determining whether the projects actually were implementing the program. Moreover, their backgrounds and life experiences were totally different from those of health center clientele. The few minority-group program analysts tended to be viewed as "sell-outs," and the others by definition, were outsiders. Inevitably, the ability of the staff to understand the desires and aspirations of low-income persons was open to question.

Viewed with understandable suspicion by community people, the Washington analysts often were not well equipped to handle provider institutions. Since the analysts lacked medical training, they were not regarded as professional colleagues and therefore peers. Given the general ethos of the OEO, its image of being staffed by youthful liberals, if not radicals, who wanted to "change the system," the program analysts were potential antagonists for provider institutions. Ironically, those analysts who were liberal and attempted to meet their data-gathering commitment were regarded as sources of harassment by practitioners in centers devoted to *quality* care.

From the local projects' perspective, the provision of information to Washington could be a waste of time. It was likely to cause disruption and delay. Also it could be an activity with potentially dangerous consequences for the project. In either case, the provision of information was not viewed as a neutral, routine operation.

Inevitably, Washington's need for data leads to local complaints regarding the volume of paperwork required by Washington. The amount and type of information demanded may appear to be irrelevant to the local project. Hence, projects tend not to devote much time and energy to the endeavor. Local project personnel

> are notoriously uninterested in data collection that does not serve their immediate purposes. Their task is to make things happen and not to stop and think of what forms should be filled out so that some other fellow can later make suspect use of them. Were local personnel to feel differently they would still have trouble appreciating the need of evaluators for consistent and disaggregated data that can later be recombined to serve new purposes. The local official, who must necessarily consult his own convenience, is likely to record data periodically as time permits and to aggregate it into larger lumps so that it will be easier to collect and store. His data practices, which seem quite sensible from his perspective, are likely to drive future evaluators wild with frustration.[3]

From this local perspective, information gathering is a burden and a necessary evil. The continuation of the flow of federal dollars is the major (if not the only real) incentive to provide Washington with data.

But information is also commodity with explosive consequences if one cannot exercise control over its use. Washington's recognition of the importance and determination of the relevance of different pieces of information created resentment in the projects.[4] Given their psychological as well as physical distance from Washington and their recognition of the value of information, projects usually tended to limit the supply of information to Washington and to be highly selective in its content, whenever possible. Colored by fears and fantasies concerning the information's ultimate use, projects viewed limitation on federal access to information as a protective device. It ensured that no one would be able to "turn the project in." One program analyst remarked:

> The centers may not see any return on the data they are required to collect for the agency. Yet, they hear us making noise about data collection and figure that there must be some reason. In their paranoid way, because they know that the federal faucet—at least in theory—can be turned on and off,

they fear that we are using the data for a "rank" ordering of centers. It's a big risk for questionable or paranoid centers to take a chance of coming out on the bottom—so data collection becomes equated with creating harm for themselves, and we're programmed to know ony certain kinds of things.

Nor are local fears assuaged by talk of using the data to devise better policies in Washington. Talk of better policies, as if it did not matter who determined them, only clouds the issues. As Pressman and Wildavsky point out, "If actors and organizations have conflicting policy preferences, then the technical methods of communication, planning, and coordination are unlikely to resolve the differences between them. More discussion and gathering of information might only result in pointing up differences between the organizations."[5]

Developing Incentives and Sanctions

Inevitably, analyses of federal policy implementation must address the issue of the incentives available to federal bureaucrats to encourage local projects to deliver the goods or services stipulated by federal grant or contract. Generally speaking, the need for imagination in the development and design of incentives is acknowledged in policy analyses, but little attention is paid to its actual development.

The corollary of the proposition that incentives can or must be developed to stimulate or encourage appropriate behavior is that sanctions, deterrents, or, as modern social science would have it, disincentives must be developed to discourage or penalize inappropriate behavior. Here, too, a passing nod to the need for their development appears to be a substitute for concerted thought about their substance.

On first glance, it would appear that the development of incentives to encourage good, if not outstanding, project performance is a simple task. The prospect of an increased budget for a project whets local appetites and may result in upgrading performance. Presumably, the availability of existing discretionary funds are an additional financial incentive to projects. Ultimately, it would appear that sensitively dispensed dollars rather than "stakhanovite" medals and ceremonies are the most likely candidates for a successful incentive scheme.

But if, as an agency staff member suggested, the agency's basic job is to get *large* amounts of dollars into *small* communities in *usable* form with a fairly broad mandate, the result may well be a series of foul-ups. Then, the agency has to mitigate the set of problems created by money.

What are the tools of mitigation? Does curtailment of the flow of federal dollars deter projects from pursuing a course of action viewed as undesirable or unacceptable to federal dollar dispensers? In effect, does manipulation of the dollar flow heighten the likelihood of compliance and serve as a warning to others?

There is a tendency to assume that modification or curtailment of the flow of federal dollars is a readily available federal sanction which will produce the desired results or, if necessary, rid an agency of an embarrassing, albatross project. This assumption appears to be at odds with bureaucratic reality. "Once the money has been given the first time, you can harass people and slow down the flow of dollars, or threaten not to re-fund them," one experienced staff member remarked. "But, that can be very embarassing to you, since you have as much at stake in the program as they have. You can use fiscal sanctions as a threat if you're smart enough to call the bluff. But fiscal sanctioning hasn't made good programs out of bad ones."

In OEO contracts and grants, the federal government technically retained all legal rights and therefore a vast amount of power. The government could claim unexpended funds; it was not required to re-fund projects; after an on-site project inspection, the government could recall all unspent dollars. All neighborhood health centers required written approval for a project's budget as well as any change in work plan or appointment of the project and medical directors.[6]

In part, the contractual retention of such enormous power was based on the necessity of ensuring project compliance with the minimal standards established by the General Accounting Office (GAO), thereby assisting the agency in meeting its minimal accountability requirements to Congress. But such retention of such broad power allowed a federal agency to steer erring or wayward projects in reform directions.

Fiscal "Tinkering" Devices. Most forms of dollar management and control are the result of agency attempts to generate piecemeal changes in projects or to prevent the continuation of an existing practice within a project—hence their characterization as "tinkering" devices. To understand more fully the extent of actual power through dollar-flow control and to explore its often self-defeating properties as a sanctioning mechanism, it is necessary to survey the range of dollar-flow control devices (short of defunding) available to the agency. These tinkering devices are line-item deletions, special conditions, and short funding.

For the most impeccable of bureaucratic reasons, agency staff could red-pencil budget requests generated by center administrators or the consumers acting through the advisory council for rat control, mental health, or an attorney to provide the advisory council with legal information. From Washington's perspective, given the broad scope of the social-change agenda, such deletions were relatively insignificant. However, at the local level, the consequences of such deletions were likely to be far more significant and have important repercussions. The deletion of two patient transportation vehicles from a rural project, for example, might deprive the center of hundreds of patients. The deletion of several outreach workers used to recruit new clientele might seriously affect affect community support for the program and, in the longer run, limit the possibilities for social change in that community. Generally speaking, all too often deletion of items proposed by the center's advisory board created a sense that federal promises of meaningful community participation lacked substance and that the reform effort was not a mutual endeavor.

Along with, or in addition to, line-item deletions, the agency could use special conditions to deal with specific unsatisfactory local situations. Special conditions required a center to show progress toward a specific goal. For example, a center might be informed through a special condition that its dental program was approved in principle, but that no agency funds would be released until a satisfactorily revised work program for the budget's dental section was submitted. Or an unresponsive delegate agency might be required to submit a neighborhood advisory council election plan or to follow specified procedures in a communitywide election.

Such special conditions were used by the agency in attempts to generate piecemeal changes or, at minimum, to attempt to prevent a local situation from deteriorating further. They were the means of keeping an issue alive without delivering an ultimatum. (Although the local delegate agency was informed of the imposition of nonstandard special conditions, the local advisory council was not necessarily made aware of Washington's additional conditions.) In the poignant words of a knowledgeable staff member, "they were imposed out of a sense of helplessness."

When Washington deemed a local situation even more intolerable or intractable, it could resort to the more drastic device of short funding. A project was promised a full operating year's allocation, but received only a three- or six-month budget approval by the agency. Before budget dollars for the succeeding intervals were approved by the agency, the project had to submit to further review. For example, one center which lacked an adequate facility to deliver services submitted an annual audit which was considered scandalous. "The center did not provide Washington with any documentation regarding usage of the facility by low-income persons. They had no registration, no eligibility, no third-party payment collections to show, and they were asking us for all kinds of things like additional funds for day care. . . . That situation made us vulnerable to the GAO," one staff member commented.

Short funding was used by the agency with the hope that a drastic clamp on the dollar flow would force project improvement rapidly. But, ironically, short funding, resorted to in the name of project upgrading, often crippled floundering projects even more. Competent staff on whom the center counted for its future success often became discouraged and left.

Highly qualified personnel were more difficult to recruit for a short-funded project. Drastic fiscal sanctions lowered center morale even further and provided more fuel for hostile critics. Other sources of federal money requiring that certain prerequisite standards of organizational capability exist became unavailable to a short-funded project. For example, one short-funded center was precluded acquiring an FHA loan guarantee for a desperately needed facility because the project failed to qualify under FHA standards of organizational capability.

Rationale for Continued Funding. With the passage of time, it became more apparent that some projects would succeed and others would not. Informants tended to use a "triage" classification: winners, hard cases, and losers. In part, the judgment that certain projects were succeeding or could be made to succeed was not determined by empirical conditions. It was consequent upon the public-relations image which the project had with the Washington office—an image which the project conveyed through the program analysts who handled the routine communications between the agency and the project. One informant remarked, somewhat cynically, "when you hear beautiful things, there's often beautiful 'PR-ing.' But, in another center, the agency believes everyone carries guns, and that image has an impact when that center is short-funded even for justifiable reasons. Then, there are some centers that get no 'PR' either way; they are soon seen as dead programs."

Whether the public-relations image of a project, the actual local conditions, or a combination of the two led to the conclusion that the project enjoyed little likelihood of success, the agency continued to fund the project. There are several explanations for this action which, at least on the surface, appears incompatible with the nature of a demonstration endeavor expending precious, limited dollars on a controversial program to produce visible, positive results.

One explanation for continued funding lies in the agency's recognition that the development of operational programs required more than one or two funding rounds. It would be necessary to allow a project several years to develop, much less display adequate service and administrative capabilities. "An action program may be the only trial a social innovation will be given, and the great capacity of a community to resist change, even when the program is an ambitious one, makes negative results more likely than positive ones."[7]

The most astute local project directors recognized that Washington's justifiable hesitancy to move rapidly against a project could serve the local projects well.

> Washington sends an on-site visiting team to evaluate the projects [for re-funding purposes]. The team may say to the project director, "you haven't

done anything." They holler, but they don't take the dollars away. By the time they turn in their report, etc., it's time for next year's grant re-funding. When the site team returns, the project director can say that there was less time to do things at the center because everyone was busy preparing for re-funding. So the team doesn't do anything again.

Another explanation was that the very plurality of demonstration situations worked against rapid recognition of failure in local situations. Often, with the advantage of hindsight, there is a propensity to assume that it was obvious when a local situation would continue to fail, that the choices were clear, and that mistakes could have been avoided. Accurate information regarding local conditions was not always readily available despite the best efforts of committeed Washington staff members. Moreover, agency efforts to demonstrate new ways of delivering comprehensive care to the poor in a wide variety of settings under the aegis of range of providers *did* create a bewildering plurality of situations. Different local conditions could be assessed in a manner similar to assigning golf handicaps—with the hope for improvement as the players practiced the game.

One obvious problem connected with the endorsement of this plurality perspective is that it could be quite difficult to determine when a project was playing the token compliance game. Projects could easily appear to be contributing a program element publicly while privately conceding only a small ("token") contribution, procrastinating in making any such contribution, or substituting a contribution of inferior quality.[8]

The need for lead time and the difficulty in determining noncompliance were explanations for continued funding which took into account the realities of local development of capabilities and information-gathering systems. It was consistent for the agency to give projects the benefit of the doubt under such a rationale.

Another set of explanations for continued funding relied on the "realities" perceived by bureaucrats regarding their own operation. Close scrutiny from Washington entailed high fiscal and policy consequences. Staff members as well as legal counsel who calculated the costs of close supervision and tight fiscal management argued that the issue was whether the agency should become *too involved* in the centers' operations.

Within the agency, there was widespread recognition that it was very easy to mismanage dollars in the health center. "It's like juggling fifty or one hundred balls at once. There are situations where there's a high crime rate, lots of hostility, and community people who can't wait to pounce on the project." Less widespread, or at least readily admitted, was the recognition that not all medical-provider delegate agencies used adequate management techniques in their own operations to make them trustworthy guarantors of demonstration funds.

One attorney posed the problem graphically with a counterquestion. "Suppose we hear complaints that people are 'ripping off' the center. How can we do policing in an area which is so ripe for graft? And if we take on the role of big-brother policer in one area, then why not in others?

Even if the agency chose to scrutinize the centers closely, there were enormous difficulties in acquiring accurate, specific information regarding noncompliance in local projects. Federal threats of close scrutiny and possible defunding tended to produce momentary harmony or a temporary closing of the ranks in the local project. Quarrels and conflicts often were compromised or, more likely, patched up temporarily until the "Feds" disappeared. Then the conflict or mismanagement tended to surface again. Such seesaw situations punctuated the history of the relationship between the agency and several of the most troubled and troublesome centers.

In addition, instituting defunding procedures for local projects was a resource-consuming activity comparable to a congressional investigation. The panoply of protections accorded to institutions signing contracts for federal dollars, while desirable from a due-process perspective, meant that efforts of agency staff as well as legal counsel were focused on formal proof of clearly illegal activities. In the best of all possible worlds, an agency should be equipped to handle this type of situation; in reality, the costs associated with formal enforcement processes were enormous and virtually unacceptable in all but the *most* egregious situations. Even then, the costs might be too high if the agency reckoned with political realities.

Yet another bureaucratic-reality explanation for continued funding lay in the recognition that some projects enjoyed political protection and were virtually untouchable. A project with significant leverage such as a Congress member with direct power over the agency's appropriations was protected against agency efforts to tamper seriously with their dollar flow. One staff member recounted:

> Kentucky was nothing more than a screening and referral service which was a real luxury and wasn't meeting the community's needs. But their Congressman is on the committee which handles OEO programs. When we tried to put pressure on the locals and threaten them, their Congressman called up to inquire about the center. When we voiced our hesitations, the Congressman said, "Well, maybe we can change the OEO." So we develop a "we can live with it" attitude—until the project created such a scandal that, aided by the Congressman's opponents in state politics, the agency began to institute unsuccessful termination proceedings.

Another more circumspect OEO official was reported to have said, "You have to understand the power that Perkins has over OEO. He might never have asked that a program in his district, run by his political cronies, be left alone. But we would try to anticipate his desires. There could be worse committee chairmen than Perkins, but we would try to do them a favor whenever we could."

Even in situations where a project was not politically protected from the outset, the threat of a sanction such as funding termination was almost guaranteed to produce political pressures of varying intensity on the agency. "The basic issue is millions of dollars," one informant maintained. "When it seems apparent that there is a withdrawal of funds in the offing, it brings in third-party intervention. When we threatened a withdrawal in the city, the Health Department intervened because they were convinced we were serious, and the Mayor's office entered because they didn't want to read the headline that there were less rather than more dollars coming to that city from Washington." Yet, another informant remarked:

> Congressmen also intervene; they like to announce and endorse projects for their district; though they may not have done anything to bring the project to the area, they won't do anything against it. So there's congressional pressure to keep the local program going; moreover, the center board may get to the congressman and say, "We're delivering votes for you," or the congressman is well aware that terminating funds will put people in the district out of work.

Each of the preceding considerations as an explanation for the agency's hesitancy to withdraw funds from projects—agency recognition of the need for substantial lead time before the project could be evaluated, the bewildering plurality of projects, the cost and policy consequences of close scrutiny from Washington, and the political protection enjoyed by projects—was grounded in reality. Each is a tenable explanation. In fact, each explanation probably could have been articulated by bureaucrats from almost any federal agency dispensing federal dollars for the delivery of social services. But these explanations must be placed in the context of the controversial nature of the demonstration endeavor and the desperate bureaucratic imperative to avoid difficulties and negative publicity.

In attempting to understand the agency's response of continual funding to failing projects, it is important to recognize that a component of the agency's dilemma was its position as the victim of its own rhetoric and promises. Heightened, untenable expectations regarding the program's success rate and its practical returns were generated by the agency's "hard sell" to Congress and the administration in order to gain adequate support. Somewhat ruefully, one agency staff member summarized this point:

> We should be able to talk about 20 to 30 percent success rate. But we're even afraid to say it might be under 50 percent. Moynihan employs such high expectation rates. Who told him to believe our rhetoric? Perhaps our judgment about the change agents or the local situation was wrong; or

perhaps it's so tough that we can't do anything; or the temper of the community's response to minority groups has changed.

But in controversial social-change demonstration efforts, broad experimental latitude in the rate of success is not permissible. The competition for funds has led to an unrealistically high expectation of success from experimental programs and low congressional tolerance of delayed practical returns.

The crux of the matter is that a social-change demonstration agency cannot argue that its function is fulfilled if it identifies the correct issue areas, asks the correct questions, and works in a constructive way or if it makes negative as well as positive findings which have intrinsic utility for future understanding and strategic choices. Much more is expected of the engineering of human conduct in politically controversial situations (which implicitly or explicitly question the distribution of resources in the system) than in exploring the nature of life in the scientists' laboratories or constructing a new weapon. A social-change demonstration agency's negative findings inevitably are equated with mistakes.

This equation of project failure or unsatisfactory performance with mistakes makes it difficult for participants in the project at the Washington or local level to admit to difficulties. At the local level, the medical providers were unaccustomed and unwilling to blame themselves. The project director at one of the oldest, most troubled, most troublesome, and non-productive centers summarized the situation: "Nobody wants to admit they're wrong. If it's an important hospital or medical association head, he won't tell the agency that he made a mistake. And the hospital [delegate agency] wouldn't be convinced that a community corporation could come closer to providing the answers."

Moreover, admissions of failure or mistake often had significant repercussions at the local or state level. They became a valuable weapon for local opponents of a project. For example, a study-group finding of problems in financial management, administration, and services in the beleaguered Mound Bayou project in Mississippi was used by the state's governor as an "overwhelming vindication of this [his] administration in vetoing the OEO grant to the Mound Bayou health program."[9]

Finally, and perhaps most important of all, OHA viewed the public identification of weaknesses in projects and the fiscal sanctioning of failing projects as an acknowledgment of its own failure. Alternatively, Washington argued, even if failing projects ought not be equated with agency failure, they would be interpreted as such by critics and competitors who would question the entire demonstration endeavor. "It's like a ball game; if the team loses, it's the manager's fault," a staff member announced. "If we prove that too many things don't work, we are not a pilot program," another informant noted.

Given the increasingly controversial nature of the program as it expanded, competed for more dollars, and became more visible, public admission of failures would be tantamount to washing the agency's dirty linen in public with the prospect of enemies and competitors beginning to ask whether the agency had other laundry hidden away. A staff member remarked:

> When you begin to defend a project, lots more things come out about your own housekeeping. Even if the negative evaluation and the termination of the project is totally justified, people in Washington begin to ask questions about the agency's operation in general—the least desirable prospects for any agency, particularly an agency which has placed itself on the frontlines by its commitment to change, more or less elusively defined.

Scandals and the Dilemmas They Pose. Scandal is the agency's albatross. Publication of its existence focuses congressional and possibly public attention onto the project and ultimately on the agency as well. Agency breast beating or protestations at that point are given short shrift.

Only in a highly limited number of situations where center mismanagement reached endemic proportions and became *highly visible* did the agency threaten to close down centers. The most appropriate course was to initiate the defunding process. But the panoply of due-process protections for the federal contractor in a defunding hearing makes this strategy a time-consuming and energy-draining endeavor which, like congressional hearings, can distract staff from vital daily work. Consequently, the agency tended to hesitate in embarking on a shift of the controversy to the adversarial forum of a hearing. Generally speaking, the agency sought a compromise although there was little real assurance that the compromise would lead to significant local reform.

Situations "on the margin," in which social change was extremely difficult to achieve despite the amount of dollars made available to the project, often became involved in such compromises. Lowndes County, Alabama offers an excellent illustration of an on-the-margin situation. Recollections by early senior staff people suggest that key policymakers did believe, at least in part, that they could "buy" social change in the area with federal dollars. After a time, no effort was made to deal with the racism and malpractice which surfaced. "Instead, there was policy decision to leave it alone; no visits from the staff for a year and a half. We tried to transfer it twice [to HEW]. When one of the senior Washington staff people went down there for the opening of the health facility, he only stayed for half an hour. It was so rushed that they had to say the opening prayer after he left."

One more optimistic staff member voiced a long-term hope which may have assisted the agency in rationalizing its position: "I'm horrified at what they're [The Lowndes County Board of Health] doing now. It's an expensive way to get things done, but it may be as fast a way to get things done as possible. You put in place a mechanism which cannot die. It's scary because it's risky and colonial, but it can't fail because it provides services. They [the community] will control that building though it may take ten years.'' Even if one chooses not to quarrel with this argument, the issue for the agency remained that a potentially scandalous situation prevailed in the project which the agency would be hard pressed to defend publicly.

Finally, the *Washington Post* published an article in which the center project director, a medical doctor, was reported to have said, ''you might say that I'm running a federal plantation; you might say my job is like my Daddy's.''[10] The consternation and uproar which the article created forced the agency to threaten publicly to terminate funds unless such practices as segregated waiting rooms for patients and other grossly offensive situations were remedied.

Another well-publicized illustration of the problems confronting a demonstration agency dealing with a scandalous situation can be found in the story of the politically protected neighborhood health center in Floyd County, Kentucky. One staff member commented:

> In Floyd County we made honest, basic errors. It's just not a good idea to do a program not impacting on how health care is delivered and financed. We had originally hoped to get the system to move with buying traditional medical care from fee-for-services doctors. They [the center in Floyd County] could have gotten away with it if they hadn't been so blatant and so defiant of our requests for reform (job development, full-time staff services, outreach which would have been more than mere transportation of patients). What happened was that the frills for any ancillary-services programs which we funded went for patronage not for substance.

Science, the prestigious journal of the American Association for the Advancement of Science, picked up on the OEO report for Floyd County and published two stories exposing the venality of the doctors and the corruption in the project. The article alleged major violations of OEO regulations, including exclusion of community members lacking political connections from jobs, training, and the policy-making process; sponsor use of the center primarily as a referral service only for physicians practicing in the county rather than as a treatment center; and the absence of adequate, and in some instances any record of, physician encounters despite evidence of reimbursement.[11]

Confronted by a low-income population mobilized through the Eastern Kentucky Welfare Rights Organization, the OEO was forced to undertake administrative action leading to termination of the grant. Several days before the required termination hearing, the agency backed down and agreed to a compromise awarding a new grant to a new board. To outside observers the new structure was unlikely to be substantially more responsive to community needs than the old one. But apparently the key political figure in the county is reported to have informed the OEO that "if he had no influence over the new program, then there would be no new program."[12]

Attempting to Ensure Long-Range Fiscal Viability:
Problems of "Fit"

Among social activists and reformers, broad issues of equity and justice are among the interesting aspects of social policy. The more mundane, seemingly routine matter of financing projects and their long-range fiscal viability pales before the intensity of emotion and commitment generated by vanguard issues of social change. In the headiness of planning and implementing social change, there is a tendency to assume that the projects will capture the public imagination or that the guardians of the public purse will be pressured to continue financial support. In any case, the dollars will continue to flow. With hindsight, it becomes apparent that this aspect of the reform euphoria is largely unconnected with the often harsh realities of long-range fiscal viability for the new institution. Such viability involves a "fit" with the larger system in which the reform institution is involved.

In the early days, the agency was far too preoccupied with identifying "impeccable" or reliable grantees for its risk capital and negotiating the terms for individual health centers to concern itself with matters of longer-term financing. More as a matter of bureaucratic formality than operational reality, some staff members discussed the maximum effective use of existing financial resources for low-income clientele available in the health delivery field. These resources, it was obvious, were public-health dollars. New, often controversial neighborhood health centers dependent on annual federal re-funding whose clientele had no capacity to generate private resources were unlikely to be considered a good risk by private investors.

To assuage the fears of the OEO General Counsel's Office, which was concerned with protecting the program from congressional inquiries regarding center funds being utilized to duplicate existing publicly funded services, the agency stipulated in both the guidelines and the awards that it could not fund services for which support was already available. The OEO funds were a "last dollar resource" to help fill gaps in existing services.[13] Project grants were target funds for groups and services considered priorities by the federal government for which other dollars were unavailable. At least theoretically, both outside funds and existing services were to be integrated into the comprehensive neighborhood health center. The last-dollar clause also meant that centers were also expected to collect third-party reimbursements for some of their eligible patients from Medicaid and Medicare.

In theory, utilizing existing reimbursements and services in the health-care delivery system would permit centers to operate as fiscally viable, self-sustaining entities (or, at least after start-up costs were absorbed, to cover 50 to 75 percent of their costs within several years). But the reality of financing a new delivery mechanism proved to be a far more complex and difficult endeavor than the theoretical discussions implied.

Joint funding is one means of utilizing existing resources. The experience of the agency suggests that although such cooperative funding is a bureaucratic desideratum, it is more or less a programmatic impossibility: "Everyone wants coordination—on his own terms. Invocation of coordination does not necessarily provide either a statement of or a solution to the problem, but it may be a way of avoiding both when accurate prescription would be too painful. Coordination means getting what you do not have. . . . Achieving coordination . . . means getting your own way."[14]

Existing agencies with public funds for health services were unwilling to pool their dollars in the centers. These agencies, like OEO, were concerned with precisely the same questions of bureaucratic survival through project recognition. Agencies which had small amounts to award would be swamped by massive infusions of OEO demonstration dollars into any jointly funded center. Agencies with large amounts of available dollars were unwilling to lose or dilute their authority by joint funding. Moreover, they were unwilling to become involved in a controversial or possible distasteful reform agenda. The acceptance by other health-services delivery agencies of the coordination-of-dollars principle would mean, in practice, their acknowledgment of OEO's claim of right to fund only those activities not covered by existing health dollars.

Another source of existing resources was the third-party reimbursements for center medical-care services when the patient was covered by Medicare or Medicaid. By insisting on the collection of diverse additional payments rightfully available to the centers, the agency hoped to generate a steady flow of funds, thereby ensuring fiscal stability and viability for the centers. The agency's position was spelled out in the guidelines:

Under the terms of Section 222(a)(4)(A), agencies now providing services to the target neighborhood can be furnished assistance in order to permit them to plan for participation in a neighborhood health services project and for the necessary continuation of such services.

Wherever another third party (such as private insurance or workmen's compensation) is responsible for payment for services rendered to any individual, the comprehensive health services project must obtain reimbursement of such funds.

Comprehensive health services projects will usually be eligible for reimbursement under the following programs:

1. As a vendor of covered services under the State welfare medical care program, in particular, to those eligible for benefits under Title XIX (Medicaid) of the Social Security Amendments of 1965.
2. As a provider of home health services and in those instances where the operating agency is a hospital, as a provider of outpatient diagnostic services to those eligible for benefits under Title XVIII, Part A (Medicare) of the Social Security Amendments of 1965.
3. As a provider of physicians' and other outpatient medical services and supplies to those eligible for benefits under Title XVIII, Part B (Supplemental Health Insurance Benefits) of the Social Security Amendments of 1965.

Where approval or certification for such reimbursement applies, the project must meet the conditions for such approval or certification as soon as possible; discussions with the appropriate local and State officials should be initiated early in the planning of the program.[15]

But the actual collection was fraught with unanticipated difficulties which reflected the problems of being a demonstration endeavor and depending ultimately on federal dollars as a source of funds. Even the incentive of allowing the centers to retain the income from fees collected in order to further the original grant-award purposes did not produce any marked increase in the rate or total amount of reimbursement.

As the GAO pointed out, certain difficulties regarding the collection of third-party reimbursements were the result of deficiencies in center management practices:

Although we did not attempt to determine the efficiency and economy of the NHCs' operations, our work revealed a number of operating inefficiencies. We estimated that one NHC would have been only 48 percent self-supporting if the full fees for all services provided during 1972 had been collected. Apparent overstaffing and low utilization rates for existing services contributed to this inefficiency.

Inaccurate and incomplete records were deficiencies common to all NHCs. Missed billing opportunities, incorrect billings, lack of control over accounts receivable, and other accounting system weaknesses were noted at several NHCs.

The five NHCs were deficient in identifying patients who were eligible for, or enrolled in, third-party reimbursement programs, principally the Medicaid program. Generally the NHCs obtained information on a person's ability to pay and eligibility for, or participation in, any medical insurance program only when he initially registered. Three of the NHCs did not have any comprehensive system to verify or periodically update the initial information. In many instances, information obtained at registration was inadequate to determine eligibility or ability to pay and no efforts were being made to make such determinations. As a consequence, fees which should have been charged were not.[16]

But other difficulties were not situation-specific. Rather, they were reflective of the more serious structural problem of fitting innovative social-service delivery programs with existing, conventional financing mechanisms. They included disagreements with state authorities over the number of persons eligible for third-party coverage, the services for which the center would be reimbursed, and the actual amounts of the reimbursement.

In 1967, Congress amended the Social Security Act to curtail Medicaid coverage of the medically indigent.[17] Congressional retrenchment signaled a parallel welfare-eligibility cutback by the states. And centers were deprived of the level of publicly subsidized reimbursement for some previously eligible, medically indigent persons.[18]

Commenting on the contribution of low-income persons who are able to pay and who live within the NHC's target area and are charged a prorated income based fee, the GAO noted: "The fees range from $3 to $25; the majority of the patients pay $3. Persons who live outside the target area are charged $7 for a physician or dentist visit plus fees for other services. Patient fees account for about 2 percent of total reimbursements received by the NHC.[19] This sum stood in stark contrast to the Medicaid reimbursement sum of over $41 per patient-visit to the center.

In addition, prorating meant, somewhat paradoxically, that the near-poor clientele of the health center might pay more for services at the center than they would at the local hospital clinic. Hospitals could supplement their income from private donations to cover the costs of caring for the near indigent, whereas centers were told that since they were a demonstration program funded by the federal government, they did not need philanthropic support.

The fact that one of the major alternative dollar sources for operating a neighborhood health center (Medicaid) was a political football and thus unreliable meant that center dependency on increasingly controversial OEO dollars was heightened. Moreover, the actual amount of Medicaid dollars recoverable by the center was open to speculation. Various state agencies had different reimbursement rates depending on prevailing local conditions. Summarizing the problem, one staff member commented:

> In one State the rate is $4 per patient-visit. It's hard to make dollars at that rate. . . . But when the senior staff in Washington see only $77,000 for reimbursements from Medicaid in that state reported by a center, they say it's unacceptable; a project should collect at least 10 percent of its budget from Medicaid and if a center gets $2.30 million, it should collect about $230,000. I looked at their encounter forms, and they captured all they could get. But Washington will say that any new program expansion including an evening clinic is tied to the collection of a greater sum from third parties.

In addition to the controversy over the number of persons eligible for Medicaid coverage and the amount actually recoverable, the issue of determining which center services were reimbursable by third parties (especially Medicaid) highlighted the problem of the meshing of reform programs with conventional financing mechanisms. Not surprisingly, in 1972 an amendment to the Social Security Act requiring state coverage of clinics with 95 percent federal funding was defeated.[20] In this area, the centers with their innovative forms of delivery and their provision of a number of supportive services often not associated with conventional medical practice but considered integral to the success of the program in a low-income community were faced with the difficulties of a reformist endeavor dealing with a conventional bureaucracy.

One staff member assigned to work on the relationship of Medicaid agencies to the center program talked about his notably limited success:

> State and local agencies are geared to doing things on a mass basis . . . and are geared to recognize a few billing categories: doctor in an office, hospital, nursing home, independent lab. They didn't understand an organization like ours which you could say partially encompassed all four. They wanted to treat us as one of the four though we weren't even a near fit. In a bureaucratic situation it's easiest to stop and do nothing when you're confused. If the state agencies hadn't been hounded by some of the grantees, they wouldn't have done anything. And then that raised the issue whether in a new demonstration the project director's priority ought to be pounding his head against the wall, especially when other federal dollars were available. The first battle was to show that we were not like Public Health Service direct federal health-care programs (because third-party intermediaries like Blue Cross and Blue Shield don't pay for direct federal services). Then we fought out the issue of unnecessary exceptions [in Medicaid billing] as well as the conditions under which the bill would be sent and what the bill would look like. States would decide to look at the centers like a hospital outpatient department (which we preferred) or like a group of physicians operating independently but with a central financing base.

According to the GAO, all NHCs, to claim Medicare reimbursement, had to be recognized as providers or provider-equivalents by the responsible administrative agency.[21] For NHCs controlled by hospitals or other organizations already having provider status, this presented no problem. However, recognition as a provider for an unassociated or freestanding NHC was not automatic. Although Medicare regulations provide for recognizing freestanding NHCs as "physician-directed clinics," some NHCs were denied recognition. The consequences of such structural fragmentation were bizarre and irrational. For example, "the Medicare program recognizes the Denver NHC as a provider; therefore, the NHC can bill for certain physician and clinical services provided to eligible Medicare patients. The Colorado Medicaid program does not recognize the NHC; therefore, the NHC can bill Medicaid only for physician visits.''[22]

Even the development of negotiated categories for defining a center's operation did not solve the problem of defining the range of reimbursable services. One county health department informed a health-center administrator that welfare could not reimburse the center for home health services provided by the community-health teams. In other situations, a center's use of outreach workers who were trained to assist the medical staff in a wide variety of functions as well as recruit patients for the center caused difficulty for state bureaucracies. Since the states were obligated to contribute matching funds to federal dollars for Medicaid, the use of outreach workers to recruit even more indigent patients who might qualify for Medicaid assistance ran counter to every state effort to trim welfare costs.

Differences between programs meant that acceptable categories for reimbursement under one program were not reimbursable under another. According to the GAO, "the Sunset Park NHC receives an all-inclusive rate under the Medicaid program for each physician or dentist visit. During 1972 the Medicaid program paid the NHC $41.06 for each fully covered Medicaid patient who visited a physician or dentist.

The Medicaid program accounts for about 97 percent of the third-party reimbursements received by the Sunset Park NHC. Less than 1 percent of the NHC's reimbursements are received from the Medicare program which does not reimburse the NHC for dental care, drugs, or preventive health services.''[23]

According to the GAO which conducted an investigation in 1972 of five HEW neighborhood-health-center programs (three of which had been OEO programs in the 1960s), some medical and medically related services were generally not covered by third-party reimbursement programs at the NHCs.[24] These services included optometry, mental health, speech therapy, nutrition, and supportive activities, such as social, nursery, and transportation services.

Whereas Medicare coverage of services is standard throughout the United States, Medicaid coverage, aside from those services required by law, varies from state to state. Both programs provide only partial coverage for certain services. For example, Medicaid in many states covered only the services provided directly by a physician or dentist. The cost of services provided by a dental hygienist, social worker, nurse, psychologist laboratory, and X-ray were not reimbursable.

"Although federal and state governments have been spending $10 billion a year for Medicaid and Medicare," one staff member who was preoccupied with issues of longer-range fiscal viability remarked, "little of this money has worked its way back to the centers to pay for operations. I don't think that centers in the 'best states' are able to collect more than 25 percent or 30 percent in Medicare and Medicaid reimbursements." Overall recovery estimates ranged from 10 to 15 percent.

In effect it became increasingly apparent that the practices of the NHCs and the available third-party reimbursement programs operated to prevent the centers from becoming self-supporting. One federal official contemplating the future of the centers summarized the situation: "As a national program, it will be impossible for neighborhood health centers to reach self-sufficiency until a federal financing mechanism is in place which will give broader entitlement both for services and eligibility.

The preceding chronicle of almost insurmountable problems connected with the establishment of long-range fiscal viability suggests that fitting a new institution into an existing system requires a more complex and sophisticated funding design than the type usually generated by inspired reformers. But the equally valid counter argument suggests that efforts to develop innovative institutions cannot rely on existing funding categories or mechanisms. Existing mechanisms fund conventional and routine activities. Demonstration programs by their very nature are unconventional and seek to break out of the very activities with which funding sources are most comfortable. To expect a fit within two, three, or even five years for many projects rests on the unwarranted assumption that funding sources are likewise undergoing changes to keep pace with the most advanced institutions in a social-service delivery system.

Conclusions

The problems connected with the headaches of dollars explored in this chapter point to the proposition that analysis of the program implementation must consider the structural handicaps of a systemic nature which programs face. These obstacles may dilute and ultimately defeat reform programs, however well intentioned or motivated individual participants in the program may be.

The headaches generated by dollars are several. A successfully expanding, controversial social-change agency will inevitably find itself confronted by a struggle with local projects to *define* the use of federal dollars. This struggle is generated by the difference between local and federal perspectives on the same demonstration operation and hence on the crucial area of dollar definition.

Although the difference in perspective between Washington and the local projects is by no means confined to demonstration projects, it does have heightened consequences for program implementation in a controversial demonstration situation. Washington has limited resources and an unreasonably short time to implement reform agenda. Hence, the need to develop a modus vivendi between Washington and the local projects is more pressing, although there is no indication that such pressure results in a more satisfactory resolution of a seemingly intractable issue.

Dollar definition is simply the first step. Dollars must not be dispensed; their flow must be monitored and controlled. If necessary, this may mean the enforcement of sanctions against projects. But fiscal tinkering devices either cannot provide the impetus for a change in project direction when desired or, more perniciously, lead to that further decline in a project which Washington hopes to avoid.

In theory, the funding of demonstration endeavors implies that precious resources should not continue to be expended on projects which are clear failures. Instead, these resources ought to be channeled into existing successful programs or new ones. Theory is often overruled by the anticipated, if not anticipatable, political consequences of publicly and voluntarily admitting to mistakes by initiating defunding procedures. Quite predictably, only in the most flagrant cases after public attention had been drawn to a situation did the agency begin to institute the time- and resource-consuming process of defunding.

Recognizing that demonstration dollars are finite, a demonstration agency may attempt to ensure the long-range fiscal viability of its projects by fitting its projects, which are controversial and often considered as poor risks by other public or private funding sources, into existing funding channels. The agency and ultimately the projects are likely to expend enormous time and energy with very limited prospects for success. Successful fitting, when it occurs, is likely to involve compromising the reform agenda in order to make projects palatable to existing stable funding sources.

Each of the three major headaches caused by dollars in the administration of the NHC program was not simply time-consuming. Struggles connected with dollars, like the struggles connected with the development of governance and accountability structures detailed in chapter 5, were all too likely to result in dilution of the reform agenda. Dollars were both the incentive and the underminer of reform.

7 Dilemmas of Demonstration Program Effectiveness

Rare indeed is the agency which develops the capacity for introspection about the nature of its endeavors and their consequences and the ability, from time to time, to stand back from the crush of events and crises in order to assess itself. For a demonstration agency, the likelihood of indulging in such seemingly leisurely activities is minimal. Reflection requires time and psychological space. Demonstration agencies are caught up in the seemingly endless complexities and conflicts generated by their distribution, definition, and monitoring responsibilities of federal dollars. As the preceding chapters detail, dollars cause headaches, and headaches can be barriers to thoughtful consideration. Reflection requires the ability to move from a high- to a low-profile position. Demonstration agencies are haunted by the imperative to achieve and maintain high visibility. Reflection requires the absence of stress. Underlying the agency's acute intermittent headaches is the chronic condition of anxiety generated by an ongoing need to prove program effectiveness.

Even if a demonstration agency possesses the sensibilities and sensitivities to anticipate and possibly head off major handicaps or disasters, it still must confront another task which is likely to compound difficulties that operate to undermine its effectiveness. These additional difficulties spring from the demands on an agency for an accounting to Congress.

Historically, such an accounting was limited to an audit of expended funds. Over time, as congressional oversight functions expanded, the audit has been replaced by a program evaluation:

> The reasons for evaluating process are obvious. First, from the standpoint of the administration of human-resources programs, it is critical to know that what presumably was paid for or deemed desirable was actually undertaken. Second, there is no point in being concerned with the impact or outcome of particular programs unless one knows that they did indeed take place, and did so with the appropriate target group. Many programs are not implemented and executed in the way originally designed for a variety of reasons. Sometimes personnel and equipment simply are not available; sometimes persons engaged in the program are prevented by political or other reasons from undertaking what they intended. Individuals who are part of the program staff may not have the motivation or know-how to carry out their tasks as outlined. There are also instances in which the intended program targets do not exist in the numbers required, cannot be identified precisely, or cannot provide the necessary cooperation.[1]

117

During the past decade, an increasing amount of attention has been paid to the design of satisfactory evaluation formats—those plans which estimate, assess, or appraise policy, including its content, implementation, and effects.[2] The trend persists despite the widespread recognition that there are "few if any illustrations of well developed and carefully conducted evaluation studies completed in time to affect directly either legislation or the short range decision making process of policymakers."[3]

Demonstration agencies along with other bureaucracies share the common fate of having their program efforts evaluated. While equity associated with reform can be a propelling force for the passage of legislation, it is an unsatisfactory basis for a longer-term commitment to a reform-oriented social policy. Equity focuses on a problem, often a distributional one. After the compelling rhetoric it often generates has subsided, problem solving surfaces as a more attractive foundation for policy. And problem solving ostensibly is amenable to scientifically oriented evaluations of progress. In turn, these evaluations lead to an understanding and amelioration, if not the elimination, of the problem.

Often, evaluation efforts, especially those performed by experts unconnected with the implementing bureaucracy and therefore less amenable to agency control, are the object of ambivalent feelings. To the extent that such evaluation efforts legitimate or defend programs, delay decisions, allow for the floating of trial balloons, can be used as offensive weapons against recalcitrant projects, or serve to reduce uncertainty, they are likely to evoke positive responses from bureaucrats.[4] But to the extent that such efforts are equated with "judicious" modification of programs and hence increase uncertainty, they provoke anxiety and fear among bureaucrats. (In all fairness, it should be noted that the theoretical need to obtain rigorous analysis is countered by the short-run need for "big splashes" with dramatic anecdotal evidence. Given these conflicting imperatives, less systematic, systematic research may well be appropriate, despite the more critical scholarly response it elicits.)

> Decision-makers respond to a host of factors besides evidence of program effectiveness. They are concerned with the political and organizational feasibility of the program; its acceptability to funders, staff, and constituents; the availability of money. They may have an ideological commitment to the program or an interest in maintaining the agency's position in the field. They may fear the unknown consequences of change and feel more comfortable in the status quo.[5]

Empirical verification of these fears is quite another matter. Rossi, quite provocatively, notes:

> In fact, I do not know of any action program that has been put out of business by evaluation research, unless evaluation itself was used as the

hatchet to begin with. Why is this the case? Why do negative results have so little impact? The main reason lies in the fact that the practitioners, first of all (and sometimes the researchers), never seriously entertained in advance the possibility that results would come out negative or insignificant. Without commitment to the bet, one or both of the gamblers usually welch.

The ways by which welching is accomplished are myriad. It is easy to attack the methodology of any study: Methodological unsophisticates suddenly become experts in sampling, questionnaire construction, experimental design, and statistical analysis, or borrow experts for the occasion. Further replication is called for. But, most often it is discovered that the goals of the program in terms of which it was evaluated are not the "real" goals after all.[6]

Local project staff also dislike the prospect of evaluation studies.

Many program staff are convinced of the program's worth and see little need for evaluation. If results of the study are positive, they knew it all along. If the results are negative, it is probably the fault of the evaluators and the grossness of their measures, which are too intensive to capture the subtle and important changes that are going on. Furthermore, if people take negative findings seriously, the consequence of the study may be to imperil the program—and possibly the staff's own jobs. It is not remarkable that they are uncooperative when they view evaluation as a sitting-in-judgment on their work. Even when defensiveness is not a salient element in their view, they often see little potential payoff from evaluation.[7]

Moreover, as Cain and Hollister point out, friction develops between local project administrators and evaluators.[8] There is likely to be a failure of agreement on the level of decision making for which the results of evaluation are to be used. Local projects are likely to want results which will assist them in their efforts. Washington's information needs may dictate the gathering of other information for evaluation purposes.

The parallel is striking between local discomfort, if not paranoia, regarding the use of information for the evaluation process and the responses elicited from local projects regarding the conveying of information for Washington's monitoring purposes (see chapter 6). The underlying theme common to both situations is the political value attached to information.

Measuring Program Impact

Agencies with a demonstration mandate operate within a political time frame. They must return to Congress annually for funding. Basically, the re-funding process involves convincing the Office of Management and the Budget (OMB) and key members of appropriate congressional committees that the program has produced some significant results. "No matter how comprehensive and ennobling the proponents of the program say it is, the program must still run a political and economic gauntlet to prove its effectiveness and value."[9] The concept of program evaluation is a compelling one. And the combination of the techniques of evaluation with an organization capable of performing the task on itself with sensitivity and insight reflects the best of all possible worlds. Such an ideal organization

> would continuously monitor its own activities so as to determine whether it was meeting its goals or even whether these goals should continue to prevail.
>
> . . . To evaluate man the organization doesn't matter unless it facilitates the accomplishment of objectives. . . . Both objectives and resources, says evaluative man, must be continously modified to achieve the optimal response to social need.[10]

Basically the program evaluation endeavor has a deceptively simple format. It consists of

1. Finding out the goals
2. Translating [them] into measurable indicators of goal achievement
3. Collecting the data on the indicators for those who have been exposed to the program
4. Collecting similar data on a control group
5. Comparing the data on program participants and controls in terms of goal criteria[11]

Less ambitious *operational* evaluation efforts scrutinize financial costs and benefits as well as agency and project efforts to follow legal standards and procedures. Newer, more ambitious impact evaluations measure the societal *impact* of a program.

Impact evaluation includes determinations of efforts to achieve stated objectives and an exploration of alternatives.

> It is concerned with gauging the extent to which a program effects a change in the desired direction. It implies that there is a set of prespecified operationally defined goals and criteria of success; measured impact refers to movement or change toward the desired objectives. These objectives may be social-behavioral ones, such as reduction of parole violations or decline in the rate of admissions to hospitals; they may be community measures, such as the frequency of crime reported to the police or reported in sample surveys by community members. . .[12]

Measuring program effectiveness requires that even if relatively little money is spent (as in a demonstration program), relatively few people are affected and the real problem is hardly even touched.[13] Impact must be measured though the state of research methodology, and politics militate against the development of a powerful design capable of rendering an unequivocal statement.

There is the historical irony of measuring impact in new programs when massive results are unlikely to occur: "New treatments can be expected to yield marginal improvements over present treatments and that cost-to-benefit ratios . . . rise dramatically. Hence, there is considerable interest in research but considerable apprehension over what it will show concerning the effects of programs."[14]

But whether of the operational or impact type, evaluation is viewed as a preeminently rational activity.[15] Set aside is the recognition that the evaluators' perspectives on various public-policy issues are not immune from prevailing preconceptions and intellectual fashions.

> For instance, the flow of research on human capital responded to, even as it first reinforced and then undermined, the simple faith in education. The research on the ineffectiveness of certain government programs reflected, even as it strengthened, a disillusionment about the potential good to be achieved by governmental action.[16]

Set aside is the recognition that evaluation, especially cost-effectiveness studies, has a conservative bias. When these studies were undertaken by liberals and radicals during the Johnson years, they appeared to be tools for pushing the pace of social change. But their utilization by these liberals and radicals obscured, as Aaron points out, the profoundly conservative tendency of formal evaluation and program analysis, demonstrated so well during the Nixon administration.[17]

As a first step, impact evaluation requires that the goals or objectives of a program be already specified or readily discoverable. Only then can measurable indicators of success or impact be developed. The logic of such a requirement is impeccable. The reality is that specific goals and objectives are likely to be unarticulated, unspecific when articulated, and possibly inconsistent when specified.

As chapter 1 makes painfully apparent, such an exercise in refinement never was undertaken either for the War on Poverty or for its specific programmatic emanations. Recognition of this deficiency led to calls by NHC supporters for more formal classification and prioritization of local project goals. "O.E.O. should require that each neighborhood health center state specific attainable objectives pursuant to the observed health and social needs of the target area, and consistent with the center's resources. . . . In this way progress will become observable.[18]

Even if some satisfactory measure of goal definition were achieved, the complexity of most programs would affect the evaluators' ability to assess the program's effectiveness and impact. Building in measures to determine which factors produced which observed effects is a difficult and controversial task.

> Some programs are not only complex in content and method, they also shift course in midstream. . . . The evaluator, even one who had the foresight to take measurements of important program variables, is faced with a dilemma. He will be able to discover the extent of change that occurred in participants on the outcome indicators, but to what does he attribute the change: the original program, the subsequent program, the transition, or some admixture of everything going on?[10]

In addition to the difficulties of achieving consensus on goals or objectives and the lack of simplicity in social reform endeavors—both of which affected the quality of evaluation research—another serious obstacle to scientific rigor in evaluation methodology exists. Extreneous nonprogram factors operate on programs and are difficult to measure.

Attributing the correct degree of change to the program is theoretically possible when control-group behavior is compared with program-participant behavior. But it is difficult to obtain control groups of persons who were unexposed to the program but on whom the same extraneous nonprogram factors operated.

> The essential condition for controls is that they be very much like the participants. The best way to assure similarity is to draw participants and controls from the same population pool and randomly assign individuals to one group or the other. Now there's the rub. In evaluation, the evaluator can rarely randomize assignments. Sometimes the program has to be offered to intact natural groups. . . . Sometimes the program is offered on a voluntary basis and serves everyone who applies. How can you find controls . . . when everyone eligible and motivated is already participating in the program? On occasion, program directors and staff reject the whole concept of control groups as a denial of service to people in need.
>
> A second-best procedure is to match participants and controls on characteristics assumed relevant to outcomes. . . . While often the best that can be done, matching procedures are frequently limited by ignorance of what variables are significant enough to require matching and by other potential biases as well.
>
> Even when the evaluator succeeds in setting up controls, problems arise in maintaining them. Program staff may undermine the control groups by accepting their members into the program when vacancies open up. . . . Further, it is sometimes hard to maintain contact and cooperation with controls when the program periodically asks them for information but offers nothing in return.[20]

To this seemingly overwhelming catalog of difficulties and obstacles in attempting to implement an effective evaluation program must be added the problem of developing an effective cost/benefit calculus. In the NHC program, the "hardware" aspect (the actual delivery of services) appeared to be the least difficult aspect of the program to document and presumably to evaluate. It was thought that more reliable indicators, or at least scientific sounding measurements, could be developed over time to determine the impact of the services on the local population, though no ready technique existed for sorting and recording measurable performance indices. But within a few years it became apparent that the evaluation of centers' actual delivery of health-care services was a far more complex endeavor than the agency ever anticipated.

The initial problem in developing a cost/benefit ratio for health services is the conceptualization of the activity. Health services may be considered as either consumption goods or investment goods, although there is no general agreement regarding their classification. If they are considered as consumption goods, they are an end, and their receipt by the consumer is the major means for assessing their adequacy. If they are considered as investment goods, health services are a means to another end, such as increased productivity in the workforce. The conceptual choice clearly is crucial to the development of the ratio and its outcome.

Independent of the conceptual choice of health as a consumption or an investment good is another important, deceptively simple, choice which will affect the ratio—the method of calculating costs. This choice is disguised as a methodological consideration, but is in reality a political one of great importance.

Generally speaking, the costs of innovation, at least initially, tend to be higher than the cost of operating in a conventional, routine manner. In the delivery of health-care services to low-income persons where the number of untended, chronic conditions is considerably higher than for the rest of the population, costs are likely to soar as soon as care is delivered to the previously excluded. However, these high costs are a liability for the agency when the administration and Congress are making judgments regarding the continuation of programs. For evaluation purposes, high costs tend to become one of the negative features of a program.

In addition to the extra costs incurred for providing health care to previously underserved or excluded population groups, costs can be inflated by the innovative aspects of a reform program. The assignment of a proper weight to these extra costs is a political as well as an economic calculus. "When OEO looked at our budget," one staff member in a center which relied on paraprofessionals recruited from the community remarked angrily, "they calculated our costs by dividing them by the number of doctors without looking at our other personnel. Of course, the costs came out high. It would be better for us to go back to the traditional model of medical care and get eighty doctors. Then we'd even get more money from Medicaid."

Even if it is apparent that the institution or service delivered does not operate in a classical market-economy type of situation, a comparison of costs with those of other institutions or similar services places the demonstration program in a meaningful context. But, as Rivlin points out, analysts who want to make better decisions on social-action programs have not progressed very far toward making the benefits of social action comparable; nor can they offer much help with the larger issue of how to allocate public resources among major types of programs.[21]

The very nature of a demonstration program makes this essential comparison of costs difficult, if not impossible, to accomplish. With what institutions or services should the demonstration program compare itself?

One method developed to make both internal comparisons across projects and comparisons between the centers and other types of health-care facilities is the medical audit (the pulling of patients' medical records at random and evaluating the quality of care from that written record). The process studies developed from these audits have focused on quality of service delivered.[22] They have been criticized for assuming a connection between quality and outcomes.

Clearly, the measurement device is still a crude one, and there are several problems with the technique. It relies on accurate, sophisticated recordkeeping. New demonstration projects, especially those utilizing relatively unskilled staff, are likely to compromise with less adequate records. Moreover, there is no readily available body of data with which findings from health centers through medical audits could be compared. Nevertheless, in the attempt to provide data for quality and cost purposes, the audit serves a useful function. But it should not be confused with the technology for outcome assessment, which "is even more rudimentary and practically non-existent for community wide comprehensive health services."[23]

The problems in establishing a cost calculus find their counterpart in the equally controversial and confused issue of estimating or determining benefits. At the broadest conceptual level, poverty-program endeavors presumably should assist in eliminating poverty or in the removal of as many people as possible from such a situation. The program's effectiveness and the benefits it distributes should, at least in theory, be measured against this criterion despite the lack of consensus on what constitutes poverty.

Clearly, for a demonstration program focusing on the delivery of health-care services to the poor, relieving immediate health difficulties or conditions may be an extremely inaccurate basis for a benefit calculus. Basic problems are connected with the fact that most health measures used in such analyses tend to focus on health conditions that impinge on income, and thus they ignore the benefits involved in the elimination of pain and of worry.[24]

At an even more concrete level, the agency had to develop a set of satisfactory definitions to the key policy-question terms which defined the scope of benefits. "Are neighborhood health centers a reasonable way to provide adequate health care which is competitive with existing delivery mechanisms in cost, quality, and acceptability to the population served?" The major terms *reasonably, adequate, competitive, cost, quality*, and *acceptability* were capable of multiple interpretations and hence multiple criteria for evaluation purposes. If the definition of the major terms

> [is] too vague, no evaluation can be done, If [it is] too specific, it never encompass[es] all the indefinable qualities that adherents insist [it has]. If [it is] too broad, any activity may be said to contribute to [it]. If [it is] too narrow, [it] may favor one segment of the organization against the others. Strategically located participants often refused to accept definitions of objectives that put them at a disadvantage or in a straightjacket should they wish to change their designation of what they do in the future.[25]

Participants who are providers may be unwilling to go beyond measuring services in order to assess consumer satisfaction, that is, to deal with how the services were delivered.

Initially, the agency was able to take the position that centers were such new and different programs and were addressing such complex issues that it would require several years before their successes and benefits could be evaluated. In the interim, the agency could only stress the consistency between current social values and the program assumption of the generally unquestioned benefits of visiting a doctor and receiving good care. "I've seen more operational centers than almost anyone," one agency staff member noted. "Nothing could be worse off than the way the situation was [before the centers were built]. On any narrow dimension of evaluation, they could come off better smelling like a rose." Another informant commented: "All we can say is that the best of medical care expertise says that such things [as are done in the neighborhood health center] should be done—and evaluation efforts can determine whether an institution is doing them."

Over time, pressures on the agency for more definitive answers to basic policy issues began to surface. One informant, summarizing the pressures, remarked: "The first year, the agency could make excuses for a program; the second year, we needed some evidence; the third year, there was no excuse." Such issues as the extent to which health status was actually affected by the delivery of services began to emerge. According to an OEO commission study,[25] positive changes in the lives of indigenous center employees appear to be more significant than in the lives of the users, and more profound improvement was reported among urban employees than rural employees.[26] Rural users reported more changes than urban ones. Comments by center workers suggest that the lives of users have changed in a positive direction whereas comments by users reveal only minimal improvement.

The extent of access to facilities and the significance of increased utilization of services were also problems. Controversy exists over whether increased utilization is an indication of poorer-quality care, better-quality care through the discovery of more individual patient disabilities, general acceptability of center care leading to "overutilization" of the facility, or simply the lack of other facilities in the target area leading to the center's becoming the repository of all the accumulated unmet needs of patients.

Ideally the answer to the benefits calculus should be determined by data from an experimental situation in which change is measured before and after program implementation. But when the emphasis is on service and the pressing demands of health-care delivery, this answer virtually is impossible to obtain.

Longitudinal outcome studies are difficult to do. Such studies require a ten- to fifteen-year time span. And this interval is a politically untenable period of grace for a demonstration program under constant pressure to provide early, premature assessments regarding its impact and benefits. Moreover, built into such a study would have to be the recognition that centers had far greater demands placed on their capacities than many conventional health-care providers because they operated in low-income communities where greater numbers of seemingly unstable problem situations existed.[27] When a center "relates to a multiproblem family which is like terminal cancer, the medical-care team winds up hacking at a set of insatiable demands," one center physician noted. The episodic examples of success which occur in such situations can be considered scientifically significant; nevertheless, they may not be proof of the general effectiveness of medical care.

Finally, such a study would have to take into account the "creaming process." "Efforts to improve the condition of the poor, when effective generally result in improving the condition of those at the top of the bottom, leaving the bottommost untouched. Those left behind may be worse off than before."[28] Impact studies of poverty programs whose purported inclusion of marginal population groups still results in exclusion and rejection of the most marginal may be unreasonable in their delineation of realistic objectives.

Even if the ideal situation or set of conditions allowing for an outcome study were readily available, the broader question would be whether conventional epidemiological measures reveal anything significant. In a moment of frankness, one senior staff member with medical training remarked, "Baseline studies assuming that medical care is related to health status are doomed to failure. The argument that the health care looks different, therefore the health status is or will be different, is misleading."

Once a demonstration agency moves outside the parameter of the direct benefits consequent on its provision of services, it moves into even murkier waters. Despite bold pronouncements by the agency, assessments of the effectiveness of its social-change endeavors often are tenuous at best.

> Even when a study has analyzed the effects of different conditions on the program outcomes, it is likely to find small differences in effects and yield only tantalizing clues about factors favorable to success. The decision-maker is rarely presented with clear and unambiguous direction, and his reluctance to leap into uncharted waters is understandable. Particularly when he has to dredge implications for action out of a long, murky report, he may fail to consider seriously even those findings that do offer guidance for change.[29]

Emphatic statements regarding the broad nature of proposed changes in the medical-care delivery system and among the poor can prove to be an embarrassment. Statements designed to elicit support and recognition for projects all too likely can be taken at face value and fashioned into behavioral standards and expected outcomes for the agency and its projects.

Evaluating the agency's broad-aim or social-change mandate raised multiple, complex, and often conflicting issues regarding the nature of social change and the lead time necessary for "beneficial" social changes to become visible and measurable. One agency appraisal of social-science evaluation efforts to determine the broad-aim successes and benefits of the NHC program complained sharply:

> The sociologists say that community participation should result in improved community relations between consumers and institutions purporting to serve them, or to achieve broader community goals but admit that research is needed to develop the understanding to make judgments about the processes. The economists say that the NHCs should have an antipoverty consequence—but the technique for relating improvements in the poverty community to the intervention of the NHC has yet to be developed.[30]

It is not surprising, given the nature of the agency's frustration in attempting to measure social change and its recognition that it had to justify its early glowing rhetoric, to discover agency appeals to general "social goods" as validation of its demonstration efforts. The agency complaint concerning social-science evaluation continues in frustration:

> Too few professional voices have been raised to suggest that the primary objectives—(1) access to an acceptable system of medical care and (2) consumer participation in public programs—are social goods that need no further justification. We should strongly resist the urge to test socially desirable objectives by their purported secondary benefits, primarily because these benefits fit an input-outcome model. While it is important to support research on the relationships between desirable inputs and their secondary outcomes, it is incumbent on evaluators and researchers to

support the notion that some socially desirable actions need no further justification. Citizen participation in public programs is one of these.[31]

Adding to the agency's frustration in attempting to find the most appropriate range of defensible justifications for its efforts were the dangers it evoked when it addressed unexpected undesirable consequences attributable to the program. In the best of all rational worlds, an agency proceeding by scientific standards of inquiry might conclude that the policy had failed and ought to be replaced. "But there are always competing explanations about why policies fail that may leave decisionmakers uncertain over whether to abandon them. One hypothesis is that the theory behind the policy is bad, and the more that is done the worse things will get. The other hypothesis is that the critical mass has not been reached. If more of the same thing were done, then the policy would ultimately show good results.[32]

Given the difficulties in determining actual benefits distributed by the program, it is not surprising to discover agency retrenchment from the optimism of the early days when the centers were likely to be paraded as models for the rest of the country. Over time, the agency began to make more cautious restatements regarding the equitable burden of proof which the agency and its projects ought to shoulder.

> Health programs for the poor should not bear the major burden of demonstrating that health services improve health or can help people out of poverty. The demonstration that new comprehensive care units with consumer participation can alter a delivery system troubled by 50 years of professional and political rivalries—solo-group, fee-prepayment, teaching-research services—(the town-gown syndrome) are objectives that each health delivery system must test and prove. But each must bear a responsibility for a share of the test.

> Unfortunately, health programs for the poor are being asked to prove themselves first, whereas other systems of delivery have barely been challenged.[33]

Additional Evaluation Burdens: Effectiveness as a Demonstration Agency

The preceding catalog of difficulties encountered in attempting to meet the evaluation mandate of measuring impact is common to both innovative and conventional programs, though clearly the pressures on the demonstration program shorten its time frame, heighten its vulnerability, and raise additional conceptual questions. In addition, there are a set of evaluation burdens specific to demonstration agencies and their programs.

Program evaluation must demonstrate proof of versatility, of replicability, and of the agency's ability to constantly shoulder innovative ideas. These additional burdens appear to be consistent with Rivlin's prescription that systematic experimentation (the trial of a model in enough places to make a difference and to determine the conditions under which it works bets) should replace the random-innovation approach.[34] On closer reflection, these burdens serve to minimize or defeat the likelihood of more systematic ambitious endeavors. In other words, Rivlin's attractive prescription, like the attempts to make individual project evaluation more scientific, is compelling on first consideration. But it suffers from a set of difficulties and handicaps which limit the likelihood of its implementation.

Program Expansion

Demonstration endeavors on the OEO scale are mounted by "heroic" bureaucracies.[35] In part, such heroism is a matter of style and impression management. But heroic endeavors often do require unusual people. Whereas heroic figures successfully undertake one or a series of feats and then, with their reputations firmly established, rest upon their laurels, heroic bureaucracies enjoy no such respite. They must continue to seek new participants for their program.

The inexorable logic of bureaucracy requires a demonstration agency, as almost any other conventional bureaucracy, to expand in order to ensure its own bureaucratic survival. "Successful" expansion involves increasing the number of reliable grantees who possess both the vision and the administrative capacity to develop and implement local programs consonant with Washington's social-change agenda. Ironically, the very imperative of expansion is likely to contain the seeds of the demonstration agency's own decline or demise.

A demonstration agency is a mover of money. "Its task is to remove a certain amount of money from its coffers in the time period alloted. Spending, to be sure, is not the prime goal of the granting organization . . . [but] the major criterion of success that is immediately available . . . is ability to spend the allotted amount."[36]

Dispensing money also involves identifying recipients. While funding agencies usually claim that they are giving dollars to projects for specific activities, in point of fact, they are granting dollars to persons who are key to the success of the program at the local level and who have the proper affiliations. These grantees had to possess the capability, interest, and commitment to develop and implement an NHC project. To the extent that such key persons are readily identifiable by the agency, the dollar-dispensing operation is facilitated.

As the agency soon discovered, the number of capable, interested, and committed prospective new grantees was far more limited than had been anticipated initially. Many of the later recipients of federal dollars tended not to share the vision and the intensity of commitment which characterized the early network of reformers; almost, by definition, therefore, they were less desirable developers and implementers of the initial reform idea. Only a limited number of individuals within any sector were interested in implementing the ideas embodied in the center program. And a larger number of the grantees were interested primarily in the federal dollars.

As the number of reliable grantees diminished, the agency's capacity to implement its social-change agenda in a dramatic manner and at an accelerated pace declined. This diminution in agency capacity to deliver must be coupled with the tyranny of congressional impatience, expressed through the allowance of a fairly short time interval to demonstrate impressive program results. To this structurally created downhill turn must be added the bureaucratic imperative of attempting to increase an agency budget by a significant amount each year to ensure its own survival. The result is a cruel paradox for a demonstration agency. The agency must continue to raise its budget request to meet a survival imperative, but the successful acquisition of increased funding may not be an adequate form of insurance if the agency has difficulty finding reliable grantees.

Demonstrating Versatility

In the best of all possible worlds, the selection of local projects ought to be based largely on agency-generated criteria for project proposals, shrewd assessments of project feasibility in specific locations, or the long-term capabilities of provider or community groups to sustain the operation of a health center. In the real world, however, as the NHC program expanded, it was clear that demonstrating that an institution such as an NHC could be developed by different providers was not adequate proof of the institution's versatility.

The agency must be able to demonstrate that its projects, however controversial, can operate in a number of different contexts. Some contexts may be quite hostile to the innovative project; other contexts may be strategically less desirable but politically necessary. In displaying its versatility, the agency may be forced to place its projects in less than optimal situations.

On a rational calculus, such a forced mix is a waste of service resources. But considerations of equity and political necessity in the distribution of resources sidestep such a calculus. The successful implementation of reform must occur in a number of fundamentally different situations: urban-rural; North-South; black-brown-yellow-white. Project distribution on geographical, ethnic, and ultimately political criteria became one of the agency's fundamental dilemmas of choice. In turn, this had long-term repercussions on program and agency effectiveness.

The pattern of the initial eight awards—the diversity among grantees and the relatively large sums of money granted (almost $10 million for the eight projects)—reflected agency beliefs that the commitment to establish viable projects meant experimentation in different settings and the infusion of large sums of money.

> The first major grant, awarded in the spring of 1965, was to aid efforts designed to deal with poverty health care problems on a comprehensive basis in an urban and a rural setting. OEO awarded a "Research and Development" grant to the Department of Preventive Medicine of Tufts University School of Medicine to develop projects at the Columbia Point Housing Project in Boston, Mass., and in a rural community in Mississippi [later identified as Northern Bolivar County]. . . . Soon thereafter, an "R and D" grant was made to strengthen the development of a citywide program administered by the Denver Department of Health and Hospitals under the leadership of Dr. Samuel Johnson and Dr. David Cowen. [An earlier OEO grant utilizing "local initiative" funds available to the Denver community action agency had helped initiate the programs; a Children's Bureau health grant also assisted.]
>
> In 1966, two grants were made to hospitals in New York City to expand the effort. One to the Beth Israel Medical Center enriched the ambulatory care program for the poor established in 1961 on the lower east side of Manhattan at the former Gouverneur Hospital; Dr. Howard Brown was project director. The other was to Montefiore Hospital to serve the East Bronx through a neighborhood storefront and a main health center; this project was developed and supervised by Dr. Harold Wise and Dr. Martin Cherkasky.
>
> In Chicago, a grant to the Chicago Board of Health and the Chicago Committee for Urban Opportunity [the local community action agency] had financed a landmark study of methods of improving health care for the poor. The report by Dr. Mark Lepper and Dr. Joyce Lashof documented the health needs of Chicago's poor and provided the basis for subsequent OEO-aided projects in the Mile Square and North Lawndale areas. In June 1966, grants to the Office of Medical Care Research of the Chicago Health Research Foundation initiated projects involving resources of Presbyterian-St. Luke's Hospital in the Mile Square area and the Mt. Sinai Hospital in the North Lawndale area; the former center was located in an old health facility and the latter in a building constructed with funds from the Sears, Roebuck Foundation.
>
> In 1966, a grant was also made to the University of Southern California to establish and develop health services in the Watts area of Los Angeles. Dr. Roger Egeberg, Dr. Robert Tranquada and Dr. Elsi Georgi provided initial leadership in this effort.[37]

While the initial grants covered a wide geographical area, it is important to note two major qualifications to the pattern. At least five of the eight projects were identified with well-known medical reformers with whom the senior staff of the agency had close ties. In effect, the initial grants were among the "safest" ever awarded by the agency. (Tufts programs were developed and run by Drs. Jack Geiger and Count Gibson of the Department of Community Medicine. The Denver project was the brainchild of Sam Johnson, who had presented a plan for what was to become the NHC concept at about the same time that Dr. Geiger began to talk about a new delivery institution. The Montifiore program was closely identified with medical reformers Drs. George Silver and Martin Cherkasky, who had connections with Yale University and Albert Einstein Medical College, respectively. The USC proposal was supported by Dr. Roger Egeberg, Dean of the USC Medical School, who later joined the Department of Health, Education, and Welfare as assistant secretary for health.)

In addition, all but one of the grants was awarded to a project in an urban area. Although more than half of the U.S. poor were known to be living in a rural area and the agency was fully cognizant of the enormous deficiencies in the delivery of medical-care services in rural areas, the pattern reflects two important realities for the agency: the network of important medical-care reformers was located in urban areas, and a significantly different magnitude of difficulties existed in the development and effective implementation of rural-area projects. Rural areas were largely unattractive to a center's potential medical staff. There were often few provider groups or educational institutions in rural areas with which the agency even could negotiate for the delivery of services. "We can't circumvent in the sense of total defiance of the existing medical-care delivery system or where there are no facilities already there. In a sense, we can't help the most desperately needy places," one staff member commented.

In addition to the scarcity of providers or willing professional recruits in rural areas, rural populations are likely to be widely scattered. The threshold population (estimated to be between 10,000 and 30,000) necessary for the "effective and efficient" operation of a center extends over a large geographical area. Almost inevitably such rural expanses lack a decent system of transportation or roads to connect the target population with the proposed center site. Because distance and travel time were so significant, in several rural projects the agency became heavily involved in funding transportation services to the center as a necessary component of medical-care delivery. While such transportation funding was viewed as necessary to the success of the demonstration program in the area, the use of funds for these activities meant that some medical services also deemed highly desirable might not be covered by the grant.

The 1967 amendments to the Economic Opportunity Act of 1964 (though politically motivated) point to the recognition that enormous deficiencies in rural medical-care delivery posed major problems to the agency.

In the amendments, rural-area health centers were exempted from the mandate for comprehensiveness of care because "the lack of even elemental health services may require simpler, less comprehensive services to be established at first."[38] This exception was, in fact, a double-edged sword. It permitted greater latitude in project approval but allowed for rural projects which had no intention of disturbing status quo medical-care delivery arrangements. The continuing pattern of agency awards reflects these realities of rural health-care innovation. As late of fiscal year 1971, only twenty-two of the eighty-two agency projects were in rural areas.

In passing, it should be noted that developing health centers in urban areas was fraught with its own attendant set of difficulties for the agency. The scope of health-care delivery and needs in major urban poverty areas was so enormous that demonstration dollars could go largely unrecognized and have a limited impact on the health-care system in the area. "We have an increasing number of centers in New York," one staff member commented, "but still there has been no major change in the New York health delivery system."

Here, then, was the one paradox in a nutshell. In rural areas a well-designed and adequately funded program with adequate staff would be highly visible and would be likely to have a larger impact on the local health-care delivery system. Thus, the agency's hoped- for results of visibility and impact would be achieved, but the prerequisite conditions often were extraordinarily difficult to realize. In the urban areas, projects might have met the prerequisite conditions for developing a center, but they might be less likely to meet the visibility and impact needs of a demonstration agency.

Closely allied with the issue of the urban-rural geographical dispersal of projects was the issue of the distribution of agency demonstration dollars among competing, ethnic low-income areas. The initial thrust of War on Poverty programs, a consequence of the large-scale ghetto uprisings in the early 1960s, had been directed at black communities. Initially, other dimensions of the complex U.S. ethnic calculus had been set aside by various OEO agencies.

Over time, various other minority groups began to pressure OEO for their share of the poverty pie. Spanish-speaking people claimed that they were not receiving their fair share. They attributed their inequitable distribution of resources to their failure to adopt militant tactics or the inaccuracy of census data with respect to the proportion of Spanish-speaking people in the United States. Agency response to pressures for dollar distribution to Spanish-speaking communities resulted in ten projects serving only Spanish-speaking or Spanish-speaking and black communities.

Operating in Spanish-speaking communities, as well as other ethnic-minority communities such as San Francisco's Chinatown, the agency found was more difficult and posed more unknowns than working in black communities. There were greater language and cultural barriers. According to one sympathetic organizer in Spanish-speaking communities, "People in Spanish-speaking communities were intimidated, especially because they had been totally excluded from the processes of government. . . . Many believed that such things were 'Anglo' type activities; these beliefs had to be overcome."

Versatility also meant establishing center programs in a number of different regions with different political settings. Satisfying this operating rule for project distribution meant moving into hostile political situations where projects were even more vulnerable than usual to hostile local political forces. In the South, for example, funding health centers to deliver medical care to indigent blacks was more likely to generate overt resistance or non-cooperation from officials than in other sections of the country. In one state, according to an agency staff member, "We bought a bankrupt hospital, and the governor said to us, 'If you want a center, that's it.' " But the rural South contained the greatest numnber of impoverished blacks as well as impoverished whites. On any calculus of need, it ranked as a high-priority region despite the extra difficulties of developing and implementing projects there.

Initially, the agency made its first Southern grant through Tufts University School of Medicine and left the site of the center unspecified in the grant to help avoid some of the political flack which the project generated. However, even if overt racism and entrenched paternalism which Washington often found personally distasteful existed, it became apparent that if the agency were to operate in the South at all, it would have to protect itself from the accusation of carpetbagging by funding local medical-provider institutions. (In passing, it should be noted that the vulnerability of NHC projects operating in hostile localities was aggravated by the agency's annual funding arrangements. Such unavoidable fiscal procedure allowed gubernatorial political interventions; as a result, the agency could anticipate costly, time-consuming efforts on its part to circumvent a hostile governor's veto.)

The dilemmas of choice posed by broad regional geographic distribution which necessitated working in hostile locales or with providers who were basically unsympathetic to the agency's reform mandate were heightened by the agency's need to expand and to cultivate powerful protectors, even at the cost of possible dilution of its reform efforts. One informant remarked in a rather cynical tone, "Once you get out of the ballgame of four or five demonstration programs, you've got to keep funding or say that you've failed. So, you end up sleeping with various congressmen." Projects with powerful political protectors were destined to be funded and not "pushed around" by the agency, however much their actual operations failed to mesh with the reform agenda.

Such politically generated and protected projects clearly would not have been funded if the agency were able to use its own more satisfactory criteria for determining project placement. But the greater amount of available dollars and the increased visibility of the program as a whole operated to force greater compromises; some of the agency's precious dollars were channeled into situations which were totally unproductive from a reform perspective.

Demonstrating Replicability

Closely identified with the dilemmas posed by displaying broad-based versatility for demonstration programs are the issues raised by the need to demonstrate the replicability of a project. The replicability imperative inevitably conflicts with what appears to be a common agency practice of "hothousing" to ensure project success. Such hothousing however, reduces the claim that the projects are replicable under fairly conventional conditions, a sine qua non for long-term acceptance of such programs.

Early in the program's history, the OHA was able to create relatively protected spaces for the centers. "We touted the development of a community-based health system as a new institution and wanted it to be credible. The centers had to be part of the larger system, but to keep the program from failing or being captured by the industry, the centers had to be insulated, at least initially," one former staff member maintained vigorously. Over time this posture became difficult to sustain as pressures to incorporate the new institution into the wider system increased.

While the agency may wish to continue to protect or "hothouse" its projects in order to create greater odds for the project's longer-range success, it cannot admit that its prototypical demonstration projects have largely symbolic importance. Such reasoning then leads to the conclusion that they may not be replicable. For example, the agency cannot admit that a project is successful because it attracts a disproportionate amount of funds compared to the dollars which would be available to other projects in other locales. But, as Rein and Miller point out, it usually happens that "whether people in similar situations get the help they need depends on local success in getting demonstration money from funding agencies. . . . A new source of social injustice emerges between those fortunate needy who happen to live in cities rich in demonstration projects and those who do not."[39] Project replicability all too likely depends on local political connections and organization in order to get the dollars, rather than any intrinsically desirable properties of a project or its ease of replicability.

Similarly, the agency cannot admit publicly to the fact that even if programs prove certain important results, the "number of replications are usually insufficient to prove statistically useful samples of experimental and comparison situations.''[40] This is, in point of fact, an admission to producing a set of ''exquisite gems.''

Finally, the agency cannot admit either that its programs are so special or difficult to execute or that only special people with certain personal and professional qualifications can engage in the demonstration effort successfully. This admission would be construed as a further denial of the widespread applicability and replicability of demonstration results, since such special persons are likely to be in short supply.

In summary, if the agency claims that its programs operate under special conditions which include manageable-scale, extensive agency protection, a relatively large amount of federal demonstration dollars, and special personnel requirements, then the agency appears to be admitting that its projects are not replicable in conventional situations. Since replicability is one of the essential promises held out by a demonstration endeavor, this admission is tantamount to political suicide. Consequently, the agency is forced to maintain a facade, promising that its projects are neither special nor unique while protesting against premature attempts to swallow them up by incorporation into the wider health-care delivery system.

Meeting Demands for Continuing Innovation

Pressures on and within a demonstration agency operate not only to expand funding capacity for an already visible set of projects which can be replicated, but also to remain constantly ''on the frontier.'' A demonstration agency is under constant pressure to create innovative new projects or to change or modify the emphasis of the existing programs it has developed in order to attract continuing congressional interest.

Social-change demonstration programs which attempt to generate broad changes requiring an extended time frame and a commitment for longer-term secure funds lack these vital components for program success. They are constrained by the structure of congressional-purse prerogatives and by the constant pressure to do new and different things as the price of their own survival. ''It's like 'publish or perish,' '' one informant ventured. But the analogy with academia falls short; a tenured academic can replay the same themes with ingenuity, but a social-change demonstration agency, lacking the privilege and security attendant on a tenure system, has the unenviable task of always remaining in the vanguard as the price of its own survival. The agency must be in the forefront of activity, especially as its program expands. It must walk the narrow, often politically defined, line between demonstrating and operating in retaining its capacity to innovate as well. The fineness of this line is well illustrated by the 1971 Presidential effort to veto OEO legislation in which the operating of programs was alleged to dilute the OEO's mission as in "incubator and tester of ideas."[41]

Because the agency must turn to new types of programs every few years in order to survive, it cannot build a source of power through bureaucratic expertise acquired by giving sustained attention to specific problems at the operational level. "The routines of yesterday are swept away, to be replaced by new ones. Anxiety is induced because they [the agency's staff] cannot get their bearings. They have trouble knowing exactly what they should be doing. The ensuing confusion may lead to inefficiencies in the form of hesitation or random behavior to cover as many bases as possible."[42]

Such systemically dictated loss of interest at projects has, of course, serious consequences for the projects themselves and, at least in theory, for the agency's ultimate purpose of reforming the existing delivery system. The frontier shifts rapidly for a demonstration program, every two or three years in most cases. Three years is a short time in the life of a fledgling institution with powerful competitors. For projects which were funded as the agency's budget expanded, the period is likely to be one or two years. If such projects lack the capacity and skills to manage "out on a limb," they are likely to be dismissed or absorbed by other agencies or medical purveyors with a further compromise of their reform properties.

The magic wand of funding moves from health area to health area and from crisis to crisis, causing one kind of facility to grow and flourish for a time, and then another. Existing projects are left with a cruel dilemma. As part of the agency's demonstration agenda, the projects should continue to improve their fledgling operation. To continue to qualify for increased funds and agency attention (even if the center is providing fairly reasonable and reliable health services at the time), the local project must try to meet the new demonstration agenda sold by the demonstration agency as the price of its own survival in Congress.

The general effect of such a dynamic is to heighten the anxiety and insecurity of the projects. "It's hard enough to launch a center," one agency staff member commented, "but when we constantly change emphases . . . and [when] we were often caught with changing signals [to the projects] . . . it's impossible." One center administrator summarized the prevailing uncertainly: "When the dust settles, are you left with something convincing and a program where you know where you will be, generally speaking, three years from now?"

Even if centers bravely attempted to follow the trail of new federal demonstration dollars earmarked for yet another innovation in the medical-care delivery system, they were likely to be handicapped in their efforts. After Congress imposed individual income-eligibility standards, the neighborhood health centers reported a downgrading in respect for patients, lower status for staff, and the appearance of other characteristics associated with institutions designed to serve the poor. This suggests a reinforcement of the two-class medical-care delivery system which the agency hoped to avoid.[43] As clearly defined poor people's health facilities, the centers were even less likely to receive federal dollars earmarked for further innovations.

Within four years of the establishment of the NHC program, a new administration was exploring the experimental funding of sizable health maintenance organizations (HMOs) based on large provider institutions. The OHA, claiming extensive experience in developing new delivery systems for low-income populations, attempted to get its share of the pie (in competition with the Department of Health, Education and Welfare). The agency's new line was that the neighborhood health centers did not put the larger medical-care delivery system on notice because centers were, in reality, a patching-up operation and would take years to become the nucleus of a delivery system. They did not affect to any significant extent the delivery structure of the larger system, nor did agency dollars service large numbers of medically indigent patients. To counter these "failings," the agency would have to look to other delivery mechanisms as a vehicle for change in the larger delivery system. Not surprisingly, hospitals with their large outpatient departments which service great numbers of the indigent became the new focus. The irony of this change of emphasis is readily apparent when one recalls the agency's hesitancy to pour dollars into hospitals in the first few years of the health-center program and its efforts at a convincing argument for this policy position.

Basically, the agency's posture became one of agreeing that coordination of existing facilities was the key to structural reform.

> The Office of Health Affairs is increasingly interested in developing several larger scale programs (for a population of 100,000-200,000 persons, predominantly poor) involving broadly based community groups and multiple health providers which will address the issue of developing more rational and coordinated networks to deliver comprehensive health care on a "community-wide" basis. . . . The result of this effort should be the creation of a multi-institution and provider network that has full responsibility and accountability for all ambulatory health care. The network should finally tie together all public and private delivery and financing systems that focus on ambulatory care. The home, the group practice, the neighborhood health center, the health department, the hospital outpatient department, and the ambulatory care facilities of the teaching hospital setting would be joined together. All the ambulatory care resources would make up a community health network that renders any point within the system accessible from any other point of entry, that ensures continuity of care as patients move through the various elements of the network, and that provides access to, and follow-up from, inpatient care facilities.[44]

In many ways, the network concept ran counter to the initial reform concepts. Networks involved large numbers of providers—a situation in which a fledgling neighborhood health center might easily be submerged. Networks involved providers who may well have ignored the agency's more dramatic efforts at reform through the centers, but who could be far more comfortable with a greater dilution of federal dollars among a number of provider "buddies" in the area. The rubric of coordination was likely to mean putting greater dollar amounts into planning grants rather than immediately operational endeavors.

Centers penalized by geography because they lacked other provider groups with which they could join to form a network could, of course, maintain and upgrade their services; but there was little likelihood that there would be federal recognition commensurate with their efforts. If the center were fortunate enough to operate in a situation where there was an uncoordinated but possible interested set of provider institutions, it might continue to benefit from agency interest, albeit on a less intense scale, as part of a network. But even the most sophisticated and successful of the neighborhood health centers often were not candidates to develop networks. When one center wanted to do a set of networks based on a prepaid group practice in the community, the reply from Washington was, "they don't have the capability; they just can't jump on the federal bandwagon because there are new federal dollars."

In effect, the change in demonstration agenda could only work to individual project detriment. There is more than a touch of irony in the rationalization for agency actions expressed by one informant who remarked, "Some of these things we [Washington] do are bitter pills for you [the centers] to swallow, but it's good for us in Washington. Since your survival [however diluted] is dependent in large part on our continued existence, the bitter pills are good for you too."

As the agency was forced to lose interest in the demonstration value of individual neighborhood health centers because the congressional focus for funding shifted, the centers were transferred to the Department of Health, Education and Welfare (an operating agency) and OHA dollars and staff were be freed for network development. In fiscal years 1971 and 1972, over $30 million of projects were transferred.

For such centers, the social-change experience was over. Under the aegis of a conventional operating agency whose constituency was composed of many of the groups which had resisted OEO health-care reforms, the centers "became peripheral and supplemental programs, eternally precarious and starved for funds."[45] They were not a major focus for the health component of the Department of Health, Education and Welfare, whose concerns and budget covered an enormous range of health-related activities. The reward for any success which a project might have enjoyed was to discourage any further innovation by placing it under the aegis of a conventional operating bureaucracy.

> If there is real promise to an innovative program that comes out of OEO, whatever it may be, part of the argument raised against the transfer by some witnesses is the ongoing agency [HEW] will in effect be so interested with that which they have always done, that what is a promising new program will atrophy in the new surroundings, and lose the zest that it showed it had the potential to produce in the old agency, that is OEO.[46]

Epilogue

The role of government in social change is as much an unresolved political issue as it ever was and, in all likelihood, ever will be. All partisans in the dialogue operate from positions fraught with unarticulated assumptions embodying value judgments. The trendiness of government as intervenor and distributor, and even redistributor, of benefits is no more. The "top-down" school has been replaced by the organizational development, "bottom-up" school. The critical eyes of scholars, students, and persons involved in the policy process have been cast on government, now viewed as part of "the problem."

If the analysis of the processes of dollar dispensing for the purchase of social change detailed in this book is accurate, the bottom-up school ought to pause for reflection, for here is an account of an endeavor in which it was assumed that an administrative solution was not always possible.

Appendix: Comprehensive Health-Services Projects' Status Report, 1970

Item	State	Location	Type[a]
1	Ala.	Lowndes	R
2		Montgomery	N
3	Alaska	Bethel	R
4	Ariz.	Phoenix	P/O
5	Calif.	Alviso	R
6		East Palo Alto	N
7		King City	R
8		Los Angeles (East)	P/O
9		Los Angeles (Watts)	N
10		San Bernardino	G
11		San Diego	R
12		San Francisco (Chinatown)	G
13		San Francisco (Mission)	N
14	Col.	Denver (East)	N
15		Denver (West)	N
16		San Luis	R
17	Conn.	Hartford	P/C
18	D.C.	Citywide	P/C
19		Upper Cardoza	N
20	Fla.	Miami	N
21	Ga.	Atlanta	N
22	Ill.	Chicago (N. Lawndale)	N
23		Chicago (Mile Square)	N
24	Ky.	Floyd County	R
25		Leslie County	R
26		Louisville	N
27	Me.	Penobscot	P/R
28		Franklin County	P/R
29	Md.	Baltimore	N
30	Mass.	Boston (Columbia Point)	N
31		Boston (Roxbury)	N
32		Boston	P/O
33		Boston (City Hospital)	O
34	Mich.	Baldwin	R
35		Detroit	N
36	Minn.	Minneapolis	P/O
37		Red Lake	R
38	Miss.	Jackson	R
39		Mound Bayou	R
40		N. Bolivar	R
41	Mo.	Kansas City	N

Appendix *(continued)*

Item	State	Location	Type[a]
42		St. Louis	N
43	Mont.	Glendive	P/R
44	N.J.	Newark	O
45	N.Y.	Albany	O
46		NYC/Brooklyn (Provident)	N
47		NYC/Brooklyn (St. Mary's)	N
48		NYC/Brooklyn (Long Island)	N
49		NYC/Brooklyn (Lutheran)	N
50		NYC/Bronx (Montefiore)	N
51		NYC/Manhattan (Gouveneur)	N
52		NYC/Manhattan (St. Luke's)	N
53		Rochester	N
54		Syracuse	N
55		West Suffolk County	G
56	N.C.	Chapel Hill	R
57	Ohio	Bellaire	R
58		Cincinnati	P/O
59		Cleveland	N
60	Okla.	Oklahoma City	P/O
61		Tulsa	N
62	Ore.	Portland	G
63	Pa.	Philadelphia (Hahnemann)	P/O
64		Philadelphia (Hartranft)	N
65		Philadelphia (Nicetown)	N
66		Philadelphia (Southeast)	N
67		Pittsburgh	N
68		Wilkes-Barre	R
69	R.I.	Providence	P/C
70	S.C.	Beaufort-Jasper	R
71		Charleston	N
72	Tenn.	Chattanooga	P/N
73		Memphis	P/G
74		Nashville	N
75	Texas	Houston	P/O
76		San Antonio	O
77	Utah	Salt Lake City	O
78	Va.	Columbia	R
79	Wash.	Renton	G
80		Seattle	G
81	W. Va.	Beckley	R
82	Wis.	Marshfield	P/R
83		Milwaukee	G

Source: Office of Health Affairs, Office of Economic Opportunity. (Washington, D.C. 1970).

[a]C = communitywide network
G = group practice
O = outpatient
P = planning
N = neighborhood health center
R = rural

Notes

Introduction

1. President Johnson called for a total victory over poverty "because it is wise, and because it is possible." Mark Arnold, "The Good War that Might Have Been," *New York Times Magazine*, September 29, 1974, p. 56.
2. Ibid.
3. Herbert Kaufman, *The Limits of Organizational Change* (University: University of Alabama Press, 1971), p. 10.
4. "Imperiled OEO Rescued Till October," *The New York Times*, July 10, 1974, p. 16.
5. Daniel Moynihan, *Maximum Feasible Misunderstanding: Community Action in the War on Poverty* (New York: Free Press, 1970), p. xiii. See also D. Moynihan, "What Is Community Action?" *Public Interest* 7 (Fall 1965):3-8.
6. See Yesheskel Hasenfeld, "Dilemmas in Innovating Social Services: The Case of the Community Action Centers," *Journal of Health and Social Behavior* 12 (September 1971). See also S.L. Kravitz, "The Community Action Programs in Perspective," in Warner Bloomberg, Jr., and Henry J. Schmidt (eds.), *Power, Poverty and Urban Policy* (Beverly Hills, Calif.: Sage Publishing, 1968).
7. Peter Marris and Martin Rein, *Dilemmas of Social Reform: Poverty and Community Action in the United States* (New York: Atherton Press, 1967). See also Aldan R. Talbot, *The Mayors Game* (New York: Harper and Row, 1967), and Herbert Kronsey, *Beyond Welfare: Poverty in the Supercity* (New York: Holt and Rinehart, 1966).
8. Eugene Bardach, *The Implementation Game: What Happens after a Bill Becomes a Law*, (Cambridge, Mass.: M.I.T. Press, 1977), p. 5.
9. Ibid.
10. Robert A. Levine, "Rethinking Our Social Strategies," *Public Interest*, Winter 1968, p. 87.
11. Ibid., p. 91. See also Bardach, *The Implementation Game*, pp. 114-119.
12. Levine, "Rethinking Our Social Strategies," p. 90. See also James Q. Wilson, "The Bureaucracy Problem," *Public Interest* 7 (Winter 1967):3-9, for a discussion of the constraints imposed by the disparity between the supply of able, experienced executives and the mandates of many public policies.
13. Bardach, *The Implementation Game*, p. 9.
14. Jeffrey L. Pressman and Aaron B. Wildavsky, *Implementation: How Great Expectations in Washington Are Dashed in Oakland or Why It's*

Amazing that Federal Programs Work at All, This Being a Saga of the Economic Development Administration as Told by Two Sympathetic Observers Who Seek to Build Morals on a Foundation of Ruined Hopes (Berkeley: University of California Press, 1973), p. 136.

15. L.B. Schorr and J.T. English, "Background, Context and Significant Issues in Neighborhood Health Center Programs," *Milbank Memorial Fund Quarterly* 46 (July 1968):293.

16. M. Rein and S.M. Miller, "Social Action in the Installment Plan," *Transaction* 3 (January-February 1969):32.

17. Pressman and Wildavsky, *Implementation*, p. 90.

18. Barney G. Glaser and Anselm L. Strauss, *The Discovery of Grounded Strategies for Qualitative Research* (Chicago: Aldine Press, 1967). See also Peter Bachrach and Martin S. Baratz, *Power and Poverty: Theory and Practice* (New York: Oxford University Press, 1970), preface.

19. Nathan Glazer, "The Limits of Social Policy," *Commentary* 58 (September 1971):53.

Chapter 1

1. Bernard Frieden and Marshall Kaplan, *The Politics of Neglect: Urban Aid from Model Cities to Revenue Sharing* (Cambridge, Mass.: M.I.T. Press, 1977), p. 33.

2. H. Aaron, *Politics and the Professors: The Great Society in Perspective* (Washington: The Brookings Institution, 1978), p. 17.

3. See Aaron, *Politics and the Professors*, chapter 2, for a summary of these changes.

4. U.S. Department of Health, Education, and Welfare, *Delivery of Health Services to the Poor* (Washington: Office of the Assistant Secretary [Planning and Evaluation], 1967), p. 34; See Avron Yedidea, " A Program for the Organization of Neighborhood Health Centers," OEO contract no. 513, September 27, 1965, for an excellent summary of the association.

5. James Blumstein and Michael Zubkoff, "Perspectives on Government Policy in the Health Sector," *Health and Society*, 1973, p. 399.

6. See Martin Rein, "Social Science and the Elimination of Poverty," *Journal of the American Institute of Planners* 33, no. 3 (May 1967), for an excellent summary of this debate.

7. See Robert H. Haveman, "Poverty and Social Policy in the 1960s and 1970s—An Overview and Some Speculations," and Lawrence M. Friedman, "The Social and Political Context of the War on Poverty: An Overview," in Robert H. Haveman (ed.), *A Decade of Federal Antipoverty Programs: Achievements, Failures and Lessons* (New York: Academic Press, 1977).

8. Adam Walinsky, Book Review of Daniel Moynihan's *Maximum Feasible Misunderstanding, New York Times Book Review*, February 2, 1969, p. 2.

9. Aaron, *Politics and the Professors*, p. 19.

10. See Aaron, p. 29. But, as Blumenthal notes, prosperity was likely to make structural weaknesses easier to deal with by sustaining general health and vigor in the economy. Richard Blumenthal, "The Bureaucracy: Antipoverty and the Community Action Program," in Allan P. Sindler (ed.), *American Public Institutions and Public Policy* (Boston: Little, Brown, 1969).

11. Aaron, *Politics and the Professors*, p. 54.

12. Blumenthal, "The Bureaucracy," pp. 135-136.

13. See General Accounting Office, *Report on Effectiveness and Administration of Comprehensive Health Services, Chicago, to Senate Committee on Labor and Public Welfare*, 89th Cong., 2d sess., p. 7.

14. Martin Rein, *Social Science and Public Policy* (New York: Penguin Books, 1976).

15. Robert Weiss and Martin Rein, "The Evaluation of Broad Aim Programs: Experimental Design, Its Difficulties and an Alternative," *Administrative Science Quarterly* 15, no. 1 (March 1970):97.

16. Karen Davis and Cathy Schoen, *Health and the War on Poverty: A Ten-Year Appraisal* (Washington: The Brookings Institution, 1978).

17. See Julius Richmond, *Currents in American Medicine* (Cambridge, Mass.: Harvard University Press, 1969), p. 12. See also George Rosen, "The First Neighborhood Health Center Movement—Its Rise and Fall," *American Journal of Public Health* 61, August 1971, and John D. Stoeckle and Lucy M. Candib, "The Neighborhood Health Center—Reform Ideas of Yesterday and Today," *New England Journal of Medicine* 280 (June 19, 1969).

18. Lisbeth Bamberger Schoor and Joseph T. English, "Background Context and Significant Issues in Neighborhood Health Center Programs," *Milbank Memorial Fund Quarterly* 46 (July 1968):291, pt. 1.

19. Davis and Schoen, *Health and the War on Poverty*, p. 165.

20. Rashi Fein, "On Achieving Access and Equity in Health Care," *Milbank Memorial Fund Quarterly* 4 (October 1972), pt. 2.

21. James Blumstein and Michael Zubkoff, "Perspectives on Government Policy in the Health Sector," *Health and Society*, 1973, p. 397.

22. Davis and Schoen, *Health and the War on Poverty*, p. 9.

23. Robert R. Alford, *Health Care Politics: Ideological and Interest Group Barriers to Reform* (Chicago: University of Chicago Press, 1975, chapter 5.

24. Martin Rein and S.M. Miller, "Social Action on the Installment Plan," *Transaction* 3 (January/February 1969):31.

25. Ibid.

26. Ibid.

27. Frances Piven, "The Demonstration Project: A Federal Strategy for Local Change," in G. Brager and F. Purcell, *Community Action against Poverty* (New Haven, Conn.: College and University Press, 1967), pp. 84, 98-100.

28. Ibid.

Chapter 2

1. K. Davis and C. Schoen, *Health and the War on Poverty* (Washington: The Brookings, 1978), p. 161.

2. See John C. Donovan, *The Politics of Poverty* (New York: Pegasus, (1967).

3. J. Pressman and A. Wildavsky, *Implementation: How Great Expectations in Washington Are Dashed in Oakland or Why It's Amazing that Federal Programs Work at All, This Being a Saga of the Economic Development Administration as Told by Two Sympathetic Observers Who Seek to Build Morals on a Foundation of Ruined Hopes* (Berkeley: University of California Press, 1973), p. 136.

4. F. Piven, "The Demonstration Project," in G. Brager and F. Purcell, *Community Action against Poverty* (New Haven, Conn.: College and University Press, 1967), p. 83.

5. Ibid., p. 186.

6. Mark Arnold, "The Good War that Might Have Been," *New York Times Magazine*, September 29, 1974, p. 57.

7. *Economic Opportunity Act of 1964*, sec. 207, and *Economic Opportunity Act of 1964 as amended (1965)* sec. 205(a).

8. *Economic Opportunity Act of 1964 as amended (1966)*, sec. 211-2.

9. *Economic Opportunity Act of 1964 as amended (1967)*, sec. 222(4).

10. H. Aaron, *Politics and the Professors* (Washington: The Brookings Institution, 1978), p. 152.

11. Aaron, *Politics and the Professors*, p. 26.

12. Office of Economic Opportunity, "A History of the OEO Comprehensive Health Services Program" (Washington, January 1971), pp. 8-9.

13. Aaron, *Politics and the Professors*, p. 34.

14. Elizabeth Anderson, Leda Judd, Jude May, and Peter New, *The Neighborhood Health Center Program: Its Growth and Problems: An Introduction* (Washington: National Association of Neighborhood Health Centers, Inc. 1976).

15. Section 314(3) of the Partnership for Health Legislation, conceived of by the Surgeon General to be a very general authority, was used to nudge

the Public Health Service gently away from its hidebound, categorical health (as opposed to comprehensive) ways. The Office of Comprehensive Health Planning, which administered Partnership for Health, attached directly to the Surgeon General's office during the initial innovative stage of administration, rather than placed in a bureau as is more normally the case, was later merged with the Division of Medical Care Administration in the newly created Health Services and Mental Health Administration (HSMHA) of HEW. The HSMHA itself was placed under the direction of Dr. Joseph English, formerly of OEO, just before Nixon took office. Budd N. Shenken, "The Introduction of the Neighboorhood Health Centers to the United States" (Draft version of paper submitted to the Organization for Economic Cooperation and Development, Directorate for Scientific Affairs, and the Department of HEW, Health Resources Administration, from the Department of Pediatrics, University of California, San Francisco, n.d.), p. 27.

16. "Comprehensive Health Service Projects (Neighborhood Health Centers): Memorandum of Understanding" (agreement signed by Elliot Richardson, Secretary, HEW, and Donald R. Reinsfeld, Director, OEO, November 2, 1970) in Office of Economic Opportunity *"A History of OEO Comprehensive Health Services Program"* (Washington, n.d.).

17. Ibid.

18. Davis and Schoen, *Health and the War on Poverty*, p. 170. See also R.A. Reynolds, p. 52, who notes that it is unclear whether this decline is attributable to the growing maturity of the centers, economies of scale, poor recordkeeping on registration figures, or direct efforts to improve efficiency on cutbacks on available services.

19. *1971 Hearings on Amendments to the Economic Opportunity Act of 1964*, House of Representatives, pp. 386-387.

20. Anderson et al., *The Neighborhood Health Center Program*, p. 18.

21. See *Local 2677, American Federation of Government Employees* v. *Phillips*, 358 F. Supp. 60 (1973) restraining OEO from terminating community-action funds. See also *Williams* v. *Phillips*, 360F. Supp. 1363 (1973) enjoining Acting OEO Director Phillips from taking action until the nominations and confirmations process has occurred.

22. See Mark Arnold, "The Good War that Might Have Been," *New York Times Magazine*, September 29, 1974, p. 66.

23. See Davis and Schoen, *Health and the War on Poverty*, pp. 170-171.

24. Ibid., p. 172.

25. "What Happened to the War on Poverty?" *National Journal*, March 3, 1979, p. 346.

26. A. Walinsky, "Book Review of Daniel Moynihan's *Maximum Feasible Misunderstanding*," *New York Times Book Review*, February 2, 1969, p. 2.

Chapter 3

1. See Julius Richmond, *Currents in American Medicine* (Cambridge, Mass.: Harvard University Press, 1969).

2. See Section 222(a)(4) of the Economic Opportunity Act of 1964 (42 U.S.C. 2809).

3. Healthright Program Guidelines'' (Washington: Office of Economic Opportunity, 1968), p. 3.

4. M. David Ermann, "The Social Control of Organizations in the Health Care Area," *Milbank Memorial Fund Quarterly, Health and Society*, Spring 1976.

5. P. Marris and M. Rein, *Dilemmas of Social Reform* (New York: Atherton Press, 1967), pp. 220-221.

6. L.B. Schorr and J.T. English, "Background, Context and Significant Issues in Neighborhood Health Center Programs," *Milbank Memorial Fund Quarterly* 46 (July 1968):290-291.

7. A. Yedidea, "A Proposal for the Organization of a Neighborhood Health Center," OEO contract no. 513, September 27, 1965.

8. Robert K. Alford, "The Political Economy of Health Care: Dynamics without Change," *Politics and Society* 3 (Winter 1972):128.

9. See D. Moynihan, *Maximum Feasible Misunderstanding* (New York: Free Press, 1970), p. xii.

10. See Robert Alford, *Health Care Politics: Ideological and Interest Group Barriers to Reform* (Chicago: University of Chicago Press, 1975), p. 222. Alford discerns a compatibility in agendas among OEO bureaucrats and market or bureaucratic reformers. Market reformers, he argues, were not threatened by the centers because they existed in areas where few physicians practiced and where there was no private market incentive to operate. Bureaucratic reformers were responsive to the centers because they used public funding and could be a further resource for bureaucratic integration and coordination efforts.

11. "Preliminary Report of the Commission on Relations with the Black Community" (Boston: Harvard Medical School, April 1969); M. Seham, "Discrimination against Negroes in Hospitals," *New England Journal of Medicine* 271 (1964):940; J.D. Snyder, "Race Bias in Hospitals: What the Civil Rights Commission Found," *Hospital Management* 96 (1963):52; M.S. Melton, "Health Manpower and Negro Health: The Negro Physician," *Journal of Medical Education* 43 (1968):798.

12. Anselm L. Strauss, "Medical Ghettos," in Amselm L. Strauss (ed.), *Where Medicine Fails* (New York: Aldine, 1970), p. 11.

13. Dr. Geoffry B. Gordon, "The Politics of Community Medicine Projects: A Conflict Analysis," *Medical Care* 7, no. 6 (November/December 1969):423.

14. Alford, *Health Care Politics*, p. 148.

15. But see Patricia Kendall, "The Relationship between Medical Educators and Medical Practitioners: Sources of Strain and Occasions for Cooperation" (unpublished manuscript, Association of American Medical Colleges, Evanston, Ill. 1965). See also "AMA Grams," *Journal of the American Medical Association* 219; no. 12 (March 20, 1972): 1627 and "Editorial," *Journal of the American Medical Association* 221; no. 2 (July 10, 1972):187, for discussions of the strain between academic medicine and medical practice.

16. The focus of community medicine is the identification and solution of health problems among groups of people. It recognizes the need to explore and control the multiple factors which lead to disease and disability. See Kurt W. Keuschle, "What Is the Role of the Ghetto Hospital in Health Care Delivery?" in John C. Norman (ed.), *Medicine in the Ghetto)* (New York: Appleton-Century-Crofts, 1969), p. 160.

17. Physicians in public-health and community programs express frustration at the medical profession's general orientation to diagnosis and cure of highly specific diseases to the neglect of preventive medicine and the social conditions which underly illness. See David Mechanic, "Sociology and Public Health Perspectives for Application," *American Journal of Public Health* 62; no. 2 (February 1972):142-151.

18. Jack Elinson and Conrad Herr, "A Socio-Medical View of Neighborhood Health Centers," *Medical Care* 8; no. 2 (March-April 1970):99-100.

19. Office of Economic Opportunity, Office of Health Affairs, "A History of OEO Comprehensive Health Services Programs" (unpublished manuscript, January 1971), p. 9.

20. Ibid., exhibit 1, "New OEO Aided Comprehensive Health Services Projects."

21. See Michael Lipsky and Morris Lounds, "Citizen Participation and Health Care: Problems of Government Induced Participation," *Journal of Health Politics, Policy and Law* 1 (Spring 1976):89-90, for an elaboration of the argument that such unresponsiveness is functional for hospitals in carrying out their duties as defined by the staff.

22. Anne R. Somers, *Hospital Regulation: Dilemma of Public Policy* (Princeton, N.J.: Princeton University Press, 1969), p. xi.

23. Elinson and Herr, "Socio-Medical View of Neighborhood Health Centers," p. 99.

24. Ibid.

25. According to *The New York Times*, June 21, 1971, p. 1, the AMA counted less than half of the nation's physicians as members.

26. Elton Rayack, *Professional Power and American Medicine: The Economics of the American Medical Association* (Cleveland, Ohio: World Publishing, 1967), p. xiv.

27. See Eugene Feingold, "A Political Scientist's View of the NHC as a

New Social Institution," *Medical Care* 8, no. 2 (March-April 1970:111.

28. U.S Congress, Committee on Government Operations, *Office of Economic Opportunity and the Medical Foundation of Bellaire*, 91st Cong. 1st sess., House Report 91-523, 1969.

29. See Feingold, "Political Scientist's View."

30. Hubert A. Easton, "Are Ghetto Physicians Welcome in the Mainstream of American Medicine?" in Norman (ed.), *Medicine in the Ghetto*, pp. 181-190.

31. Feingold, "Political Scientist's View," p. 111.

32. D. Moynihan, *On Understanding Poverty* (New York: Basic Books, 1968) p. 33. See Robert Coles, "The Poor Don't Want to Be Middle Class, *New York Times Magazine*, December 19, 1965, p. 56, for a characterization of the confusion prevailing at the time.

33. See Michael Harrington, "The Politics of Poverty," in I. Howe and J. Larner (eds.), *Poverty: The View from the Left* (New York: William Morrow, 1968), pp. 15-21, an excellent summary of this earlier social-science perspective.

34. Melvin Moguloff, "The Emerging Concept of Neighborhood Planning: Its Significance for Community Wide Planning" (prepared for California Health and Welfare Association, n.d.).

35. R. Reynolds, "Improving Access to Health Care among the Poor," *Health and Society*, Winter 1976, p. 69.

36. Alan A. Altshuler, *Community Control: The Black Demand for Participation in Large American Cities* (New York: Western Publishing Co., 1970) p. 124.

37. See Herbert E. Klarman, "National Policies and Local Planning for Health Services," *Health and Society*, Winter 1976, for an interesting discussion regarding the use of geographical boundaries for local health services.

38. Aaron Wildavsky, "Doing Better and Feeling Worse: The Political Pathology of Health Policy," *Daedalus* 106, no. 1 (Winter 1977):112, characterizes this as the "notch" effect.

39. Rashi Fein, "On Achieving Access and Equity in Health Care," *Milbank Memorial Fund Quarterly* 50, no. 4 (October 1972):161, pt. 2.

40. See Mollie Orshansky, "Counting the Poor: Another Look at the Poverty Profile," *Social Security Bulletin* 28 (January 1965).

41. Frances Piven and Richard A. Cloward, *Regulating the Poor: The Functions of Public Welfare* (New York: Vintage Books, 1971).

42. Alice M. Rivlin, *Systematic Thinking for Social Action* (Washington: The Brookings Institution (1971), p. 10.

43. Office of Economic Opportunity, "Comprehensive Neighborhood Health Services Guidelines" (Washington, 1968), p. 13. The OEO poverty guidelines for FY 1968 are:

Family Size	Nonfarm	Farm
1	$1,600	$1,100
2	2,000	1,400
3	2,500	1,700
4	3,200	2,200
5	3,800	2,600
6	4,200	3,000
7	4,700	3,300
8	5,300	3,700
9	5,800	4,000
10	6,300	4,400
11	6,800	4,700
12	7,300	5,100
13	7,800	5,400

44. Comptroller General of the United States, *Effectiveness and Administration of the Comprehensive Health Services Program under Title II of the Economic Opportunity Act of 1964*, (Report to Congress, Washington, 1969), pp. 53-56.

45. Reynolds, "Improving Access to Health Care among the Poor," p. 53.

Chapter 4

1. F. Piven and R. Cloward, *Regulating the Poor* (New York: Vintage Books, 1971), p. 264.

2. See Lyndon Baines Johnson, "Memoirs of LBJ: The War on Poverty and the 1964 Campaign," *The New York Times*, October 1971, for Johnson's expressed concern that the program results be visible quickly.

3. M. Rein and S.M. Miller, "Social Action on the Installment Plan," *Transaction* 3 (January/February 1969):31.

4. H.J. Geiger, "Of the Poor, By the Poor, or For the Poor: The Mental Implications of Social Control of Poverty Programs," in Feingold, "A Political Scientist's View of Neighborhood Health Centers as a New Social Institution," *Medical Care* 8, no. 2 (March-April 1970).

5. D. Moynihan, *On Understanding Poverty* (New York: Basic Books, 1968), p. 110.

6. Moynihan, *On Understanding Poverty*, p. 11.

7. Marion K. Sanders, "The Doctors Meet the People," *Harper's* 236, no. 1412 (January 1968):54.

8. OEO Comprehensive Health Services Neighborhood Health Services Guidelines, (Washington, 1968 and 1969), p. 3.

9. Ibid., pp. 6-7.

10. Ibid., p. 8.

11. Ibid., p. 7.

12. U.S. Department of Health, Education, and Welfare, *Delivery of Health Services to the Poor* (Washington, 1967), p. 9.

13. General Accounting Office, "Effectiveness and Administration," p. 46.

14. Office of Economic Opportunity, "Comprehensive Neighborhood Health Services Guidelines" (Washington, 1968 and 1969), p. 5.

15. General Accounting Office, "Effectiveness and Administration," pp. 46-51.

16. See an excellent summary in Martin Rein, "Social Science and the Elimination of Poverty," *American Institute of Planners Journal* 33, no. 3 (May 1967):146-163.

17. See H. Kaufman, *Limits of Organizational Change*) University: University of Alabama Press, 1971), p. 48.

18. M. Sanders, "The Doctors Meet the People," *Harper's* 236 (January, 1968):54.

19. General Accounting Office, "Effectiveness and Administration," pp. 72-74.

20. Office of Economic Opportunity, "Comprehensive Neighborhood Health Services Guidelines," p. 11.

21. Guy Benveniste, *Bureaucracy* (San Francisco: Boyd and Fraser, 1977) and Guy Benveniste, *The Politics of Expertise* (Berkeley, Calif.: Glendessery Press, 1972).

22. Dale Marshall, *The Politics of Participation in Poverty* (Berkeley: University of California Press, 1971), p. 4. See also John Franklin Bibby and R.H. Davidson, *On Capitol Hill* (New York: Holt, Rinehart, and Winston, 1967); Sar Levitan, "Planning the Anti-Poverty Strategy," *Poverty and Human Resources* 6 (January-February 1967): 5-16; and J.C. Donovan, *The Politics of Poverty* (New York: Pegasus, 1967), p. 86.

23. Rein and Miller, "Social Action on the Installment Plan," p. 31.

24. R. Alford, "Political Economy of Health Care," *Politics and Society* 3 (Winter 1972):155-156.

Chapter 5

1. A. Wildavsky, "Doing Better and Feeling Worse: The Political Pathology of Health Policy," *Daedalus* 106, no. 1 (Winter 1977):113.

2. Dr. Geoffry B. Gordon, "The Politics of Community Medicine Projects: A Conflict Analysis," *Medical Care* 7 (November-December 1969):425.

3. See generally Eliot Friedson, *Professional Dominance: The Social Structure of Medical Care* (New York: Atherton Press, 1970).

4. See Martin Rein, "Policy Analysis and the Interpretation of Beliefs," *Journal of the American Institute of Planners* 27, no. 5 (September 1971).

5. Gordon, "Politics of Community Medicine Projects," p. 426.

6. Office of Economic Opportunity, "Comprehensive Neighborhood Health Services Guidelines" (Washington, 1968 and 1969), pp. 7-8.

7. Comptroller General of the United States, *Effectiveness and Administration of the Comprehensive Health Services Program under Title II of the Economic Opportunity Act of 1964* (Report to the Congress, Washington, 1969), p. 68.

8. Ibid., pp. 68-69.

9. "Comprehensive Health Services Projects—Urban and Rural," *Journal of the American Medical Association* 211, no. 12 (March 23, 1970):5.

10. Eugene Feingold, "A Political Scientist's View of Neighborhood Health Centers as a New Social Institution," *Medical Care* 8, no. 2 (March-April 1970):113.

11. G.M. Hochbaum, "Consumer Participation in Health Planning: Toward Conceptual Clarification" (Paper presented at American Public Health Association meeting, November 1968), p. 6.

12. Gerald Sparer, George Dines, and Daniel Smith, "Consumer Participation on OEO-Assisted Neighborhood Health Centers," *American Journal of Public Health* vol. 60, June 1970.

13. See especially R. Alford, *Health Care Politics* (Chicago: University of Chicago Press, 1975) and M. Lipsky and M. Lounds, "Citizen Participation and Health Care," *Journal of Health Politics, Policy and Law* 1 (Spring 1976):88-90.

14. Lipsky and Lounds, ibid., p. 93.

15. Gordon, "Politics of Community Medicine Projects," p. 420.

16. Daniel Moynihan, *Maximum Feasible Misunderstanding: Community Action in the War on Poverty* (New York: Free Press, 1970), p. 169. See also Richard Blumenthal, "The Bureaucracy: Antipoverty and the Community Action Program," in Allan P. Sindler (ed.), *American Public Institutions and Public Policy* (Boston: Little, Brown, (1969).

17. Alan A. Altshuler, *Community Control: The Black Demand for Participation in Large American Cities* (New York: Western Publishing Co., 1970).

18. A. Yedidea, "A Proposal for the Organization of a Neighborhood Health Center," OEO contract no. 513, September 27, 1965, pp. 13-14.

19. Ibid.

20. Ibid.

21. H.J. Geiger, "Community Control of Community Conflict?" reprinted from *NTRDA Bulletin*, November 1969.

22. Office of Economic Opportunity, "Comprehensive Neighborhood Health Services Guidelines," p. 6.

23. Jameson Doig, "Accountability in the Administration of Public Policy," *Policy Studies Journal* 5 (Autumn 1976):86-96.

24. Feingold, "A Political Scientist's View," *Medical Care* 8, no. 2 (March-April, 1970):110.

25. Office of Economic Opportunity, "Comprehensive Neighborhood Health Services Guidelines," p. 6.

26. Ibid.

27. Altshuler, *Community Control*, introduction.

28. Guy Benveniste, *Bureaucracy* (San Francisco: Boyd and Fraser, 1977), p. 139.

29. See Stanley J. Brody, "Maximum Participation of the Poor: Another Holy Grail," *Social Work* 15, no. 1 (January 1970), for an account of election mobilization efforts by the Philadelphia CAP agency.

30. Lipsky and Lounds, "Citizen Participation and Health Care," pp. 90-92.

31. Ibid.

32. Alford, *Health Care Politics*, p. 221.

33. M.S. Davis and R.E. Tranquada, "A Sociological Evaluation of the Watts Neighborhood Health Center," *Medical Care* 7, no. 2 (March-April 1969):105-117.

34. See S.M. Miller, M. Rein, P. Roby, and A. Van Steenwijk, "Creaming the Poor," *Transaction* 7, no. 8 (June 1970).

35. Lipsky and Lounds, "Citizen Participation and Health Care," p. 108.

36. Steven Jonas, "A Theoretical Approach to the Question of 'Community Control' of Health Services Facilities," *American Journal of Public Health* 61, no. 5 (May 1971):917-918.

37. E. Anderson, L. Judd, J. May and P. New, *The Neighborhood Health Center Program, Its Growth and Problems: An Introduction* (Washington: National Association of Neighborhood Health Centers, Inc., 1976), pp. 22-23.

38. Lipsky and Lounds, "Citizen Participation and Health Care," pp. 94-95.

39. Office of Economic Opportunity, "A History of the OEO Comprehensive Health Services Program" (Washington, n.d.), p. 10.

40. Jonathan Black, "X-Raying a Hospital: Prognosis Is Hostility," *Village Voice*, November 1970, cited in Notkin and Notkin, "Community Participation in Health Services," *Medical Care Review* 27 (December 1970):11.

Chapter 6

1. Office of Economic Opportunity, "A History of the OEO Comprehensive Health Services Program" (Washington, n.d.), pp. 4-5.

2. See Frank Levy, Arnold Meltsner, and Aaron Wildavsky, *Urban Outcomes* (Berkeley: University of California Press, 1974), p. 228, for the argument that despite this need, the absence of data in a manageable form and the absence of criteria which establish the relevance of available information lead bureaucrats to simplify the conception of the environment and to devise operational procedures that greatly decrease the need for information.

3. Jeanne Nienaber and Aaron Wildavsky, *Buying Recreation: Budgeting and Evaluation in Federal Outdoor Recreation Policy or Money Doesn't Grow on Trees* (New York: Basic Books, 1973), p. xiv.

4. See Graham T. Allison, *Essence of Decision: Explaining the Cuban Missile Crisis* (Boston: Little, Brown, 1971).

5. Jeffrey Pressman and Aaron Wildavsky, *Implementation: How Great Expectations in Washington Are Dashed in Oakland or Why It's Amazing that Federal Programs Work at All, This Being a Saga of the Economic Development Administration as Told by Two Sympathetic Observers Who Seek to Build Morals on a Foundation of Ruined Hopes* (Berkeley: University of California Press, 1973), p. 137.

6. Office of Economic Opportunity, "Special Conditions for CHS Grants," August 25, 1971, point 12.

7. R. Weiss and M. Rein, "Evaluation of Broad Aim Programs," *Administrative Science Quarterly* 15, no. 1 (March 1970):103.

8. F. Bardach, *The Implementation Game* (Cambridge, Mass.: M.I.T. Press, 1977), p. 98.

9. "Health Projects Get Funding Plan," *New York Times*, November 14, 1972, p. 17.

10. "The Agonies of Change in Lowndes County," *Washington Post*, August 16, 1971.

11. Robert Bazell, "Health Care: What the Poor People Didn't Get from Kentucky Project," *Science* 172, no. 3982 (April 30, 1971):459.

12. Robert Bazell, "OEO Hedges on Kentucky Program," *Science* 174, no. 4004 (October 1, 1971):458.

13. Office of Economic Opportunity, "Comprehensive Neighborhood Health Services Guidelines" (Washington, 1968 and 1969), p. 6.

14. J. Pressman and N. Wildavsky, *Implementation* (Berkeley: University of California Press, 1973), pp. 134-135.

15. Office of Economic Opportunity, "Comprehensive Neighborhood Health Services Guidelines," p. 8.

16. Comptroller General of the United States, *Implementation of a Policy of Self Support by Neighborhood Health Centers* (Report to the Subcommittee on Health of the Committee on Labor and Public Welfare, U.S. Senate, Washington, 1973), p. 25.

17. The 1967 amendments to the Social Security Act limited the definition of medically needy to 133 percent of the income level set for public assistance by the state.

18. The cutbacks meant that "Generally speaking, only one-fourth to one-third of the medically indigent [would] qualify for health services under Medicare or Medicaid, another one-fourth receive welfare health assistance, but one-third to one-half of the people in a poor community [might] have no coverage at all." "Comprehensive Health Services Projects—Urban and Rural" Office of Economic Opportunity, (Washington, n.d.), p. 7.

19. Comptroller General of the United States, *Implementation of a Policy of Self Support by Neighborhood Health Centers*, p. 20.

20. K. Davis and C. Schoen, *Health and the War on Poverty* (Washington: The Brookings Institution, 1978), p. 171.

21. Comptroller General of the United States, "Implementation of a Policy of Self Support by Neighborhood Health Centers," p. 20.

22. Ibid., p. 15.

23. Ibid., pp. 24-25.

24. Ibid., p. 17.

Chapter 7

1. I. Bernstein and H. Freeman, *Academic and Entrepreneurial Research: The Consequences of Diversity in Federal Evaluation Studies* (New York: Russell Sage 1975), p. 19.

2. See James E. Anderson, *Public Policy Making* (New York: Praeger, 1975), pp. 132-160, for an account.

3. Joseph Whaley, J. Scanlon, H. Duffy, J. Fukumoto, and L. Vogt, *Federal Evaluation Policy: Analyzing the Effects of Public Programs* (Washington: Urban Institute, 1973), p. X. But, as Weiss notes, "A full cycle of the program has to operate before such data can be collected, or if longer term effects are to be assessed (as is often desirable), even more time must elapse." C. Weiss, "A Treeful of Owls," in C. Weiss, (ed.), *Evaluating*

Action Programs: Readings in Social Action and Education (Boston: Allyn & Bacon, 1972), p. 10.

4. Guy Benveniste, *Bureaucracy* (San Francisco: Boyd and Fraser, 1977), p. 142-143.

5. Weiss, "A Treeful of Owls," p. 11.

6. Peter Rossi, "Booby Traps and Pitfalls in the Evaluation of Social Action Programs" in C. Weiss (ed.), *Evaluating Action Programs*, p. 227.

7. C. Weiss, "A Treeful of Owls," p. 7.

8. Glen G. Cain and Robinson G. Hollister, *The Methodology of Evaluating Social Action Programs* (Madison, Wis.: Institute for Research on Policy, 1969), p. 5.

9. M. Rein and S.M. Miller, "Social Action on the Installment Plan," *Transaction* 3 (1969):31.

10. Wildavsky, "The Self Evaluating Organization," pp. 509-510.

11. Rashi Fein, "An Economist's View of the Neighborhood Health Center as a New Institution," *Medical Care* 8, no. 2 (April 1970):104.

12. Weiss, "A Treeful of Owls," p. 6.

13. Bernstein and Freeman, *Academic and Entrepreneurial Research*, p. 19.

14. Rossi, "Booby Traps and Pitfalls," pp. 225-226.

15. See Alice M. Rivlin, *Systematic Thinking for Social Action* (Washington: The Brookings Institution, 1971), pp. 86-119.

16. Henry J. Aaron, *Politics and the Professors: The Great Society in Perspective* (Washington: The Brookings Institution, 1978), p. 157.

17. Ibid., p. 33.

18. Cecil G. Sheps and Donald L. Madison, "Evaluation of Neighborhood Health Centers: A Plan for Implementation" (prepared for the Office of Economic Opportunity, Washington, July 1967), p. 70-71.

19. Weiss, "A Treeful of Owls," p. 7.

20. Ibid., pp. 9-10.

21. Rivlin, *Systematic Thinking for Social Action,* p. 64.

22. See Mildred A. Morehead, Rose S. Donaldson, and Mary R. Seravalli, "Comparison between OEO Neighborhood Health Centers and Other Health Care Providers of Ratings of Quality Health Care," *American Journal of Public Health* 61 (July 1971):1306. See also Mildred A. Morehead, "Evaluating Quality of Medical Care in the Neighborhood Health Center of the Office of Economic Opportunity," *Medical Care* 8 no. 2 (March-April 1970):118. Although Morehead focused on performance in specific clinical areas, she notes that certain "principles relating to the organization and functioning of group practice (team approach, comprehensive care, baseline preventive services, continuity of care, coordination, adequate medical records, ancillary personnel and education activities) are *implicit* [*emphasis added*] among the items selected for review" (p. 119).

23. Gerald Sparer and Joyce Johnson, "Evaluation of OEO Neighborhood Health Centers," *American Journal of Public Health* 61, no. 5 (May 1971): 932.

24. Mildred A. Morehead, "Evaluating the Quality of Medical Care in the Neighborhood Health Center Program of OEO" (Paper presented at the Medical Care Section of American Public Health Association meeting, 1969), p. 19.

25. Jeanne Nienaber and Aaron Wildavsky, *Buying Recreation: Budgeting and Evaluation in Federal Outdoor Recreation Policy or Money Doesn't Grow on Trees* (New York: Basic Books, 1973), p. xiv.

26. J.H. Langston, *Study to Evaluate the OEO NHC* (Rockville, Md.: Geomet, Inc., 1972), p. 53.

27. Office of Economic Opportunity, Office of Health Affairs, memorandum, untitled and undated, p. 3. "The early projects undertook to update census data for their service area. Later projects included a health interview survey to provide baseline demographic data utilization patterns and broad disability measures."

28. S.M. Miller, Pamela Roby, and Alwine Van Steenwijk, "Creaming the Poor," *Transaction*, (June 1970):39.

29. Weiss, "A Treeful of Owls," p. 11.

30. G. Sparer, G. Dines, and D. Smith, "Consumer Participation on OEO-Assisted Neighborhood Health Centers," *American Journal of Public Health* 60 (June 1970):5.

31. Ibid.

32. J. Nienaber and A. Wildavsky, *Buying Recreation* (New York: Basic Books, 1973), p. xiii.

33. Gerald Sparer, "Memo on Evaluation on OEO Neighborhood Health Centers," Washington, n.d., p. 2.

34. Rivlin, *Systematic Thinking for Social Action*, p. 91.

35. Frank Levy, Arnold Meltsner, and Aaron Wildavsky, *Urban Outcomes* (Berkeley: University of California Press, 1974), p. 231. The authors use this term to describe "poverty agencies" which they view as operating under a Galbraithian model of seeking clientele and encouraging demands on the bureaucracy.

36. J. Pressman and A. Wildavsky, *Implementation* (Berkeley: University of California Press, 1973), p. 137.

37. *A History of the OEO Comprehensive Health Services Program* (Washington, 1971), p. 182. But see Morehead, *"Medical Care,"* p. 130, for the claim that project location in a rural area did not consistently affect its position in the rank order of centers.

38. Office of Economic Opportunity, "Comprehensive Neighborhood Health Services Guidelines, March 1968 and 1969, p. 9.

39. Rein and Miller, "Social Action on the Installment Plan," p. 32.

40. Weiss and Rein, "The Evaluation of Broad Aim Programs," *Administrative Science Quarterly* 15 (March 1970):97.

41. Excerpts from the President's Veto Message of OEO. *The New York Times*, December 10, 1971, p. 22.

42. A. Wildavsky, "The Self Evaluating Organization," *Public Administration Review* 32 (September-October 1972):513.

43. R. Alford, *Health Care Politics* (Chicago: University of Chicago Press, 1975), pp. 149-150.

44. Office of Economic Opportunity, "Criteria for a Community Health Network" (Washington, August 1970), pp. 1-3.

45. Alford, *Health Care Politics*, pp. 149-150.

46. *Economic Opportunity Amendments of 1971, Hearings before the Committee on Education and Labor*, House of Representatives, 92d Cong. 1st sess., p. I, p. 372.

Bibliography

Books and Monographs

Aaron, Henry J. *Politics and the Professors: The Great Society in Perspective.* Washington: The Brookings Institution, 1978.

Alford, Robert R. *Health Care Politics: Ideological and Interest Group Barriers to Reform.* Chicago: University of Chicago Press, 1975.

Allison, Graham T. *Essence of Decision: Explaining the Cuban Missile Crisis.* Boston: Little, Brown, 1971.

Altshuler, Alan A. *Community Control: The Black Demand for Participation in Large American Cities.* New York: Western Publishing Co. (Pegasus paperback), 1970.

Anderson, Elizabeth; Judd, Leda; May, Jude; and New, Peter. *The Neighborhood Health Center Program: Its Growth and Problems: An Introduction.* Washington: National Association of Neighborhood Health Centers, Inc., 1976.

Anderson, James E. *Public Policy Making.* New York: Praeger, 1975.

Bachrach, Peter, and Baratz, Martin S. *Power and Poverty: Theory and Practice.* New York: Oxford University Press, 1970.

Bardach, Eugene. *The Implementation Game: What Happens after a Bill Becomes a Law.* Cambridge, Mass.: M.I.T. Press, 1977.

Bendix, Richard, and Lipset, Seymour Martin (eds.). *Class, Status, and Power.* New York: Free Press, 1966.

Benveniste, Guy. *Bureaucracy.* San Francisco: Boyd and Fraser, 1977.

_____ . *The Politics of Expertise.* Berkeley, Calif: Glendessery Press, 1972.

Bernstein, Ilene, and Freeman, Howard. *Academic and Entrepreneurial Research: The Consequences of Diversity in Federal Evaluation Studies.* New York: Russell Sage, 1975.

Bibby, John Franklin, and Davidson, R.H. *On Capitol Hill.* New York: Holt, Rhinehart, and Winston, 1967.

Bloomberg, Warner, and Schmidt, Henry J. (eds.). *Power, Poverty and Urban Policy.* Beverly Hills, Calif.: Sage Publications, 1968.

Blumenthal, Richard. "The Bureaucracy: Antipoverty and the Community Action Program." In Allan P. Sindler (ed.), *American Public Institutions and Public Policy.* Boston: Little, Brown, 1969.

Brager, George A., and Purcell, Francis P. *Community Action against Poverty.* New Haven, Conn.: College and University Press, 1967.

Braybrooke, David, and Lindbloom, Charles E. *A Strategy of Decision: Policy Evaluation as a Social Process.* New York: Free Press, 1963.

163

Cain, Glen G., and Hollester, Robinson G. *The Methodology of Evaluating Social Action Programs*. Madison: University of Wisconsin, Institute for Research on Policy, 1969.

Clark, Kenneth, and Hopkins, Jeannette. *A Relevant War against Poverty*. New York: Harper, 1968.

Couto, Richard A. *Poverty, Politics and Health Care: An Appalachian Experience*. New York: Praeger, 1975.

Davis, Karen, and Schoen, Cathy. *Health and the War on Poverty: A Ten-Year Appraisal*. Washington: The Brookings Institution, 1978.

Donovan, John C. *The Politics of Poverty*. New York: Pegasus, 1967.

Edelman, Murray. *The Symbolic Uses of Politics*. Urbana: University of Illinois Press, 1967.

Frieden, Bernard J., and Kaplan, Marshall. *The Politics of Neglect: Urban Aid from Model Cities to Revenue Sharing*. Cambridge, Mass.: M.I.T. Press, 1977.

Friedson, Elliott. *Professional Dominance: The Social Structure of Medical Care*. New York: Atherton Press, 1970.

Greer, Scott. "Professional Self-Regulation in the Public Interest: The Intellectual Politics of PSRO." In Scott Greer, Ronald Hedlund, and James L. Gibson (eds.), *Accountability in Urban Society* (vol. 15, Urban Affairs Annual Reviews). Beverly Hills, Calif.: Sage Publications, 1978.

Harrington, Michael. *The Other America: Poverty in the United States*. New York: Macmillan, 1963.

Haveman, Robert H. (ed.). *A Decade of Federal Antipoverty Programs: Achievements, Failures and Lessons*. New York: Academic Press, 1977.

Hollister, Robert M.; Kramer, Bernard M.; and Bellin, Seymour S. (eds.). *Neighborhood Health Centers*. Lexington, Mass.: Lexington Books, D.C. Heath, 1974.

Howe, Irving, and Larner, Jeremy (eds.). *Poverty: The View from the Left*. New York: William Morrow, 1968.

Kershaw, Joseph A. with Courant, Paul. *Government against Poverty*. Washington: The Brookings Institution, 1970.

Kosa, John, and Zola, Irving. *Poverty and Health: A Sociological Analysis*. Cambridge, Mass.: Harvard University Press, 1975.

Kronsey, Herbert. *Beyond Welfare: Poverty in the Supercity. New York: Holt and Rinehart, 1966.*

Langston, J.H. Study to Evaluate the OEO Neighborhood Health Center Program at Selected Centers. Final Report, 3 vols. Rockville, Md.: Geomet, Inc., 1972.

Levine, Robert A. *The Poor Ye Need Not Have with You: Lessons from the War on Poverty*. Cambridge, Mass.: M.I.T. Press, 1970.

Levitan, Sar. *Programs in Aid of the Poor*, 3rd ed. Baltimore, Md.: Johns Hopkins Press, 1976.

––––––. *The Great Society's Poor Law: A New Approach to Poverty*. Baltimore, Md.: Johns Hopkins Press, 1969.

Levitan, Sar, and Taggart, Robert. *The Promise of Greatness*. Cambridge, Mass.: Harvard University Press, 1976.

Levy, Frank; Meltsner, Arnold; and Wildavsky, Aaron. *Urban Outcomes*. Berkeley: University of California Press, 1974.

Lynn, Laurence A., Jr. (ed.). *Knowledge and Policy: The Uncertain Connection* (Study Project on Social Research and Development, vol. 5). Washington: National Academy of Sciences, 1978.

Marris, Peter, and Rein, Martin. *Dilemmas of Social Reform: Poverty and Community Action in the United States*. New York: Atherton Press, 1967.

Marshall, Dale. *The Politics of Participation in Poverty*. Berkeley: University of California Press, 1971.

Mayer, Robert R. "Social Science and Institutional Change," Chronograph of National Institute of Mental Health. Washington: DHEW, 1979.

Moynihan, Daniel. *Maximum Feasible Misunderstanding: Community Action in the War on Poverty*. New York: Free Press, 1970.

––––––. (ed.). *On Understanding Poverty: Perspectives from Social Science*. New York: Basic Books, 1968.

Nelson, Richard R., and Yates, Douglas, (ed.). *Innovation and Implementation in Public Organizations*. Lexington, Mass.: D.C. Heath, 1978.

Nienaber, Jeanne, and Wildavsky, Aaron. *Buying Recreation: Budgeting and Evaluation in Federal Outdoor Recreation Policy or Money Doesn't Grow on Trees*. New York: Basic Books, 1973.

Norman, John C. (ed.). *Medicine in the Ghetto*. New York: Appleton-Century-Crofts, 1969.

Piven, Frances Fox, and Cloward, Richard A. *Regulating the Poor: The Functions of Public Welfare*. New York: Vintage Books, 1971.

Pressman, Jeffrey. *Federal Programs and City Politics: The Dynamics of the Aid Process in Oakland*. Berkeley: University of California Press, 1975.

Pressman, J., and Wildavsky, Aaron. *Implementation: How Great Expectations in Washington Are Dashed in Oakland or Why It's Amazing that Federal Programs Work at All, This Being a Saga of the Economic Development Administration as Told by Two Sympathetic Observers Who Seek to Build Morals on a Foundation of Ruined Hopes*. Berkeley: University of California Press, 1973.

Rayack, Elton. *Professional Power and American Medicine: The Economics of the American Medical Association*. Cleveland, Ohio: World Publishing, 1967.

Regier, Marilyn C. *Social Policy in Action: Perspectives on the Implementation of Alcoholism Reforms*. Lexington, Mass.: Lexington Books, D.C. Heath, 1977.

Rein, Martin. *Social Science and Public Policy*. New York: Penguin Books, 1976.

Reissman, Frank, and Popper, Hermine I. "The Evolutionary Revolution." In Frank Reissman (ed.), *Up from Poverty*. New York: Harper & Row, 1968.

Richmond, Julius. *Currents in American Medicine*. Cambridge, Mass.: Harvard University Press, 1969.

Rivlin, Alice M. *Systematic Thinking for Social Action*. Washington: The Brookings Institution, 1971.

Rose, Stephen M. *The Betrayal of the Poor: The Transformation of Community Action*. Cambridge, Mass.: Schenkman, 1972.

Rourke, Francis E. *Bureaucracy, Politics and Public Policy*, 2d ed. Boston: Little, Brown, 1976.

Seligman, Ben B. (ed.). *Poverty as a Public Issue*. New York: Free Press, 1965.

Sindler, Allan. *American Political Institutions and Public Policy*. Boston: Little, Brown, 1969.

Somers, Anne R. *Hospital Regulation: Dilemma of Public Policy*. Princeton, N.J.: Princeton University Press, 1969.

Strauss, Anselm L. "Medical Ghettos." In Anselm L. Strauss (ed.), *Where Medicine Fails*. New York: Aldine, 1970.

Sunquist, James L. (ed.). *On Fighting Poverty: Perspectives from Experience*. New York: Basic Books, 1969.

Talbot, Alan R. *The Mayors Game*. New York: Harper & Row, 1967.

U.S. Department of Health, Education, and Welfare. *Delivery of Health Services to the Poor*. Washington, 1967.

Weiss, Carol H. *Evaluating Action Programs: Readings in Social Action and Education*. Boston: Allyn & Bacon, 1972.

Whaley, Joseph S.; Scanlon, John W.; Duffy, Hugh G.; Fukumoto, James S.; and Vogt, Leona M. *Federal Evaluation Policy: Analyzing the Effects of Public Programs*. Washington: The Urban Institute, 1973.

Journals

Alford, Robert. "The Political Economy of Health Care: Dynamics without Change." *Politics and Society* 3 (Winter 1972).

Arnold, Mark. "The Goodwar that Might Have Been." *New York Times Magazine*. September 29, 1974.

Bailey, R.M. "Philosophy, Faith, Fact and Fiction in Production of Medical Services." *Inquiry* 8 (March 1970).

Bazell, Robert J. "OEO Hedges on Kentucky Program." *Science* 174, no. 4004 (October 1, 1971).

———. "Health Care: What the Poor People Didn't Get from the Kentucky Project." *Science* 172, no. 3982 (April 30, 1971).

Berman, Paul. "The Study of Micro and Micro-Implementation." *Public Policy* 26, no. 2 (Spring, 1978).

Blumstein, James, and Subkoff, Michael. "Perspectives on Government Policy in the Health Sector." *Health and Society*, 1973.

Borgatta, E.F. "Research Problems in Evaluation of Health Service Demonstration." *Milbank Memorial Fund Quarterly* 44, no. 4 (October 1966), pt. 2.

Brody, Stanley J. "Maximum Participation of the Poor: Another Holy Grail." *Social Work* 15, no. 1 (January 1970).

Brown, H.J. "Delivery of Personal Health Services and Medical Sources for the Poor." *Milbank Memorial Fund Quarterly* 46 (1968):203-223.

Bryant, Thomas E. "Goals and Potential of Neighborhood Health Centers." *Medical Care* 8 (March and April 1970).

Burke, Edmund. "Citizen Participation Strategies." *Journal of American Institute of Planners* 34, no. 5 (September 1968).

Coles, Robert. "The Poor Don't Want to be Middle Class." *New York Times Magazine*, December 19, 1965.

Colombo, T.J.; Saward, E.W.; and Greenlock, M.R. "The Integration of an OEO Health Program into a Prepaid Comprehensive Group Practice Plan." *American Journal of Public Health* 59 (April 1969):641-650.

Davis, M.S., and Tranquada, R.E. "A Sociological Evaluation of the Watts Neighborhood Health Center." *Medical Care* 7, no. 2 (March-April 1969):105-117.

Doig, Jameson W. "Accountability in the Administration of Public Policy." *Policy Studies Journal* 5 (Autumn 1976).

Donabedian, Avedis. "An Evaluation of Pre-Paid Group Practice." *Inquiry* 6 (September 1969).

Dutton, Diana. "Explaining the Low Use of Health Services by the Poor: Costs, Attitudes or Delivery Systems?" *American Sociological Review* 43 (June 1978).

Elinson, Jack, and Herr, Conrad. "A Socio-Medical View of Neighborhood Health Centers." *Medical Care* 8, no. 2 (March-April 1970).

Elmore, Richard. "Organization Models of Social Program Implementation." *Public Policy* 26, no. 2 (Spring 1978).

Ermann, M. David. "The Social Control of Organizations in the Health Care Area." *Milbank Memorial Fund Quarterly, Health and Society*, Spring 1976.

Fein, Rashi. "On Achieving Access and Equity in Health Care."
    Milbank Memorial Fund Quarterly 4 (October 1972), pt. 2.

————— . "An Economist's View of the Neighborhood Health Center as a
    New Institution." *Medical Care* 8, no. 2 (March-April 1970).

Feingold, Eugene. "A Political Scientist's View of Neighborhood Health
    Centers as a New Social Institution." *Medical Care* 8, no. 2 (March-
    April 1970).

Geiger, H.J. "Of the Poor, By the Poor, or For the Poor: The Mental
    Health Implications of Social Control of Poverty Programs."
    Psychiatric Research Reports 21 (April 1967):55-65.

Ginsburg, Eli, and Solow, Robert (eds.). "The Great Society: Lessons for
    the Future." *Public Interest* 34 (Winter 1974) (special issue).

Glazer, Nathan. "The Limits of Social Policy." *Commentary*,
    September 1971.

Goldberg, G.A.; Trowbridge, F.L.; and Buxbaum, R.C. "Issues in the
    Development of Neighborhood Health Centers." *Inquiry* 6, no. 1
    (1969):37-48.

Gordon, Geoffrey B. "The Politics of Community Medicine Projects: A
    Conflict Analysis." *Medical Care* 7 (November-December 1969).

Greenberg, George; Miller, Jeffrey; Mohr, Lawrence; and Vladeck, Bruce.
    Developing Public Policy Theory: Perspectives from Empirical
    Research." *American Political Science Review* 71 (1977).

Hester, James, and Sussman, Elliott. "Medicaid Prepayment: Concept
    and Implementation." *Health and Society*, Fall 1974.

Jonas, Steven. "A Theoretical Approach to the Question of 'Community
    Control' of Health Services Facilities." *American Journal of Public
    Health* 61, no. 5 (May 1971).

Kasanof, D. "Antipoverty Medicine: Atlanta to Watts." *Medical Eco-
    nomics*, July 8, 1968, pp. 123-143.

Klarman, Herbert E. "National Policies and Local Planning for Health
    Services." *Health and Society* (Winter 1976).

Kovner, Anthony; Katz, Anthony; Kahane, Stanley; and Sheps, Cecil.
    "Relating a Neighborhood Health Center to a General Hospital: A
    Case Study." *Medical Care* 7 (March-April 1969).

Levine, Robert A. "Rethinking Our Social Strategies." *Public
    Interest*, Winter 1968.

Levitan, Sar. "Planning the Anti-Poverty Strategy." *Poverty and Human
    Resources* 6 (January-February 1967).

Lewis, Charles. "A Longitudinal Study of Potential Change Agents in
    Medicine—A Preliminary Report." *Journal of Medical Education* 44
    (November 1969).

Lipsky, Michael, and Lounds, Morris. "Citizen Participation and Health
    Care: Problems of Government Induced Participation." *Journal of
    Health Politics, Policy and Law* 1, no. 1 (Spring 1976).

Mansfield, Edwin. "Contribution of R&D to Economic Growth in the United States." *Science* 175 (February 1972).

Mechanic, David. "Sociology and Public Health Perspectives for Application." *American Journal of Public Health* 62 (February 1972).

Medical Care for Low Income Families." Proceedins of the 10th Annual Symposium on Hospital Affairs, December 8-9, 1967. *Inquiry* 5 (March 1968).

Melton, M.S. "Health Manpower and Negro Health: The Negro Physician." *Journal of Medical Education* 43 (1968).

Menke, Wayne G. "Professional Values in Medical Practice." *New England Journal of Medicine* 28, no. 17 (April 24, 1969).

Miller, S.M.; Rein, Martin; Roby, Pamela; and Van Steenwijk, Alwin. "Creaming the Poor." *Transaction* 7, no. 8 (June 1970).

Miller, S.M.; Rein, Martin; Roby, Pamela; and Bertram Gross "Poverty, Inequality and Conflict." *Annals of the American Academy* 373 (September 1967).

Morehead, Mildred A. "Evaluating Quality of Medical Care in the Neighborhood Health Center of the Office of the Economic Opportunity." *Medical Care* 8, no. 2 (March-April 1970).

Morehead, Mildred A.; Donaldson, Rose S.; and Seravalli, Mary R. "Comparison between OEO Neighborhood Health Centers and Other Health Care Providers of Ratings of Quality of Health Care." *American Journal of Public Health* 61 (July 1971).

Moynihan, Daniel. "What Is Community Action?" *Public Interest* 7 (Fall 1965).

Notkin, Herbert, and Notkin, Marilyn S. "Community Participation in Health Services: A Review Article." *Medical Care Review* 27 (December 1970).

Ovshansky, Mollie. "Counting the Poor: Another Look at the Poverty Profile." *Social Security Bulletin* 28 (January 1965).

Rein, Martin. "Policy Analysis and the Interpretation of Beliefs." *Journal of the American Institute of Planners* 27, no. 5 (September 1971).

_____ . "Community Action Programs: A Critical Reassessment." *Poverty and Human Resources Abstracts*, May-June 1968.

_____ . "Social Science and the Elimination of Poverty." *Journal of the American Institute of Planners* 33, no. 3 (May 1967).

Rein, Martin, and Miller, S.M. "Social Action on the Installment Plan." *Transaction* 3 (January-February 1969).

Reynolds, Roger A. "Improving Access to Health Care among the Poor—The Neighborhood Health Center Experience." *Health and Society*, Winter 1976.

Rosen, George. "The First Neighborhood Health Center Movement—Its Rise and Fall." *American Journal of Public Health* 61 (August 1971).

Sanders, Marion K. "The Doctors Meet the People." *Harper's* 236 (January 1968).

Schorr, L.B., and English, J.T. "Background, Context and Significant Issues in Neighborhood Health Center Programs." *Milbank Memorial Fund Quarterly* 46 (July 1968).

Seham, M. "Discrimination against Negroes in Hospitals." *New England Journal of Medicine* 271 (1964).

Snyder, J.D. "Race Bias in Hospitals: What the Civil Rights Commission Found." *Hospital Management* 96 (1963).

Sparer, Gerald; Dines, George; and Smith, Daniel. "Consumer Participation on OEO-Assisted Neighborhood Health Centers." *American Journal of Public Health* 60 (June 1970).

Stoeckle, John D., and Candib, Lucy. "The Neighborhood Health Center—Reform Ideas of Yesterday and Today." *New England Journal of Medicine* 280 (June 19, 1969).

Torres, Paul R. "Administrative Problems of Neighborhood Health Centers." *Medical Care* 9 (November-December 1971).

Tranquada, R.E. "A Health Center for Watts." *Hospitals* 41 (December 16, 1967):42-47.

Walinsky, Adam. "Book Review of Daniel Moynihan's *Maximum Feasible Misunderstanding.*" *New York Times Book Review*, February 2, 1969, p. 2.

Weiss, C.H. "The Politicization of Evaluation Research." *Journal of Social Issues* 26, no. 4 (November 4, 1970):57-68.

Weiss, Robert, and Rein, Martin. "The Evaluation of Broad Aim Programs: Experimental Design, Its Difficulties and an Alternative." *Administrative Science Quarterly* 15 (March 1970).

Wildavsky, Aaron. "Doing Better and Feeling Worse: The Political Pathology of Health Policy." *Daedalus* 106, no. 1 (Winter 1977).

_____ . "The Self Evaluating Organization." *Public Administration Review* 32 (September-October 1972).

Wilson, James Q. "The Bureaucracy Problem." *The Public Interest* 7 (Winter 1967).

Wise, H.B.; Torrey E. Fuller; McDade, Adrienne; Perry, Gloria; and Bogred, Harriet; "The Family Health Worker." *American Journal of Public Health* 58 (October 1968):1828-1838.

Zahn, S. "Neighborhood Medical Care Demonstration Program." *Milbank Memorial Fund Quarterly* 46, no. 3 (July 1968):309-328, pt. 1.

Zwick, Daniel. "Some Accomplishments and Findings of the Neighborhood Health Center." *Milbank Memorial Fund Quarterly* 50 (October 1972).

Unpublished Manuscripts and Monographs

Blum, H., and Showstack, E. "A National Health Policy." Conference on National Health Policy Issues, San Francisco, February 1976.

Hochbaum, G.M. "Consumer Participation in Health Planning: Toward Conceptual Clarification." Paper presented at American Public Health Association meeting, November 1968.

Moguloff, Melvin. "The Emerging Concept of Neighborhood Planning: Its Significance for Community Wide Planning." Prepared for California Health and Welfare Association, n.d.

Myers, Vincent, and Visco, Eugene "Methods Development for an Exploration of the Anti-Poverty Impacts of the Comprehensive Health Services Projects (Neighborhood Health Centers)." Final report for the Office of Economic Opportunity. Rockville, Md.: Geomet, Inc., January 1972.

Shenken, Bud N. "The Introduction of the neighborhood Health Centers to the United States." Draft version of paper submitted to the Organization for Economic Cooperation and Development, Directorate for Scientific Affairs, and the Department of HEW, Health Resources Administration, from the Department of Pediatrics, University of California (San Francisco), n.d.

Shenken, Bud, and Pritchard, Isabel. "Organizing Primary Care in America: Using the Neighborhood Health Centers to Improve Our Policy Choices." Manuscript prepared for the National Center for Health Services Research, 1976.

Sheps, Cecil G., and Madison, Donald L. "Evaluation of Neighborhood Health Centers: A Plan for Implementation." Prepared for the Office of Economic Opportunity, Washington, July 1967.

Sparer, Gerald; Dines, George B.; and Smith, Daniel. "Consumer Participation in OEO Assisted Neighborhood Health Centers." Paper presented at American Public Health Association meeting (Medical Care Section), November 13, 1969.

Yedidea, A. "A Proposal for the Organization of a Neighborhood Health Center." OEO contract no. 513, September 27, 1965.

Government Documents

Comptroller General of the United States. "Better Use Should Be Made of Physicians and Dentists in Health Centers." Report to Congress, Washington, 1979.

———. "Review of Economic Opportunity Programs: Report to the Congress of the United States along with Related Agency Comments by the U.S. Department of the Interior." 91st Cong. 1st sess. Washington: Government Printing Office., March 1979.

———. "Implementation of a Policy of Self Support by Neighborhood Health Centers." Report to the Subcommittee on Health of the Committee on Labor and Public Welfare, U.S. Senate, Washington, 1973.

_____ . "Effectiveness and Administration of the Comprehensive Health Services Program under Title II of the Economic Opportunity Act of 1964." Report to Congress, Washington, 1969.

Office of Economic Opportunity. "Special Conditions for CHS Grants," August 25, 1971.

_____ . "Comprehensive Neighborhood Health Services Guidelines," March 1968 and 1969.

_____ . "Comprehensive Health Services Projects—Urban and Rural," Washington, n.d.

_____ . "A History of the OEO Comprehensive Health Services Program," Washington, n.d.

U.S. Congress, Committee on Government Operations. "Office of Economic Opportunity and the Medical Foundation of Bellaire." 91st Cong., 1st sess. House Report 91-523, 1969.

Index

Index

43-45, 99, 110, 111, 112, 113;
Chicago report of, 54-57, 59-60,
71-72
Ghettos, revised perspective of, 39
Gibson, Count, 32, 132
Gouveneur Hospital, 34
Governance, structure of NHC, 75-
87
"Gradualists," 7
Grants, planning versus opera-
tional, 57-58. *See also* Dollars

Hanft, Ruth, 11
Head Start, 17
Health, Education and Welfare
(HEW), Department of, 12, 14,
15, 62, 65; and Health Maintenance Organization, 58, 138;
and Partnership for Health
Amendments, 16; transfer of
health centers to, 17-20
Health-care services, deliverers of,
22; community corporations,
22-24, 27; health departments,
37-39; hospitals, 32-34; medical
schools, 30-32; practitioners,
34-37; provider institutions, 23,
24-29
Health-care services, persons eligi-
ble for, 39-45
Health-care system, reform of, 3-10
Health departments, participation
of, in NHC program, 37-39
Health Maintenance Organization
(HMO), 58, 138
Health status, poverty and, 1
Hollister, Robinson G., 119
Holloman, John, 35
Hospitals, participation of, in NHC
program, 32-34

Incentives and sanctions, development of, 98-108

Income eligibility requirements,
40-42
Information, provision of, to
Washington, 95-98
Innovation, meeting demands for
continuing, 136-140
Institutions, existing health-care
provider, 23, 24-29

Job Corps, 17
Johnson, Lyndon B., 1, 14, 121
Johnson, Sam, 37, 132
Jonas, Steven, 83

Kaiser Medical Foundation, 37
Kennedy, Edward, 15
Kennedy, John F., 1

Lashof, Joyce, 34
Long Island College Hospital, 31
Longitudinal outcome studies, 126

Martin Luther King Neighborhood
Health Center, 63-64
Maximum feasible participation,
concept of, 75-76, 78
Medicaid, Medicare, 3, 6, 14, 36,
94; and third-party reim-
bursements, 108, 109-114
Medical audit, 124
Medical Foundation of Bellaire, 37
Medical group practices, participa-
tion of, in NHC program, 36-37
Medical schools, participation of,
in NHC program, 30-32
Medical societies, local, participa-
tion of, in NHC program, 35-36
Medicare. *See* Medicaid, Medicare
Miller, S.M., 135
Money. *See* Dollars
Montifiore Hospital, 32, 132
Mount Sinai Hospital, 33-34
Moynihan, Daniel, 75

About the Author

Isabel Marcus received the B.A. from Barnard College and the M.A., Ph.D., and J.D. from the University of California at Berkeley. She is an assistant professor in the Department of Government and a visiting assistant professor in the School of Law at the University of Texas at Austin. She has also been a visiting assistant professor at the University of Texas LBJ Graduate School of Public Affairs. Dr. Marcus is a licensed attorney and an arbitrator for the Federal Mediation and Conciliation Service.